THE WORKS OF SHAKESPEARE

EDITED FOR THE SYNDICS OF THE
CAMBRIDGE UNIVERSITY PRESS
BY
JOHN DOVER WILSON

# KING RICHARD II

# KING RICHARD II

CAMBRIDGE
AT THE UNIVERSITY PRESS
1971

PUBLISHED BY
THE SYNDICS OF THE CAMBRIDGE UNIVERSITY PRESS

Bentley House, 200 Euston Road, London, NW1 2DB
American Branch: 32 East 57th Street, New York, N.Y. 10022

ISBNs:
0 521 07552 1 *clothbound*
0 521 09495 X *paperback*

*First edition* 1939
**Reprinted* 1951, 1961, 1966
*First paperback edition* 1968
*Reprinted* 1971

*Places where editorial changes or additions introduce variants from the first edition are marked by a date [1950] in square brackets.

*First printed in Great Britain at the University Press, Cambridge*
*Reprinted in Great Britain by Hazell Watson & Viney Ltd,*
*Aylesbury, Bucks*

# CONTENTS

# KING RICHARD II

*Richard II* comes down to us in a good text, upon which Dr A. W. Pollard has written a masterly bibliographical essay, and has been happy in its modern editors, among whom the name of Herford stands preeminent. The character of its central figure has moreover laid a spell upon most of the great critics, a spell scarcely less potent than that of the Prince of Denmark, with which it has often, somewhat misleadingly, been compared. The concentration of nineteenth-century criticism upon character-problems has, however, here as elsewhere, led to a distorted view of the play as a whole, a view which merits reconsideration, while recent discoveries in regard to the sources seem likely to revolutionize our ideas of the genesis not only of *Richard II* itself but of the Histories that succeed it. These matters form the staple of the ensuing introduction, the main purpose of which is, as in the case of *Hamlet* and *King John*, rather to reconstruct, so far as is now possible, the Elizabethan attitude towards the play than to add one more interpretation of the characters of Richard and Bolingbroke to the ever-growing collection of modern analyses.

## I. King Richard on the Stage and in History, Modern and Elizabethan

### (*a*) *The date of the play*

Fortunately we can date *Richard II* with more precision than most of Shakespeare's other plays. It was entered in the Stationers' Register by the publisher Andrew Wise on 29 August 1597 and was printed for him shortly after by Valentine Simmes, in what is now known as the First Quarto. These transactions have all the appearance of regularity and trade respectability, and there is no reason to doubt that Wise had procured his copy of the play from Shakespeare's company, the Lord Chamberlain's Servants, in the ordinary way of business[1]. Further, an acting company of that time is unlikely to have allowed a popular play, such as *Richard II* undoubtedly was, to circulate among the reading public until its financial possibilities as a theatre-piece showed signs of exhaustion. We may therefore legitimately suppose that by the summer of 1597 the play had been for some time in the company's repertory. The earliest recorded performance was, in fact, a private one, and took place in Canon Row, on 9 Dec. 1595, at the house of Sir Edward Hoby, an active member of parliament and the son of the diplomatist, Sir Thomas Hoby, who is best known as the translator of Castiglione's *Courtier*. In view of the play's later association with the rising of the Earl of Essex, it is well to emphasize the highly respectable circumstances of this performance. Our record of it is an invitation dated 7 Dec. 1595 (preserved among the Hatfield papers and recently discovered by Sir Edmund Chambers) from Hoby to Sir Robert Cecil, which runs as follows:

> Sir, findinge that you wer not convenientlie to be at London to morrow night, I am bold to send to knowe whether Teusdaie [Dec. 9] may be anie more in your grace to visit poore Channon rowe, where, as late as it shal please you, a gate for your supper shal be open, & K. Richard present him selfe to your vewe. Pardon my boldnes that ever love to be honored with your presence; nether do I importune more then your occasions may willingly assent unto; in the meanetime & ever restinge At your command, Edw. Hoby[2].

As the paper is endorsed 'readile,' we may assume that

[1] v. A. W. Pollard, *King Richard II: a new quarto*, pp. 7–10.

[2] E. K. Chambers, *William Shakespeare*, ii. pp. 320–1. I have added a little punctuation to clarify the sense.

Robert Cecil, already associated with his father Burghley as secretary of state, accepted the invitation and witnessed the performance of what cannot, therefore, at that date have been considered a treasonable drama. Notice too, in passing, the picture which Hoby calls up, of cooks and players (including no doubt Shakespeare) all agog for the great man's entertainment, waiting into the night for the porter's word of his arrival at the gate.

There is nothing to show that the 'K. Richard' thus presented to the view of the Queen's leading statesman had not previously been seen by others; and it is exceedingly unlikely that Hoby would have engaged the players to give a play, of which he knew nothing, before such a guest and on such a subject, or that they would have offered one not already tried out on the public stage. Moreover, the terms of Hoby's letter suggest, I think, that Cecil had himself heard of the play, and may have even perhaps expressed a desire to see it. Certainly, *Richard II* took London by storm when it first appeared. We have it on the authority of Queen Elizabeth herself that it was acted forty times, an unusually long run for an Elizabethan play, and a run to which we can assign no other date than 1595–6[1]. Yet if Shakespeare's tragedy had become the talk of the town before December 1595, its reputation could not at that time have been anything but recent. Indeed, we can be positive that the play, as we now have it, was first performed sometime in 1595, because, as will later appear, one of Shakespeare's main sources in the writing of it was Samuel Daniel's poem, *The Civil Wars between the two houses of Lancaster and York*, the first four books of which were entered in the Stationers' Register on 11 Oct. 1594 and published with the date 1595 on the title-page[2]. And this fits in well enough with the date which I hazarded for the extant text of *King John*, inasmuch as the two plays are so closely allied, both in general atmosphere and in detail,

[1] v. below, pp. xxxii–xxxiii. [2] v. below, pp. xlii–xliii.

that it is difficult not to believe that they were composed at the same period[1]. *Richard II* then, though assuredly not 'the author's first attempt at historical drama' as Swinburne asserted, is comparatively early, and belongs to the opening stages of the second period of Shakespeare's career, which began with the formation of the Lord Chamberlain's company in 1594 and their acting before the Queen, with Shakespeare as one of their leading men, during the Christmas season of that year.

### (*b*) *Style and symbolism*

In 1595 Shakespeare was already thirty-one years of age; yet he was still, in the opinion of most critics, 'in standing water between man and boy' as regards his art. A mixture of styles has been noted by many in the verse of the play; attributed by some to revision, and by others to a struggle between the influence of Greene and that of Marlowe. 'The author of *Selimus*,' Swinburne writes, 'is visibly contending with the author of *Faustus* and *Edward II* for the mastery of Shakespeare's poetic and dramatic adolescence[2].' There is probably something in this, yet too much has been made of it. It is dangerous to differ on matters poetic from critics who are them-

[1] v. *King John* (New Shakespeare), Introd. p. lvi. While still believing that *King John* slightly preceded *Richard II*, I am now inclined to date it at the beginning of 1595, instead of late in 1594, because it contains one or two passages which seem to have been suggested by Daniel's poem. Cf. notes below 2. 1. 44–63, 47–9, 61–3. The striking parallels between *Richard II* and *The Troublesome Reign* may be explained as due either to proximity of the dates of *Richard II* and *King John* or to *The Troublesome Reign* and the play used by Shakespeare for his *Richard II* being written by the same author. Cf. notes 1. 3. 134–5; 1. 4. 39; 2. 1. 40–68; 3. 3. 113; and on *2 Hen. IV*, 118–20 [1950].

[2] A. C. Swinburne, *Three Plays of Shakespeare*, 1909, p. 60.

selves poets; but when Sir Henry Newbolt, who in collaboration with Dr J. C. Smith[1] has given us a very interesting edition of the play, follows Swinburne in his introduction, I cannot in turn follow him.

> In this play [he writes], if we turn from the characters to the speeches which they utter, a striking peculiarity is noticeable: the method absolutely halts between two totally different styles, the verse being partly blank verse and partly rhymed. These two styles being means of expression vitally related to the feeling or thought with which they deal, the inconsistency involved in their mixed use is a very serious one. Its effect is to produce on each occasion not a discord perhaps, but a sudden and violent change of key. As the change is always at the end of a speech or scene, and from the stronger to the weaker form, an anticlimax or sense of loss results, though this is no doubt exactly the opposite of what the author was feeling after[2].

The facts are acutely observed; but I doubt whether the critic would have felt either a violent change of key or a sense of loss had he been content to judge the play by comparison with other plays of the same period rather than with the later tragedies. Too often do we wrong the younger dramatist by setting him over against his elder, the author of *Hamlet* or of *Antony and Cleopatra*. *Richard II* is not an immature *Hamlet*; it is a play in a wholly different manner, and that manner almost perfect of its kind. The kind is evident when we turn to *Love's Labour's Lost*, which belongs approximately to the same stage of the dramatist's development[3]. The 'mixture of styles' noted in *Richard II* is to be found there also, and as in *Richard II* the rhymes tend to recur at the end of the speeches, a fact which not only pre-

[1] Who has been good enough to read this volume in proof and to make many helpful suggestions.

[2] *Richard II*, Oxford, 1912, pp. xxiii–xxiv.

[3] Sir E. K. Chambers dates it 1595; in my provisional survey I give Christmas 1593 as the date of its first draft and conjecture a later revision about 1597.

cludes the theory of revision as an explanation, but makes it certain, to my thinking, that the alternation of styles is intentional, not involuntary. *Love's Labour's Lost* is, in short, a comedy in deliberately patterned speech, and *Richard II*, as clearly, a tragedy after the same manner.[1]

This conclusion, if sound, has a bearing not only upon our critical appreciation of the play but also upon its stage-production. The realization of its pattern-character has recently led to the rediscovery, after three hundred years, of *Love's Labour's Lost* as a lovely and significant stage-spectacle[2]. It is obvious what a stylized production might make of a play so full of pageantry and symbolism as *Richard II*. Even the brawling of the nobles and the casting of their gages, at the opening of act 4, an episode irritating to the modern reader hoodwinked by naturalistic conceptions of drama, would fall into place as a detail in the design. As for symbolism, three writers have lately independently drawn attention to the sun-image, which dominates the play as the swastika dominates a Nazi gathering[3]. For Shakespeare the sun stood in general as the symbol of royal majesty[4]; but it appears that 'the sun emerging from a cloud' was also a personal emblem of King Richard himself, and is actually one of the three badges embroidered upon the robes of

[1] These observations do not apply to act 5, which presents special problems of its own (v. pp. lxviii–lxxvi). The probability is that the old play upon which Shakespeare worked contained rhymed verse, and this may have influenced him in revision. But to regard it as the cause of the elaborate verse patterns of the early acts would be absurd.

[2] I have particularly in mind the remarkable revival by Mr Tyrone Guthrie at the Old Vic in the summer of 1936.

[3] v. Paul Reyher, 'Le Symbole du Soleil dans la tragédie de Richard II' (*Revue de l'Enseignement des Langues Vivantes*, June, 1923); C. Spurgeon, *Shakespeare's Imagery*, 1935, pp. 233–8; Wolfgang Clemen, *Shakespeares Bilder*, 1936, pp. 77–8.

[4] Cf. *Troil.* 1. 3. 89–94; Spurgeon, *op. cit.* pp. 235–6.

his effigy in Westminster Abbey[1]. Whether the dramatist was conscious or not of this fact, he certainly employs sun-imagery with peculiar force and frequency in the play[2], and theatrical producers might well take a hint from it[3]. *Richard II* ought to be played throughout as ritual. As a work of art it stands far closer to the Catholic service of the Mass than to Ibsen's *Brand* or Bernard Shaw's *Saint Joan*.

It is remarkable that the one writer to see this is Walter Pater, whose essay on *Love's Labour's Lost* is also the only critique with any understanding of that play which appeared during the nineteenth century. So far from feeling the style of *Richard II* mixed or inconsistent, he finds it perfectly adapted to the purpose and mood of the poet.

> In no other play perhaps is there such a flush of those gay, fresh, variegated flowers of speech—colour and figure, not lightly attached to, but fused into, the very phrase itself....With him [i.e. Richard] blank verse, infinitely graceful, deliberate, musical in inflexion, becomes indeed a true 'verse royal,' that rhyming lapse, which to the Shakespearian ear, at least in youth, came as the last touch of refinement on it, being here doubly appropriate[4].

The style of this may strike the modern ear as itself too flowery, but it expresses the truth of the matter. 'In fact,' he declares,

[1] Fairholt, *Costume in England*, i. 123 (cited by Reyher *op. cit.*). Newbolt (note on 2. 4. 21–2) writes 'Richard's badge was the sun obscured by clouds,' an unhappy misstatement. Cf. also V. H. Galbraith in *History*, XXVI, 238–9 [1950].

[2] Cf. 2. 4. 21–2; 3. 2. 36–53; 3. 2. 217–18; 3. 3. 62–7; 3. 3. 178–9; 4. 1. 260–2; 4. 1. 283–4, and notes on these passages.

[3] For example, a representation of the rising sun behind the royal seat in the lists at Coventry might assist the imagination of moderns unaccustomed to the suggestions of medieval heraldry.

[4] *Appreciations* (3rd ed.), p. 194.

the play of *Richard II* does, like a musical composition, possess a certain concentration of all its parts, a simple continuity, an evenness in execution, which are rare in the great dramatist....It belongs to a small group of plays, where, by happy birth and consistent evolution, dramatic form approaches to something like the unity of a lyrical ballad, a lyric, a song, a single strain of music[1].

Pater's perceptions, moreover, are in striking accord with those of a great modern bibliographer, based upon an exact and comprehensive survey of the textual minutiae of the First Quarto. 'The impression,' writes Dr Pollard,

which a very close study of the play has made on me (I mention it for what it is worth) is that Shakespeare wrote it at top speed, the words often coming to him as fast as he could set them down, and that some passages he could hardly have troubled himself to read over[2].

I am inclined to believe, as will later appear, that Shakespeare may have fallen in love with, and lingered over, act 4; but it is the pulse of the spirit, not the ticking of the clock, which is in question. In other words, the tragedy of King Richard the Second has all the air of being composed in a single mood, as Shakespeare's 'mind and hand went together' in the easy production of a task conceived in delight and untroubled in gestation.

There are critics who dislike *Richard II*. Dr Johnson, for example, is strangely cold about this gorgeous dramatic essay on the Divine Right of kings; and can discover little in it either 'to affect the passions or enlarge the understanding.' But whether one likes or dislikes the play, none can deny that Shakespeare himself took keen pleasure in the writing of it. And because of the author's enjoyment, and of what Pater calls the drama's 'simple continuity,' *Richard II* possesses a unity of tone

[1] *Appreciations* (3rd ed.), pp. 202–3.
[2] *King Richard II: a new quarto*, pp. 97–8.

and feeling greater than that attained in many of his greater plays, a unity found, I think, to the same degree elsewhere only in *Twelfth Night*, *Antony and Cleopatra* and *The Tempest*, plays which were likewise, one may conjecture, composed without interruption and under a single impulse of passionate inspiration. The absence of comic elements suggests that this unity was, in part at least, deliberate. In *Richard II* Shakespeare, as most critics believe, is pitting himself against the author of *Edward II*. It may, therefore, be not entirely fortuitous that here and in *Richard III* alone he eschews 'such conceits as clownage keeps in pay.'

Pater is no less suggestive on the ritualistic character of *Richard II* than he is on its unity of tone; and what he wrote in 1889 under this head is the more interesting that it was inspired by memories of a production in the late 'fifties by Charles Kean, in whose hands, he tells us, 'the play became like an exquisite performance on the violin.' Perhaps Kean's elaborate stage-realism and his striving after archaeological accuracy, which gave, in Pater's enthusiastic words, not only 'the very person of the king, based on the stately old portrait in Westminster Abbey,' but also 'a scenic reproduction, for once really agreeable, of the London of Chaucer,' would have seemed to us, with our more enlightened notions of the staging of Shakespeare, both tiresome and distracting[1]. But what caught Pater's imagination above all, and held it for thirty years, was the actor's interpretation of the part of Richard himself, more particularly in the parliament scene, and that must have come near to Shakespeare's own intention. The remarkable passage that follows, for example, may be attributed as much to Kean as to Pater.

In the Roman Pontifical, of which the order of Coronation is really a part, there is no form for the inverse process,

[1] Kean also took great liberties with the text, v. p. lxxxvii.

no rite of 'degradation,' such as that by which an offending priest or bishop may be deprived, if not of the essential quality of 'orders,' yet, one by one, of its outward dignities. It is as if Shakespeare had had in mind some such inverted rite, like those old ecclesiastical or military ones, by which human hardness, or human justice, adds the last touch of unkindness to the execution of its sentences, in the scene where Richard 'deposes' himself, as in some long, agonising ceremony, reflectively drawn out, with an extraordinary refinement of intelligence and variety of piteous appeal, but also with a felicity of poetic invention, which puts these pages into a very select class, with the finest 'vermeil and ivory' work of Chatterton or Keats[1].

This goes to the heart of the play, since it reveals a sacramental quality in the agony and death of the sacrificial victim, as it were of the god slain upon the altar, which we to-day can only begin to understand by reading a book like *The Golden Bough*.

### (*c*) *The significance of Richard's fall to the contemporaries of Shakespeare*

To the contemporaries of Shakespeare Richard was no ordinary man; and it is by failing to realize this that modern criticism, despite all its penetrating, and for the most part just, analysis of his human qualities, leaves every thoughtful reader and spectator of the drama baffled and dissatisfied. Richard was a king, and a good deal more. First of all he stood in the eyes of the later middle ages as the type and exemplar of royal martyrdom; of a king not slain in battle, not defeated and killed by a foreign adversary, not even deposed owing to weakness or tyranny in favour of his heir, but thrust from the throne in his may of youth by a mere usurper, under colour of a process at law utterly illegal, and then foully murdered. One may catch something of this aspect of his tragedy by turning to the 'form of prayer with fast-

1 *Appreciations*, p. 198.

ing,' for 'the day of the martyrdom of the Blessed King Charles I,' which was printed in the Book of Common Prayer until half-way through the nineteenth century[1], or by remembering the passionate devotion which the memory of Mary Queen of Scots inspired until an even later date. Richard combined the personal attractiveness of Mary with the wrongs of Charles, and moreover belonged to a period when men were far more swayed by the glamour of kingship and the tendency to canonize those they admired, than they have been during the last three centuries. Not that the admiration was universal; there were, as ever in such cases, two parties, the idolaters and the defamers. As long as the house of Lancaster, which triumphed in Richard's fall, ruled the country, it was of course treasonable for Englishmen to take his side. But from the first on the continent, where thought was free, the reading public, already rejoicing in Boccaccio's most popular book, *De Casibus Illustrium Virorum* (1360–74), which Shakespeare's Richard seems to be describing in the well-known lines:

> For God's sake let us sit upon the ground,
> And tell sad stories of the death of kings—
> How some have been deposed, some slain in war,
> Some haunted by the ghosts they have deposed,
> Some poisoned by their wives, some sleeping killed;
> All murdered,

had found in Richard's own 'casus' a peculiar appeal; so much so indeed that no fewer than three different

[1] Our latter-day 'royalist,' Mr T. S. Eliot, is still found referring to the execution of Charles I as 'the Martyrdom' sans phrase, in a recent publication; v. *Seventeenth Century Studies in honour of Sir Herbert Grierson*, p. 242. On the other hand a Catholic historian like Mr Hilaire Belloc, who speaks of Richard II as the 'sacramental man,' and of his dethroning as 'sacrilege,' shows that the medieval conception of Richard is not yet extinct (v. *History of England*, iii. 90–1).

contemporary accounts of it, favourable to Richard, have come down to us in the French tongue, while yet a fourth of similar sympathies, though in Latin not French, reposes in the library of Gray's Inn[1]. One of the French chronicles exists in some twenty or more MS. copies to be found in various continental libraries.

This widespread interest may, it is suggested, have been due in part to anti-English feeling among French patriots during the latter half of the Hundred Years' War[2]. But that the 'sad story' was also valued for its own sake is proved by the persistence of its popularity, which, when the accession of the Tudors healed the dynastic breach, found voice in England itself, so that the tragedy of Richard appears, not it is true very sympathetically told[3], in *The Mirror for Magistrates*, 1559–63. This well-known book, an immense corpus of such 'casus,' was a continuation and enlargement of Lydgate's *Falls of Princes*, which in turn was itself an adaptation of Boccaccio's original collection. Moreover, the most remarkable fact about the four original pro-Richard chronicles is that they already, as we shall see later, give utterance to that mystical conception of the martyred king which we find in Shakespeare, and compare his betrayal with that of Christ and his enemies with Pilate and Judas, much as the play itself does. Nor is it certain that they are not in this nearer the truth than the orthodox modern historian who has on the whole accepted the Lancastrian version of the revolution of 1399. The

[1] Reprinted with a valuable introduction by M. V. Clarke and V. H. Galbraith as 'The Deposition of Richard II' (*Rylands Library Bulletin*, vol. xiv, Jan. 1930).

[2] P. viii of Preface to *Chronicque de la Traïson et Mort de Richart Deux roy Dengleterre* (ed. by B. Williams, 1846); v. below.

[3] 'I would (quoth one of the cumpany),' runs the prose preface, 'gladly say sumwhat for King Richard. But his personage is so sore intangled as I thinke fewe benefices be at this day' (p. 110, ed. L. B. Campbell, 1938).

official story, embodied in the Parliament Roll, was being denounced by a scholar in 1824 as 'a gross fabrication of Henry IV for purposes of state[1]'; and a recent study of the evidence by Professor Galbraith and Miss Clarke comes to very much the same conclusion[2].

Yet the fall of Richard fascinated the late medieval and Elizabethan world as much by its magnitude and its unaccountableness as by its pathos and the sacrilege that brought it to pass.

> Down, down I come, like glist'ring Phaethon:
> Wanting the manage of unruly jades,

are words which Shakespeare places in his mouth, and some critics have taken them as the key-note of the play. But though in their sun-imagery they express the splendour of the catastrophe, like that of Lucifer from the empyrean, they do not touch its mystery, of which all at that period who studied the young king's career were conscious, and which is one of the main impressions that Shakespeare's play still leaves upon our minds. This mystery was closely associated with the supposed workings of Fortune, a Roman deity which continued to exercise under Providence a potent influence over men's thought during the middle ages, and was conceived of by Elizabethan England far more concretely than by the England of our own day, despite its daily race-meetings, its football pools and its almost universal habit of gambling. The symbol and attribute of Fortune was, of course, her wheel, which is hardly ever absent from any of the countless pictures and references to her in medieval art and literature. Shakespeare makes no mention of the wheel in *Richard II*, though he employs the less familiar figure of Fortune's buckets in the deposition scene[3].

[1] v. *Archaeologia*, xx. 138.
[2] v. note 1, p. xviii.
[3] Cf. 4. 1. 184–9 and note.

His reticence, however, is part of his subtlety. For the wheel is constantly in his mind throughout the play. Indeed, it determines the play's shape and structure, which gives us a complete inversion[1]. The first act begins immediately after the death of the Duke of Gloucester, when, as Froissart notes, Richard was 'hygh uppon the whele[2],' and exhibiting all the hybris and tyranny expected of persons in that position, while, at the same time, his opponent, Bolingbroke, is shown at the lowest point of his fortune, at the bottom. But from the beginning of act 2 the wheel begins to turn mysteriously of itself, or rather by the action of Fortune. The will of the King seems paralysed; he becomes an almost passive agent. Bolingbroke acts, and acts forcibly; yet he too appears to be borne upward by a power beyond his volition.

This last is an important point, since it rules out those indications of deep design which some subtle critics, following Coleridge, think they discover in the character of the usurper from the very beginning, but which I feel sure were not intended by Shakespeare. Circumstance drives Bolingbroke on from point to point: he takes what Fortune and Richard throw in his path. The attitude of the nobles towards him in 2. 3 shows that they regard him as a claimant to the throne, and by that time the larger horizon has begun to open out before him. But this is quite a different thing from entertaining deep designs. Bolingbroke is an opportunist, not a schemer[3].

[1] Cf. *The Goddess Fortuna in Medieval Literature*, by H. R. Patch, 1927, and *The Medieval Heritage of Elizabethan Tragedy*, by W. Farnham, 1936, pp. 415–18.

[2] Berners' *Froissart*, vi. 307 (Tudor Translations).

[3] The passage depicting Bolingbroke as a deep politician occurs in Coleridge's 1818 notes. In the lectures of 1811–12 he took a different view. 'In Bolingbroke,' he then declared, 'we find a man who in the outset has been sorely injured: then, we see him encouraged by the grievances of his country, and by the strange mismanagement of the government, yet

And when, the hand of Death upon him, he looks back over the events that had led to his accession, and solemnly declares:

> Though then, God knows, I had no such intent,
> But that necessity so bowed the state
> That I and greatness were compelled to kiss[1],

the deep note of contrition proves the sincerity of the words. In fact Shakespeare followed Daniel, who himself accepted the judgment of the historians of his time upon this matter. As we shall see, Daniel considered that Bolingbroke

> Was with occasion thrust into the crime,

for which Fortune was more responsible than the criminal, while the relations between the two cousins throughout the play are already defined, as a recent scholar has noted, in the following passage from Holinshed, which is itself borrowed from Hall[2]:

> This suerlie is a verie notable example, and not vnwoorthie of all princes to be well weied, and diligentlie marked, that this Henrie duke of Lancaster should be thus called to the kingdome, and haue the helpe and assistance (almost) of all the whole realme, which perchance neuer thereof thought or yet dreamed; and that king Richard should thus be left desolate, void, and in despaire of all hope and comfort, in whom if there were anie offense, it ought rather to be imputed to the frailtie of wanton youth, than to the malice of his hart: but such is the deceiuable iudgement of man, which not regarding things present with due consideration,

at the same time scarcely daring to look at his own views, or to acknowledge them as designs. He comes home under the pretence of claiming his dukedom, and he professes that to be his object almost to the last; but, at the last, he avows his purpose to its full extent, of which he was himself unconscious in the earlier stages' (T. M. Raysor, *Coleridge's Shakespearean Criticism*, ii. 188–9). Cf. below note 1. 1. 30–3.

[1] 2 *Henry IV*, 3. 1. 72–4.
[2] Farnham, *op. cit.*

thinketh euer that things to come shall haue good successe, with a pleasant & delitefull end. But in this deiecting of the one, & aduancing of the other, the prouidence of God is to be respected, & his secret will to be woondered at[1].

The second great attraction, then, of the story of Richard of Bordeaux and Henry, Duke of Lancaster, for the men of the fifteenth and sixteenth centuries, was that it afforded, in its spectacle of the 'dejecting of the one and advancing of the other,' a perfect example of the mysterious action of Fortune, working of course under the inscrutable 'providence of God,' according to the quasi-mechanical symbolism under which they conceived that action. And this in turn constituted one of the main appeals of *Richard II* for the spectators who first witnessed it. For, though the operations of Fortune were most evident and potent in the lives of the great, everything human was subject to them. It is a point which did not escape Pater, who has seen so much in this play. 'His grief,' he writes of Richard, 'becomes nothing less than a central expression of all that in the revolutions of Fortune's wheel goes *down* in the world[2].' Shakespeare's play was a mirror, not only for magistrates, but for every son of woman; and when on Shakespeare's stage the 'dejected' king gazed into the glass—incomparable symbol for that age!—what he saw there was the brittleness both of his own glory and of all earthly happiness.

In the third place, the reign of Richard II possessed a peculiar significance in the history of England, as the Elizabethans understood that history. In itself, and for the two protagonists who brought it to an end, a striking example of a turn of Fortune's wheel, it marked the beginning of a much greater revolution in the story of the nation's fortunes. Shakespeare and his contem-

[1] Holinshed, *Chronicles*, ed. 1587, vol. iii. p. 499/2/50.
[2] *Appreciations*, p. 199.

poraries, rejoicing in the Tudor peace and looking back with horror to the period of civil strife, known as the Wars of the Roses, which preceded the accession of Henry VII, were haunted by fears of a return of such anarchy, and found its origin in the events of the last few years of Richard II's reign. And rightly so; for the deposition and murder of Richard not only shocked the conscience of Christendom, they struck at the legal basis of the monarchical, that is to say the whole constitutional, system of England. As Professor Galbraith puts it, 'The procedure of deposition as well as the act itself was a cause of the "disorder, horror, fear, and mutiny" of the fifteenth century[1].'

In *King John* Shakespeare had dealt, for the one and only time, with the question of the relations between this country and the Papacy, which was one of the two main problems of Tudor England. In *Richard II*, which I think followed immediately after, he now handles the other and, in Tudor eyes, still more important problem, the problem of government, or rather of the Governor or Prince. Writing on 'the nature of Tudor despotism,' Neville Figgis, our chief authority on the history of the idea of kingship in England, remarks:

> The exaltation of the royal authority was due to the need of a strong government. The crime of the Lancastrian dynasty had been, not that it was capricious or self-seeking or oppressive, but that it was weak, that law and order were not maintained and private war was once again becoming prevalent. It is as 'saviours of society' that the Yorkists and afterwards the Tudors win their position. In the statutes of liveries and in the Star Chamber is to be found the *raison d'être* of Tudor despotism. Government must be effective, private oppression must be punished, great offenders must be forced to submit to the authority of the Crown. That is the general sentiment. In a word, obedience must be enforced. The very causes, which drove men to support the Tudors at all, drove them also to insist on the

[1] Clarke and Galbraith, *op. cit.* p. 33.

paramount importance of obedience, and to proclaim the iniquity of rebellion[1].

In that age men could not think of government except as embodied in a single person. Indeed, only a very small proportion of the human race is capable of thinking otherwise to-day. Dangers for government and order might therefore arise from three causes: from weakness of character on the part of the monarch, from the accession of a monarch with a weak claim to the throne, and from the turbulence and ambition of the great nobles surrounding him, who might take advantage of either of the two weaknesses just mentioned or of some other occasion. Except for the abortive insurrection of Essex at the end of her reign, Elizabeth had little trouble from her nobles, who were for the most part 'new men' and close adherents of her dynasty from motives of self-interest. But the other two dangers made a special appeal to the fears of her subjects. Not only was her own title, as also her legitimacy, open to question, but being unmarried she had no heir, so that the succession was left at hazard. Writing on *The State of England, Anno Dom.* 1600[2], a contemporary lawyer, Sir Thomas Wilson, enumerates no fewer than twelve different 'competitors that gape for the death of that good old Princess the now Queen.' Moreover, though history in retrospect depicts her as a strong character and a great statesman, to her contemporaries, who judged her conduct from day to day and could neither see her reign as a whole nor appreciate to the full the difficulties that faced her, she probably appeared a weak and vacillating woman. In any event, as we shall see, there is plenty of evidence that her courtiers spoke of her not infrequently as 'Richard II' and that she herself was conscious of their doing so.

[1] *Divine Right of Kings* (2nd ed.), p. 88.

[2] Edited from the manuscripts among the State Papers in the Public Record Office by F. J. Fisher (*Camden Miscellany*, vol. xvi. p. 2).

All this being so, the Elizabethans felt much the same interest in the Lancastrian and Yorkist period, culminating in 'the glorious union of Henry VII,' as Englishmen of the eighteenth and the nineteenth centuries felt in the Civil Wars and the 'Glorious Revolution of 1688.' And just as the reign of Charles I marked the beginning of the one struggle, so that of Richard II marked the beginning of the other. The period 1398–1485 was, moreover, a self-contained one, was sufficiently remote to be safe to write about, and possessed something of an epical quality, inasmuch as it embraced the martyrdom of a king, the efforts of a usurper to establish his rule, the brilliant episode of Henry V's victories over the foreign foe, the downfall of government and the reign of chaos during the quarrels of the rival dynasties, and finally the restoration of order at the hands of a new dynasty, heir to the claims of both houses. It is not surprising, therefore, that no fewer than three elaborate accounts of this critical period have come down from the sixteenth century. The first is that earliest of Tudor histories, Hall's *Chronicle* (1548), which set the tone for all the histories that followed[1]; the second is the poem already spoken of, a poem in eight books, entitled *The Civil Wars between the two houses of Lancaster and York* (1595–1609) by Samuel Daniel; and the third is the dramatic cycle of Shakespeare's English Histories, composed during the years 1590–9.

What Englishmen, in the age of the Tudor peace, thought about the Wars of the Roses, and the usurpation of Henry Bolingbroke in connexion with them, finds eloquent, if quaint, expression on the very title-page of Hall's book, which runs:

*The vnion of the two noble and illustre famelies of*

[1] Cf. C. L. Kingsford, *Prejudice & Promise in XVth century England*, p. 3: 'Hall's presentment of past history appealed naturally to those who came after him, and was embedded firmly in the opinion of the time.'

*Lancastre & Yorke, beyng long in continuall discension for the croune of this noble realme, with all the actes done in both the tymes of the Princes, both of the one linage & of the other, beginnyng at the tyme of kyng Henry the fowerth, the first aucthor of this deuision, and so successiuely proceading to the reigne of the High and Prudent Prince Kyng Henry the Eight, the indubitate flower and very heire of both the saied linages.*

And I do not know of any better text to set in the forefront of this, the first (though not the first written) of Shakespeare's series of historical plays upon the same theme, than Hall's title and the following words with which his book opens, and which, as we shall find, were themselves inspired by a passage in Froissart:

What mischiefe hath insurged in realmes by intestine deuision, what depopulacion hath ensued in countries by ciuill discenciō, what detestable murder hath been cōmitted in citees by seperate faccions, and what calamitee hath ensued in famous regiōs by domestical discord & vnnaturall controuersy: Rome hath felt, Italy can testifie, Fraunce can bere witnes, Beame[1] can tell, Scotlande maie write, Denmarke can shewe, and especially this noble realme of Englande can apparantly declare and make demonstracion. For who abhorreth not to expresse the heynous factes comitted in Rome, by the ciuill war betwene Julius Cesar and hardy Pōpey by whose discorde the bright glory of the triūphant Rome was eclipsed & shadowed? Who can reherce what mischefes and what plages the pleasant countree of Italy hath tasted and suffered by the sedicious faccions of the Guelphes and Gebelynes? Who can reporte the misery that daiely hath ensued in Fraunce, by the discorde of the houses of Burgoyne and Orliens: Or in Scotland betwene the brother and brother, the vncle and the nephew? Who can curiously endite the manifolde battailles that were fought in the realme of Beame[1], betwene the catholikes and the pestiferous sectes of the Adamites and others? What damage discencion hath dooen in Germany and Denmarke, all christians at this daie can well declare.

[1] i.e. Bohemia.

And the Turke can bere good testimony, whiche by the discord of christen princes hath amplified greatly his seigniory and dominion. But what miserie, what murder, and what execrable plagues this famous region hath suffered by the deuision and discencion of the renoumed houses of Lancastre and Yorke, my witte cannot comprehende nor my toung declare nether yet my penne fully set furthe.

For what noble man liueth at this daie, or what gentleman of any auncient stocke or progeny is clere, whose linage hath not ben infested and plaged with this vnnaturall deuision. All the other discordes, sectes and faccions almoste liuely florishe and continue at this presente tyme, to the greate displesure and preiudice of all the christian publike welth. But the olde deuided controuersie betwene the fornamed families of Lācastre and Yorke, by the vnion of Matrimony celebrate and consummate betwene the high and mighty Prince Kyng Henry the seuenth and the lady Elizabeth his moste worthy Quene, the one beeyng indubitate heire of the hous of Lancastre, and the other of Yorke was suspended and appalled in the person of their moste noble, puissāt and mighty heire kyng Henry the eight, and by hym clerely buried and perpetually extinct. So that all men (more clerer then the sonne) maie apparantly perceiue, that as by discord greate thynges decaie and fall to ruine, so the same by concord be reuiued and erected. In likewise also all regions whiche by deuisiō and discencion be vexed, molested and troubled, bee by vnion and agrement releued pacified and enriched.

Exactly the same note is being struck by Daniel, sixty-three years later, in the Epistle Dedicatory to the third edition of his *Civil Wars* (1609), a passage of which is worth quoting for its emphasis upon succession in the direct line and the uncertainties of Elizabeth's reign as compared with that of James I:

And, whereas [Daniel writes] this Argument was long since vndertaken (in a time which was not so well secur'd of the future, as God be blessed now it is) with a purpose, to shewe the deformities of Ciuile Dissension, and the miserable euents of Rebellions, Conspiracies and bloudy Reuengements, which followed (as in a circle) vpon that breach of the due course of Succession, by the Vsurpation of *Hen.* 4; and thereby to make the blessings of Peace, and the happinesse of an established Gouernment (in a direct Line) the better to appeare: I trust I shall doo a gratefull worke to my Countrie, to continue the same, vnto the glorious Vnion of *Hen.* 7: from whence is descended our present Happinesse.

Daniel never completed his poem. Neither did Shakespeare round off his cycle. Perhaps the idea of so doing did not come to the dramatist until his task was well under way. For the cycle, as everyone knows, is in two parts of four plays each, followed by a final play detached from the rest, viz. (*a*) *Richard II*, *Henry IV*, parts i and ii, *Henry V*, (*b*) *Henry VI*, parts i, ii and iii, *Richard III*, and (*c*) *Henry VIII*. The plays in the (*b*) section were undertaken first, but when those in (*a*) were written they were carefully linked on to the others, so as to compose a continuous series. *Henry VIII* was, however, clearly an afterthought, if it was not an old play refurbished for a particular occasion; and there is nothing to connect it with *Richard III*. Why did these two great literary undertakings remain unfinished? The death of Elizabeth provides at least one answer. With the peaceful accession of James I the problem of the succession was settled. A new dynasty was established upon the throne, a dynasty founded not upon civil war and the rise of a noble house, but upon legal right so strong that it was recognized in a foreign branch of the royal line. The address of the Translators to His Majesty which stands as preface to the Authorized Version of the Bible, 1611, has often been condemned for fulsomeness by modern writers. But the following passage from the opening paragraph shows that the gratitude they express to James for his mere existence was not all flattery:

For whereas it was the expectation of many, who wished not well vnto our Sion, that vpon the setting of that bright *Occidentall Starre* Queene Elizabeth of most happy memory, some thicke and palpable cloudes of darkenesse would so haue ouershadowed this land, that men should haue bene in doubt which way they were to walke, and that it should hardly be knowen, who was to direct the vnsetled State: the appearance of your Maiestie, as of the *Sunne* in his strength, instantly dispelled those supposed and surmised mists, and gaue vnto all that were well affected, exceeding cause of comfort; especially when we beheld the gouernment established in your Highnesse, and your hopefull Seed, by an vndoubted Title, and this also accompanied with Peace and tranquillitie, at home and abroad.

Whether Shakespeare wrote his hundred and seventh sonnet in relation to these events is disputed. But the four crucial lines

> The mortal moon hath her eclipse endured
> And the sad augurs mock their own presage;
> Incertainties now crown themselves assured
> And peace proclaims olives of endless age,

bear a striking similarity to the words and sentiments of the Translators. In any case, with the death of the last of the Tudors, the reign of Henry VII, which neither Daniel nor Shakespeare managed to deal with, though it represented the climax of their historical undertakings, lost its interest for a time[1]. And upon the accession of a family, 'of an undoubted title' crowned with 'olives of endless age,' the taste for poems and dramas on the troublous times of the fifteenth century disappeared with the political anxieties which had stimulated it. When Shakespeare desired to write history in future, he turned to Plutarch, where he found dimly reflected, as in some magic crystal, a new and hitherto hardly suspected political problem, which was after his death to bring civil strife back to England,

[1] Bacon's *Historie of the Reigne of King Henry the Seventh*, written in 1621, was the return by a ruined and disillusioned statesman to his Elizabethan student-projects; but it seems to have led to a revival of interest in Tudor (though not in Lancastrian) history.

Change the complexion of her maid-pale peace
To scarlet indignation and bedew
Her pasture's grass with faithful English blood.

I mean, of course, the conflict between the Crown and the Commons, the Governor and his people, an issue already felt in *Julius Caesar* and evident in *Coriolanus*.

## (*d*) *Richard II and Queen Elizabeth*

But while Elizabeth lived, the older anxieties governed men's thoughts and in their fears that her reign might be the prelude to yet another period of anarchy, they naturally bent eagerly enquiring eyes upon the events of the reign of Richard II which had led up to the earlier period of trouble and particularly upon the actions of the usurper Henry IV, who was, as Hall taught them, 'the first aucthor of this deuision.'

There are [writes Sir Edmund Chambers] many indications of an analogy present to the Elizabethan political imagination between the reign of Richard II and that of Elizabeth herself. A letter of Sir Francis Knollys on 9 January 1578 excuses himself for giving unwelcome counsel to the queen. He will not 'play the partes of King Richard the Second's men'; will not be a courtly and unstatesmanlike flatterer. Clearly the phrase was familiar. Henry Lord Hunsdon similarly wrote at some date before 1588, 'I never was one of Richard II's men.' More cryptic is a letter from Raleigh to Robert Cecil on 6 July 1597, 'I acquaynted my L: generall [Essex] with your letter to mee & your kynd acceptance of your enterteynemente, hee was also wonderfull merry att y^e consait of Richard the 2. I hope it shall never alter, & whereof I shalbe most gladd of as the trew way to all our good, quiett & advancement, and most of all for her sake whose affaires shall therby fynd better progression.' All these allusions are of course in perfect loyalty, the utterances of devoted, if critical, officials[1].

[1] *William Shakespeare*, i. 353.

Others, however, might employ the analogy for different ends. *Thomas of Woodstock*, the only other extant Elizabethan play on the subject[1], is patently unsympathetic to Richard, its theme being the glorification of his uncle the Duke of Gloucester, whose murder was the first link in the chain of events that led to the King's downfall. And that this play was not unconnected with contemporary politics may be surmised from the fact that the Earl of Essex traced his descent from the same duke, which remote alliance with the blood royal constituted his sole claim to the crown. Moreover, after the summer of 1597 (when for a brief space Essex, Raleigh and Cecil were in accord), as the Earl fell by degrees into disfavour and began to entertain seditious thoughts towards his royal mistress, he seems to have identified himself more and more in imagination with Bolingbroke, and to have contemplated with increasing equanimity the possibility of Elizabeth's deposition in his favour. In January, 1599, one John Hayward was foolish enough to publish a prose history entitled *The First Part of the Life and Raigne of King Henrie IIII* with an epistle dedicatory to Essex in which the Earl is described as 'magnus et presenti iudicio et futuri temporis expectatione'; words that suggest an heir to the throne at the least. Apart from this the book seems innocent enough to the modern eye; but it was considered seditious by the authorities, and suppressed.

The most remarkable of all occurrences, however, connecting the fortunes of Elizabeth and Essex with those of Richard and his rival, was the performance at the Globe theatre, by the express wish of the Earl's supporters, who added an honorarium to their other per-

[1] *Jack Straw* (1593) deals with the Peasants' Revolt, 1381, and has nothing to do with the Deposition. The entry in Simon Forman's *Booke* concerning a *Richard II*, seen in 1611, does not describe this play. For the authenticity of the *Booke* see *R.E.S.* July 1947.

suasions, of a play *Richard II* generally assumed to be Shakespeare's, on the eve of the attempted rebellion, which took place on 8 February 1601, and came, as all men know, utterly to grief. The transaction at the Globe was discussed at length in the trial that followed; but Shakespeare was not among the Globe players brought to book, and there is no evidence that he and his company suffered in any way for their part therein. On the contrary, they are found playing at Court before the Queen on the day preceding Essex's execution. Anyone who knew the play, as Cecil did, would have been able to acquit its author of treasonable intent. Nevertheless, the Queen herself appears to have nourished a grudge against it. At least that seems the natural deduction from the famous story told by William Lambarde, keeper of the Tower records. While he was visiting her at Greenwich on 4 August 1601, and presenting her

with his Pandecta of all her rolls, bundells, membranes, and parcells that be reposed in her Majestie's Tower at London ...her Majestie fell upon the reign of King Richard II, saying, 'I am Richard II, know ye not that?'

*W. L.* Such a wicked imagination was determined and attempted by a most unkind Gent. the most adorned creature that ever your Majestie made.

*Her Majestie.* He that will forget God, will also forget his benefactors; this tragedy was played 40$^{tie}$ times in open streets and houses[1].

Unhappily no theatrical records of Shakespeare's company have come down to us; but from Henslowe's *Diary* it appears that the longest run for a play belonging to their rivals, the Admiral's Servants, was thirty-one performances spread over two and a half years[2]. Queen Elizabeth, therefore, in mentioning the forty performances of *Richard II*, was emphasizing something quite out of the common. She refers, we must suppose, not to

1 Chambers, *William Shakespeare*, ii. 326–7.
2 Chambers, *Elizabethan Stage*, ii. 148.

the revival in 1601, which was for one occasion only (and when, as the players averred to those who urged them to act it, the drama was so 'stale' that 'they should get nothing by playing' it[1]), but to the original performances in 1595–6, at which time, it was asserted in official notes concerning Essex drawn up in 1600, 'the Erle himself' was 'often present at the playing thereof,... with great applause giving countenance and lyking to the same[2].'

It is to be presumed also that the deposition scene, which was not printed until after Elizabeth's death, had been acted on all these occasions. As Sir Edmund Chambers remarks, it 'was evidently given at the 1601 performance'; and I agree with him that 'it was probably given in 1595 also.[3]' Certainly it is unlikely that Sir Edward Hoby would have offered a maimed and deformed play when he desired 'K. Richard' to 'present himselfe to' the view of Sir Robert Cecil[4]. Furthermore, had the scene been forbidden by the Censor, the players could hardly have acted it with impunity, as they appear to have done, in 1601. Clearly, the whole play, as we now have it, received the Censor's endorsement in 1595—as why should it not, at a time before suspicions had begun to attach themselves to the Earl of Essex and while he yet stood high in the Queen's favour?—and was acted from the original 'allowed book' at the revival six years later. Not that the deposition scene contained anything in the least seditious; on the contrary, its whole tenour might seem to appeal for the sympathy of the audience on behalf of the distressed King. And I believe this obvious fact may have stood the Chamberlain's Servants in good stead during the trial of Essex. Yet, what in normal times would seem quite innocuous might take on a dangerous complexion when treason was

1 *William Shakespeare*, ii. 326.

2 *Ibid.* i. 354, ii. 323.

3 *Ibid.* i. 355.

4 v. above, p. viii.

abroad. That Shakespeare's *Richard II* exhibited the spectacle of a monarch being actually dethroned, and that monarch popularly regarded as the prototype of the Queen, was enough to render it 'good propaganda,' as the modern political jargon goes, in the eyes of the hot-heads of Essex's party, who would remember perhaps the private comments by their leader upon it after seeing it in 1595. And that the same spectacle had been cut out by the Censor of books, who was a different functionary from the Censor of plays, when the drama came to be printed in the autumn of 1597, is, perhaps, an indication that by that date the authorities were beginning to grow nervous about the intentions of the headstrong Earl, and more conscious of the analogy between Richard and Elizabeth[1]. Or may it have been decided that what was safe enough to perform in loyal and Protestant London might prove too exciting for heady wits to read at the universities or in the Catholic north?

The foregoing paragraphs are offered as an explanation of a situation which has hitherto baffled enquirers by presenting a series of apparently irreconcilable contradictions. How came a play which is patently loyalist in tone, if critical of Richard's actions, to be used for seditious ends? Why was a scene, allowed by one censor, considered dangerous by another? How was it that the Chamberlain's men, having enacted a play at the request of conspirators and for seditious purposes, escaped scot-free from the vengeance of the authorities? The probability that *Richard II* was well known to these authorities, and particularly to Cecil, in 1595, and known to have had nothing whatever to do with the disaffection of Essex, taken together with the progressive deterioration of the relations between Essex and Elizabeth during the years 1597–1601, is sufficient, I think, to account for all the circumstances.

[1] v. above, p. xxx.

### (*e*) *Richard and Bolingbroke*

Whatever, then, Shakespeare's personal attitude towards Essex may have been, the association of his *Richard II* with the Earl's schemes was an accidental one, and has no relevance either to the purpose of the dramatist or to our understanding of the play. The play is, nevertheless, steeped in Elizabethan political notions, and unless we grasp them we are likely to miss much that the author intended us to perceive. Not that he was attempting anything in the nature of a political argument. On the contrary, the political situation he dealt with was merely the material for drama. He takes sides neither with Richard nor with Bolingbroke; he exhibits without concealment the weakness of the King's character, but he spares no pains to evoke our whole-hearted pity for him in his fall. Indeed, it is partly because it succeeds in holding the balance so even that *Richard II* is a favourite play with historians. It develops the political issue in all its complexity, and leaves judgment upon it to the spectator. Shakespeare's only prejudices are a patriotic assertion of the paramount interests of England above those of king or subject, an assertion which, following a hint in Froissart, he places upon the lips of the dying John of Gaunt, and a quasi-religious belief in the sanctity of an anointed monarch; and it is part of his dramatic setting that these two prejudices or ideals are irreconcilable under the historical circumstances with which the play deals.

Another reason why the modern historian tends to delight in *Richard II* is that, unlike most of Shakespeare's other chronicle-plays, the events it relates are with minor exceptions regarded as historically correct. Thus we have our greatest imagination at work, in the disinterested spirit of true art, upon a series of facts, admirably adapted for dramatic treatment, which are still for the most part attested by modern history. And how closely Shakespeare's diagnosis of Richard's character tallies with that of a typical historian of our time may be seen from the following extract from Sir Charles Oman's *Political History of England*, 1377–1485:

> Richard's temper on any given occasion was incalculable. Energy and apathy, over-confidence and abject depression came to him at the inappropriate moments....He was a creature of moods, and his moods always visited him at the wrong time. If he had not been thoughtless, arrogant, and overbearing in 1398, he might have reigned for many a year. If he had shown common resolution in 1399, he might have made a fair fight for his crown: it was by deserting his army at Milford that he ruined himself. Later events showed that he possessed many friends, and that they would have defended him if he had given them the chance. It was not the deaths of Gloucester and Arundel that doomed him to destruction, but his vain boasting, his petty interferences with the liberties of his subjects, his fits of passion, his senseless acts of injustice to men of minor importance....Yet few tyrants have shed so little blood—if few have made so many foolish boasts concerning their prerogative. Richard cannot be called cruel, nor was he a notorious evil liver, nor a thriftless weakling. Nevertheless he fooled away the crown which kings intellectually, as well as morally, his inferiors preserved to their death-day.... No sovereign was ever more entirely the author of his own destruction[1].

There, except for his poetry—a large exception—and for other slighter variations and small differences of emphasis, stands Shakespeare's Richard as Coleridge saw him.

And yet, if we follow Coleridge and most modern critics in isolating the figure of Richard from the dramatic composition of which it is only a part, and ignoring the political prepossessions of the audience for whom the play was written, we miss much, perhaps most, that Shakespeare intended. For his Richard, as

[1] *Political History of England*, 1377–1485, pp. 150–1.

often happens with his characters for one reason or another, is to be viewed on a double plane of vision: at once realistically as a man, and symbolically as the royal martyr whose blood, spilt by the usurper, cries out for the vengeance which tears England asunder for two generations[1]. Looked at merely from within the framework of the play of which he is the central figure, he seems the rather contemptible person that Coleridge has depicted; seen in the secular perspective of the whole cycle, his personal failings, the *ἁμαρτία* of his peculiar tragedy, become the occasion of something much larger than himself, the deposition and death of the Lord's anointed. For that break in the lineal succession of God's deputies-elect meant the beginning of political chaos.

> Take but degree away, untune that string,
> And hark what discord follows!

is the moral of Shakespeare's series of English chronicles as of everything else he wrote that touches political issues.

And what is true of Richard is true also of the lesser characters in the play. The prophetic voice of Gaunt, for example, pronounces judgment not only upon the spendthrift King, whose deposition it foretells[2], but also by implication upon Bolingbroke, the son who lifts

> An angry arm against God's minister[3],

and becomes the sacrilegious instrument of his deposition. As I have said above, Bolingbroke is not rightly understood, until he is regarded as in part at least the puppet of Fortune. And, successful as he is in *Richard II*, we feel even here that he has been caught up into the tragic net by usurpation, so that it is with no surprise we find him at the beginning of the sequel not only renewing his vow to go on a crusade in expiation of his guilt,

[1] For the historical or legendary ingredients from which Shakespeare's Richard was composed v. below, pp. lviii–lix.
[2] 2. 1. 108. [3] 1. 2. 40–1.

but pronouncing himself 'shaken' and 'wan with care.' Indeed, the whole play is as full of foreboding as it is of patriotic sentiment. Civil war is already implicit in the strife between Bolingbroke and Mowbray, with which it opens, and in the wrangling of the nobles before Richard's deposition, while it is explicit in the prophecy of the Bishop of Carlisle (4. 1. 129–49) and in the scarcely less significant words of Richard to Northumberland at 5. 1. 55–68. Thus when Richard's tragedy is ended, we are left with the feeling that England's has only just begun.

Yet the foreboding has almost entirely evaporated in the Histories that immediately follow. When Shakespeare came to give us the *Henry IV* we know, his mood had changed. In 1595 he had evidently no inkling that Sir John Falstaff was waiting for him round the corner.

## II. The Sources of *Richard II*.

'This play,' declared Dr Johnson in 1765, 'is extracted from the Chronicle of Holingshead, in which many passages may be found which Shakespeare has, with very little alteration, transplanted into his scenes; particularly a speech of the bishop of Carlisle in defence of King Richard's unalienable right, and immunity from human jurisdiction.' The same view, rather less absolutely expressed, is still current, and was endorsed in 1930 by Sir Edmund Chambers, who writes in his *William Shakespeare: a study of facts and problems*[1]:

> The main source of *Richard II* was the *Chronicle* of Holinshed, in the second edition of 1587, since 2. 4. 8 uses a passage not in that of 1577[2]. For a few historical points

[1] i. 356.

[2] This point was first made by Clark and Wright in 1868 (v. p. v, Clarendon Press ed. and cf. note 2. 4 *Material* below). They also suggest that 'the committal of the Bishop of Carlisle to the custody of the Abbot of Westminster'

other chroniclers may have been drawn upon. Two features not in Holinshed, the introduction of Queen Isabel, and the attribution of a soliloquy to Richard just before his murder, are common to *Richard II* and the first edition of Daniel's poem [*The Civil Wars*, 1595], but the treatment, both of these topics and of the rest of the action, is so different as to make an influence either way unlikely.

Most modern editors have adopted this standpoint without question, have printed the relevant portions of Holinshed in an appendix for the purpose of comparison, and have attributed all divergences therefrom in the play, apart from the trifling instances referred to in the note at the foot of these pages, to the invention of Shakespeare himself. Of the various chroniclers readily available at that time, viz. Stow, Hall, Grafton and Holinshed, the last named gives the fullest account of the period covered by the play, and there can be no doubt at all that for the historical facts and names with which it deals he was the principal source. It is also obvious that the events related by Holinshed could not be followed exactly, but would require modification and rearrangement in the interest of dramatic construction. Nevertheless, as is now clear, the germ of a good deal which has hitherto been set down to the poet's unaided invention can be traced to sources other than Holinshed, including certain important events of the play, the characters of Gaunt, Gloucester and the Queen, and a number of details, some of considerable dramatic significance, such as the complexion of Richard and the comparison between his betrayal and that of Christ. These sources had, as a matter of fact, been indicated in books and articles[1]

(4. 1. 152) must, and the 'little touch' about York's old age at the end of 5. 2 may, have been derived from other sources, the second probably from Hall.

[1] Introduction to *Richard II* by Charlotte Porter (William Shakespeare, First Folio Edition, Crowell, New York, 1903–10). The British Museum contains no copy of this, and I have been unable to see it, my information

which appeared in America and France before the publication by Sir Edmund Chambers of his *William Shakespeare* (1930) in this country, but of whose existence, as his bibliographies show, he was not aware[1].

The point of departure for the new investigations was a re-examination of the old and teasing question of the relations between the treatment of Richard's reign in the play and that in Daniel's *Civil Wars*, an important problem, since, as has been seen above, the dating of the play depends upon its settlement. The resemblance between the two, first noted by Charles Knight in his *Pictorial Edition of the Works of Shakespeare*, 1838–45[2], has been a source of debate ever since: some critics such as Delius, Grant White, Clark and Wright, and Gollancz suppose that Daniel borrowed from Shakespeare; others agree with Knight in ascribing the debt to Shakespeare; while, as we have just seen, Sir Edmund Chambers, with characteristic scepticism, follows Moorman[3] in refusing to admit influence either way, at least as far as the first edition of *The Civil Wars* is concerned.

That the last attitude, at any rate, is wrong may be easily proved. Relating the legendary incident at court

concerning it being derived from Dr R. M. Smith's book mentioned below.

Introduction to *Richard II* by Hardin Craig (Tudor Shakespeare, Macmillan, New York, 1912).

R. M. Smith, *Froissart and the English Chronicle Play* (Columbia Univ. Press, New York, 1915).

Paul Reyher, *Notes sur les sources de 'Richard II'* (Librairie Henri Didier, Paris, 1924).

[1] The oversight is the more remarkable that R. M. Smith's book had already been drawn upon by C. L. Kingsford for his interesting pioneer chapters on 'Fifteenth-century History in Shakespeare's Plays' in his *Prejudice & Promise in XVth Century England*, 1925.

[2] v. Histories, vol. i. pp. 82–3.

[3] F. W. Moorman, 'Shakespeare's History Plays and Daniel's Civil Wars' (*Shakespeare Jahrbuch*, 1904).

which led to the murder of Richard, Holinshed, copying Hall word for word, writes:

king Henrie, sitting on a daie at his table, sore sighing, said; Haue I no faithfull freend which will deliuer me of him, whose life will be my death, and whose death will be the preseruation of my life? This saieng was much noted of them which were present, and especiallie of one called sir Piers of Exton[1].

Shakespeare's brief scene at 5. 4 is clearly based on this, as the question beginning 'Have I no friend' shows. I quote it for comparison:

*Exton.* Didst thou not mark the king, what words he spake?
'Have I no friend will rid me of this living fear?'
Was it not so?
*Servant.* These were his very words.
*Exton.* 'Have I no friend?' quoth he—he spake it twice,
And urged it twice together, did he not?
*Servant.* He did.
*Exton.* And, speaking it, he wishtly looked on me,
As who should say, 'I would thou wert the man
That would divorce this terror from my heart,'
Meaning the king at Pomfret.... Come, let's go,
I am the king's friend, and will rid his foe.

And here is Daniel's 1595 version, far less dramatic than Shakespeare's, as befits a narrative poem, but closer to Shakespeare's than to Holinshed's. After speaking of Henry's determination to end the dangers to himself and to the commonwealth from the continued existence of the imprisoned Richard, he goes on (iii. 57):

He knew this time, and yet he would not seeme
Too quicke to wrath, as if affecting blood;
But yet complaines so farre, that men might deeme
He would twere done, and that he thought it good;
And wisht that some would so his life esteeme
As rid him of these feares wherein he stood:
And therewith eies a knight, that then was by,
Who soone could learne his lesson, by his eie.

[1] Holinshed, *Chronicles*, ed. 1587, vol. iii. p. 517/1/8.

The links here between poem and play are the verbal echoes 'rid,' 'fear' ('fears'), 'wishtly' ('wisht'), and—most striking of all—the fact that in both Henry catches the eye of Exton: links that are absent from the chroniclers and, as far as I can discover, from all other possible sources[1]. That Daniel borrowed from Shakespeare, or Shakespeare from Daniel (as well as from Holinshed), is indisputable.

But when we come to ask on which side the debt lay, we find ourselves entangled in yet another problem, a small bibliographical puzzle concerning the first edition of *The Civil Wars*. Once again let Sir Edmund Chambers voice the accepted view. Writing on the date of *Richard II*, he says:

> Some evidence for a date of production in 1595 is furnished by Samuel Daniel's *Civil Wars between Lancaster and York*. This was registered on 11 October 1594. Two editions appeared in 1595, and the second of these contains parallels to *Richard II*, which are not in the first. Obviously both might have preceded the play, but on the whole it seems more likely, especially on the analogy of Daniel's handling of his *Cleopatra*, that he made these alterations after seeing it[2].

Unhappily, Sir Edmund is here wrong in his facts. There are not two editions of *The Civil Wars* in 1595, but two issues with slight typographical differences, confined to the title-page[3], and though Daniel later revised

[1] R. M. Smith, *op. cit.* p. 153, observes the coincident use of 'rid' while Hardin Craig (note on 5. 4. 7) has drawn attention to all three links.

[2] *William Shakespeare*, i. 351.

[3] Mr Sellers of the British Museum (v. next footnote) has been good enough to compare the two issues of 1595 afresh, and informs me that 'there is not the minutest difference anywhere but on the title-page.' It is important to notice that though the 1595 edition contains 'Fowre Bookes,' Daniel rearranged these four into five books in the 1601 and subsequent editions, the original book 3 becoming books 3 and 4, so that book 4 had to be renumbered.

the poem more than once, his changes first appeared in the successive editions of 1601, 1609 and 1623[1]. Nor do the changes made in 1601 in any way indicate borrowings from the play. Some of those introduced in the far more drastic revision of 1609 do, however, suggest that Daniel had in the meantime been reading Shakespeare's play, perhaps led thereto by the fact that Shakespeare like himself had fallen into error over the age of Queen Isabel, an error he acknowledges in the preface to that edition. And here, as a matter of fact, we come upon the cause of all the misunderstanding. For Richard Grant White, in his 1859 edition of Shakespeare, cited two passages[2] written by Daniel (actually in 1609) as examples of Shakespeare's influence, erroneously assigned them to the alleged 'second edition of 1595[3],' concluded thereupon that the debt was all on Daniel's side, and so led critics astray for eighty years, including the highly sceptical and cautious Sir Edmund Chambers himself. But the great majority of the parallels between the play and the poem, and all the more important ones, are to be found in Daniel's original and genuine 1595 text; and as *Richard II* was not printed before 1597, it can hardly be doubted that Shakespeare was the debtor and that the play, as we have it, cannot have been written before the appearance of the poem at the end of 1594 or the beginning of 1595[4]. Daniel's *Civil Wars* is,

[1] Cf. H. Sellers, *Bibliography of Samuel Daniel* (Trans. of the Oxford Bibliographical Soc. vol. ii. pt. i) and Hardin Craig, *op. cit.*

[2] v. notes 1. 1. 9–14; 5. 6. 38–44.

[3] R. G. White, a careful writer, was himself, I suspect, first shown the wrong turning by Charles Knight who had quoted the first of his two selected examples as evidence that Shakespeare was borrowing from Daniel.

[4] The book was entered in the Stationers' Register on 11 Oct. 1594, and probably appeared soon afterwards. It was, and is, a practice of printers to give to books published towards the end of a year, the date of the year following, so

therefore, one of the sources to be reckoned with; and I have printed below (pp. 99–106) his exquisite description of the entry of captive Richard into London and of the interview that follows with his Queen, so that the reader may compare his version with Shakespeare's. When he does so, he will, I think, agree that here, at least, Shakespeare did not manage to wrest the laurel from his teacher[1].

Another source is Berners' translation of *The Chronycle of Syr John Froissart*. Shakespeare's debt to Daniel is established by Miss Porter and Professor Hardin Craig in the publications referred to above. A third American student, Dr R. M. Smith, while amplifying their evidence, claims that Daniel in his turn was indebted to Froissart. It remained for Professor Reyher of the University of Nancy to demonstrate that, quite apart from any indirect influence through Daniel, Froissart was an immediate source for *Richard II*. It would indeed be strange if the fourth and final book of that immortal work with its detailed and vivid account, from the hand of a contemporary and to some extent an eyewitness, of the stirring events of Richard's last years, an account moreover accessible in the stately English of

as to secure the appearance of freshness (cf. W. W. Greg, *Modern Language Review*, xxx. 81–2).

[1] It has been suggested to me that the parallels between *Richard II* and *The Civil Wars* might be explained on the theory that Daniel had seen the pre-Shakespearian *Richard II* on the stage, inasmuch as 5. 4, the scene I make use of as evidence above, occurs in the very act which I contend on pp. lxviii–lxxiv was most hastily revised by Shakespeare. But other passages, such as Carlisle's speech (v. note 4. 1. 121–9), would have served my purpose equally, while the fact that Shakespeare is sometimes only explicable by reference to Daniel (v. note 2. 1. 44–63) and that *King John* shows parallels with *The Civil Wars*, for which no analogies exist in *The Troublesome Reign* (v. note 2. 1. 61–3) persuades me that my line of communication is secure in this quarter.

Berners, had not been drawn upon for the play. And many have ventured to suggest a connexion[1]. Yet no one succeeded in proving it before 1924. Professor Reyher, however, goes even further than this. He suggests that the sources of *Richard II* include not only Holinshed, Hall, Daniel's *Civil Wars* and Berners' *Froissart*, but other French chroniclers contemporary with, or slightly later than, Froissart, and in particular the remarkable apologia for Richard entitled *La Chronicque de la Traïson et Mort de Richart Deux roy Dengleterre*[2], which I shall call *Traïson* for short, and

[1] Critics as long ago as Steevens found echoes of Froissart in the play (v. note 5. 5 *Material*). Mr Ivor John (Arden Shakespeare, ed. 1912, p. xi) notes that the deposition scene owes something apparently to Froissart, but as he states on the next page that 'the debt to any historical source other than Holinshed is trivial' he evidently attached small importance to it. Kingsford (*Prejudice & Promise*, p. 4) also writes 'Throughout the greater part of the play Shakespeare follows Holinshed very closely, though with some additions from Froissart, derived through the medium either of Berners's translation or of Samuel Daniel's *Civil Wars*.' But in this he is merely following R. M. Smith. Newbolt again (p. xxix) has 'little doubt that Shakespeare had some knowledge besides' Holinshed 'to draw upon—possibly something learned at school, or something gleaned from Froissart and other books.' But he does not particularize and shows no consciousness that Shakespeare's Gaunt is from the pages of Berners. Cf. however notes 4. 1 *Material*, 4. 1. 255–7.

[2] Ed. by B. Williams for the English Historical Society, 1846. Professor Reyher was not the first to draw attention to *Traïson* as a possible source for *Richard II*, since a writer in the *New Shakespeare Society's Transactions* for 1883 pointed out that the story of Richard's bastardy referred to at 4. 1. 255–7 (v. note) must have been derived therefrom and the point is repeated in Newbolt and Smith's note on the same passage. Newbolt (Introd. p. xlii) also refers to Créton as the ultimate source of the Pierce of Exton story, though supposing that it came to Shakespeare through Holinshed.

which exists in several versions, among them one called *La Chronicque de Richard II* (1377–99)[1], purporting to be written by one 'Jean Le Beau, formerly Canon of St Lambert of Liége.' I do not presume to discuss the relation of these to the metrical *Histoire du Roy d'Angleterre Richard II* by Jean Créton, who was 'present with Richard, whom he much admired, on his expedition to Ireland in 1399, and is a first-rate witness for the year of his fall[2].' But Professor Reyher thinks this too was consulted for *Richard II*, and I fancy that further study of it than I have time to give would show that it was drawn upon to an even larger extent than he allows. Both these works were known to Shakespeare's contemporaries. Daniel knew *Traïson*, and a copy of it, used by Holinshed and described by him as 'an old French pamphlet belonging to Iohn Stow[3],' is to be found among Stow's papers in the Harleian Library at the British Museum. Similarly a copy of Créton's *Histoire*, described by Holinshed as 'a French pamphlet which belongeth to Master Iohn Dee[4],' is preserved in the archbishop's library at Lambeth, bearing Dee's signature and the date 1575[5]. Yet, though these chronicles were widely read on the continent and exist in a large number of copies, being anti-Lancastrian in tendency they are

[1] Printed as Sup. ii in vol. xv of Buchon's *Collection des Chroniques Nationales Françaises*, 1826.

[2] Oman, *History of England*, 1377–1485, p. 499. Créton's *Histoire* is accessible in Buchon, vol. xiv, and is edited by John Webb with an introduction and an English translation in *Archaeologia*, vol. xx, 1824.

[3] Holinshed, *op. cit.* iii. 488/2 marg.

[4] *Ibid.* iii. 497/1 marg.

[5] The British Museum possesses another MS. of Créton's *Histoire* (Harleian MS. 1319), illustrated with beautiful illuminations, one of which is reproduced as frontispiece to the present edition. This is the text printed by Webb in *Archaeologia*, vol. xx.

naturally scarce in England[1]. This taint probably made the Tudor chroniclers somewhat suspicious of them; for, though they consulted them, they used them but sparingly[2].

The links which Professor Reyher notes between *Richard II* and *Traïson* are not at first sight overwhelming, and leave it open to question whether the coincidences might not be explained by reference to other sources (v. notes on 4. 1. 239–42, 256; 5. 2 *Material* below). Nevertheless, I think his claim is substantiated by further parallels, to be noted presently, which he has not himself observed. One of these, the manner of Gloucester's death, a point of which Shakespeare makes a good deal, proves in fact that the version actually used for the play was one represented by Jean Le Beau's *Chronique*, which though often following the former so closely as to be virtually a copy, departs from it in this and other particulars. Froissart, Holinshed, *Woodstock* and all the rest of the authorities, so far as I am aware, agree in attributing the duke's death to smothering by towels in a feather-bed. But Le Beau reads 'le roi envoya son oncle à Calais, et là fut décollé,' which appears in *Traïson* as 'le Roy enuoya son oncle a Calaiz et la le fist mourir[3].' But if I have still been able to glean a few ears of corn in Professor Reyher's field, the harvest is his; and I, together with all future editors of *Richard II*, rest deeply in his debt.

Finally, his researches have thrown fresh light upon the relations between Shakespeare's play and that remarkable drama on the fortunes of Richard's uncle,

[1] v. Williams, *op. cit.* pp. v–ix.

[2] Kingsford (*Prejudice & Promise*, pp. 4–5) observes, however, that Hall had drawn upon *Traïson*, which he speaks of as written by 'one who seemeth to have great knowledge of Richard's affairs.'

[3] v. note 1. 1. 101–3, Buchon, vol. xv. Sup. ii. p. 10, and *Traïson*, p. 9.

Thomas of Woodstock, Duke of Gloucester, which has come down to us in a playhouse manuscript without title, and, because the events it deals with immediately precede our play, has been called by some students 1 *Richard II*, though others name it *Thomas of Woodstock*. The latter title, shortened for convenience to *Woodstock*, seems to me the better, inasmuch as it begs no question as to the connexion between the two plays. *Woodstock*, one of the collection of fifteen playbooks preserved in the Egerton MS. 1994 at the British Museum[1], was printed with an introduction by Professor Wolfgang Keller in the *Shakespeare Jahrbuch* for 1899, and reproduced in typographical facsimile by the Malone Society in 1929, under the editorship of Miss Frijlinck, who contributes a lengthy introduction. The collection, of which it forms one item, was evidently a repertoire made, some suppose by the actor William Cartwright, about the middle of the seventeenth century. Most of the plays belonging to it are late, and Mr W. J. Lawrence argues that since *Woodstock* contains a marginal stage-direction (ll. 2093–4) 'fflorish Cornetts,' it cannot have been written earlier than 1619, at which date the use of such instruments became the fashion in the theatre[2]. The discovery, however, by Miss Frijlinck that the hand which wrote this direction is different from that of the main body of the manuscript, is evidently concerned with a revival of the play, and is identical with the one found in another playbook about 1600[3], casts doubts upon Mr Lawrence's facts, and in any case relieves us from the necessity of supposing that the manu-

[1] For a description of the collection and an essay on the play itself v. F. S. Boas, 'A Seventeenth Century Theatrical Repertoire' in *Shakespeare and the Universities*, 1923. The text of *Thomas of Woodstock* was first printed by Halliwell in 1870 [and was edited by A. P. Rossiter, 1946].

[2] *Shakespeare's Workshop*, p. 73.

[3] Malone Society Reprint, pp. xv, xvi.

script as a whole is late. Indeed, there can be little doubt that Professor Keller who fixed the first production as somewhere in the early 'nineties, between 2 *Henry VI* and *Richard II*, was correct. Miss Frijlinck sums the matter up thus:

The play belongs to the class of history plays which were in great vogue in the years following the defeat of the Armada, when there was an unusual public interest in the presentation of historical figures and subjects on the stage. It bears a very close relation to 1 and 2 *Henry VI* and in particular to *Edward II*. The author was a follower of Marlowe in his treatment and choice of plot, the conflict between the king and the nobles; on the one side a weak and frivolous king and his unworthy favourites, on the other the patriotic lords; this symmetrical grouping also marks *Woodstock* as an early play. There is a great similarity in the defiance of the nobles, even in the vocabulary (wanton king, base flatterers, minions, upstarts); there is the same complaint about the fantastic and costly dress of the favourites; there is another parallel in the preparation for the murder....As *Woodstock* belongs to this series of closely related plays it is possible that it was also one of the plays belonging to Pembroke's company of players; this would agree with the date of an early play between 1590 and 1593[1].

In view of the well-known resemblances between *Edward II* and *Richard II*, those noted by Miss Frijlinck between Marlowe's play and *Woodstock* are of great importance. Indeed, there can be little question that this turbulent drama by an unknown playwright was in some sense a link between the plays of his mighty rivals. And in the light of the numerous parallels between *Woodstock* and *Richard II* which Professor Reyher has added to those already cited by Professor Keller[2], it becomes even a question how far those between Shakespeare and Marlowe are due to immediate imitation by the former at all.

[1] Malone Society Reprint, pp. xxiv–xxv.
[2] *Op. cit.*

Sir Edmund Chambers observes that *Woodstock*, which he labels 1 *Richard II* in his *Elizabethan Stage*[1], 'might conceivably be a first part of Shakespeare's source, if he had one[2].' The difficulty with this suggestion, as Miss Frijlinck remarks, is that the two plays overlap and contradict each other to some extent. If *Richard II* were written as a sequel to *Woodstock*, or even if Shakespeare's play were based upon an older play written for this purpose, it is not easy to see how Greene who is slain and mourned at the end of part i can have reappeared alive and well at the beginning of part ii. In *Woodstock* again the Duchess of Gloucester appeals to Gaunt to avenge her husband, and he promises to do so; in *Richard II* she makes the same appeal and is refused. And there are other contradictions, such as the differing accounts of the manner of Gloucester's death, just noticed. Furthermore, *Richard II* is far more historically exact than *Woodstock*, whose author knows no chronicle but Holinshed's and pays scant respect to that. And yet there is no doubt at all that *Woodstock* was one of the major influences in the making of *Richard II*; it vies with that of Daniel's *Civil Wars* and even with that of the chroniclers referred to above.

Direct echoes, first observed by Keller, such as:

> & thoᵘ no king but landlord now become
> to this great state that terroʳd christendome.
>
> *Woodstock*, 2826–7.
>
> Landlord of England art thou now, not king.
>
> *Richard II*, 2. 1. 113.

both spoken by Gaunt to Richard; and:

> rent out oʳ kingdome like a pelting ffarme.
>
> *Woodstock*, 1888.
>
> Like to a tenement or pelting farm.
>
> *Richard II*, 2. 1. 60.

1 *Elizabethan Stage*, iv. 43.
2 *William Shakespeare*, i. 352.

and again:

> they would not taxe & pyll the commons soe.
>
> *Woodstock*, 466.
>
> The commons hath he pilled with grievous taxes.
>
> *Richard II*, 2. 1. 246.

and yet again:

> I haue a sad presage comes sodenly
> that I shall neuer see these brothers more
> on earth I feare, we neuer more shall meete.
>
> *Woodstock*, 1399–1401.
>
> Farewell—if heart's presages be not vain,
> We three here part, that ne'er shall meet again....
> Farewell at once, for once, for all, and ever.
>
> *Richard II*, 2. 2. 144–5, 150.

are only the most obvious of a large number of parallels, which exhibit the unconscious processes of memory rather than deliberate imitation. The man who drafted *Richard II* knew *Woodstock* well; had even perhaps played in it himself. Such knowledge is enough to explain all the resemblances, without positing any community of authorship. *Woodstock* is a source of *Richard II*, not part of an original play upon which it was based.

Such then were the principal sources from which the material for Shakespeare's history-play were derived: the chronicle of Holinshed, and to a lesser degree that of Hall, Berners' *Froissart*, *Traïson* or the *Chronique* of Le Beau, and probably Créton's poem, Daniel's *Civil Wars*, and the play of *Thomas of Woodstock*. Additional and more detailed evidence for these ascriptions will be found in the notes below[1]. Here, taking them each in turn, something may be said on what the play owes to them in the matter of character, plot-structure and general atmosphere.

Holinshed furnishes the plain hempen warp upon which the colourful historical tapestry we call *Richard II*

[1] v. especially the notes on '*Material*' at the head of the different scenes.

was woven; of that there can be no question. Most of the 'facts' and names come from him; he gives the fullest account of the great events in the opening scene at Windsor, in the lists at Coventry, and before Flint Castle; while he supplies much of the material which, re-assembled for dramatic ends, made up the culminating scene at Westminster. And though most of the characters, even that of Bolingbroke, turn blank faces towards us from his pages, he is clearly interested in that of Richard, concerning which he throws out many hints, not always consistent one with another, of which Shakespeare made good use. He relates, for instance, how at the parliament of 1397 Sir John Bushy, in addressing the King,

did not attribute to him titles of honour, due and accustomed, but inuented vnused termes and such strange names, as were rather agreeable to the diuine maiestie of God, than to any earthlie potentate. The prince being desirous inough of all honour, and more ambitious than was requisite, seemed to like well of his speech, and gaue good eare to his talke[1].

He tells us that after crushing his old enemies, banishing Warwick, executing Arundel and having Gloucester murdered at Calais:

he was in good hope, that he had rooted vp all plants of treason, and therefore cared lesse who might be his freend or his fo, than before he had doone, esteeming himselfe higher in degree than anie prince liuing, and so presumed further than euer his grandfather did, and tooke vpon him to beare the armes of saint Edward, ioining them vnto his owne armes. To conclude, whatsoeuer he then did, none durst speake a word contrarie therevnto[2].

He gives examples of his extravagance, of his 'insolent misgouernance and youthful outrage,' of his acts of tyranny, his licentiousness, his 'inordinate desires,' his

[1] Holinshed, *Chronicles*, ed. 1587, vol. iii. p. 490/2/58.
[2] *Ibid*. p. 492/2/64.

'lack of wit,' his 'evil gouernment' generally; and describes him as 'an vnaduised capteine, as with a leden sword would cut his owne throat[1].' This is Shakespeare's Richard at the opening of the play, the Richard who proclaims:

Not all the water in the rough rude sea
Can wash the balm off from an anointed king.
The breath of worldly men cannot depose
The deputy elected by the Lord,
For every man that Bolingbroke hath pressed
To lift shrewd steel against our golden crown,
God for his Richard hath in heavenly pay
A glorious angel; then, if angels fight,
Weak men must fall, for heaven still guards the right.

On the other hand, Holinshed speaks of his 'gentle nature,' of his 'utter despaire' and 'sorrowfullie lamenting his miserable state,' when the tide begins to flow against him, while I have already quoted[2] the passage in which he ascribes the King's downfall to the influence of fate rather than to his own fault. There is not much in Shakespeare's Richard which cannot be traced to such hints in Holinshed, though to do so is like reducing a gorgeous blossom to its elements through chemical analysis. But to appreciate the debt in full the whole of the reign should be read in the chronicle, and not just the story of the downfall, garnished with snippets from other portions, such as is furnished by most editors, and even in Boswell-Stone's otherwise useful compilation.

Holinshed draws so often, and generally almost verbatim, from his predecessor Hall, whose chronicle appeared in 1548, that there would be no need to believe the play dependent in any way upon the latter but for two scenes (5. 2; 5. 3) which relate the revelation of the conspiracy by Aumerle, and are shown by Reyher, following a clue first noticed by the Clarendon editors,

[1] *Ibid*. p. 496/1.
[2] v. pp. xxi–xxii.

to be based upon the earlier chronicler[1]. Once, however, the direct connexion with Hall is established, it is legitimate to notice other resemblances. Thus, while adopting Holinshed's account of the origin of the quarrel between Bolingbroke and Mowbray, the play follows Hall's reading of the characters of the two men rather than his successor's; in particular, scenes 1. 1 and 1. 3 probably owe not a little to Hall's reference to Mowbray as 'in deede bothe a depe dissimuler and a pleasaunte flaterer.' But the most striking parallel between Hall and the play, as already noticed, is the fact that both begin at the same point, viz. the quarrel just referred to, and that in a sense Hall furnished the frame and stretched the canvas for the whole Shakespearian cycle, *Richard II* to *Richard III*.

The *Froissart* of Lord Berners is a far more important source than Hall, and its influence is even more pervading than Reyher, who first directed proper attention to it, has realized. For example, the only satisfactory authority he can discover for the reasons which Richard gives for the banishment of Bolingbroke and Mowbray (1. 3. 123–53) is the Parliamentary Roll[2], which states precisely those reasons in the account it gives of the King's decision as approved by parliament. And he asks how Shakespeare can have come to a knowledge of these matters. The answer is: through Froissart, who furnishes a long and lively account of private deliberations between Richard and a few intimates on the subject of the quarrel of the two nobles, in which the sentence he later delivers is urged upon the King and the danger of civil war, unless he took such action, strongly emphasized[3]. Yet the remainder of the scene is drawn from Holinshed and owes

[1] notes 5. 2 *Material* (ii), 5. 3 *Material* (ii).
[2] *Rolls of Parliament* iii. 383.
[3] v. note 1. 3. 123–53 for the passage in question. Hardin Craig notes the passage in Berners but does not draw the deduction that he is a direct source for the play.

nothing to Froissart, who appears to have been unaware that the intending combatants came to the lists at all. And in this connexion an interesting little point may be made in passing. The speeches (1. 3. 124–53) in which Richard declares his sentence, and gives the reasons therefor, contain, twice over, the expression 'upon pain of life,' a formula not found elsewhere in Shakespeare, though he uses 'on pain of death' nine times, one of them occurring at line 43 of this very scene. It is not, I think, very uncommon, but I have not seen it in any of the sources for *Richard II* except Berners, who often employs it, though he does not have occasion to use it in the passage just referred to and though he sometimes also uses the more ordinary form of words. It may be coincidence, but it is surely a striking one that in the thirty lines based upon Froissart the very phraseology of his translator should be resorted to, and that when in another part of the scene the same notion is to be expressed it is given in Holinshed's words.

The most important contribution, however, which Froissart makes to the play is, as Reyher notes, in the character of John of Gaunt (so different from that of his perplexed and irresolute brother York[1]), and in his attitude to his nephew, the King. Even the famous death-bed scene, so often hailed as an instance of how Shakespeare's invention can, when he wills, soar clear of the sources on which his plays are grounded, is seen to be derived from Berners. In the chapter headed 'Howe the duke of Lancastre dyed' Froissart first tells of a message which came to Bolingbroke in exile in France, 'that the physi-

[1] v. note 2. 1. 1–4 on the contrast between the brothers and cf. notes 2. 1. 163, 212. Mr G. M. Young describes York (in a private letter) as 'the first civil servant in our literature, a man of one idea, that H.M. Government must be carried on. When he sees his way clear, he is active enough; but some superior authority is needed to make the way.'

cions and surgyons in Englande sayd surely, howe that the duke his father had on hym a paryllous sycknesse, whiche shulde be his dethe[1].' Here is the germ of Gaunt's melancholy prognostication at I. 3. 219–32, and the news of his sickness at I. 4. 54–64. Berners then continues:

So it fell that aboute the feest of Crystmasse, duke Johan of Lancastre, who lyved in great dyspleasure, what bycause the kynge had banysshed his sonne out of the realme for so litell a cause, and also bycause of the yvell governynge of the realme by his nephewe kynge Rycharde: for he sawe well that if he longe perceyvered and were suffred to contynewe, the realme was lykely to be utterly loste: with these ymagynacyons and other, the duke fell sycke, wheron he dyed, whose dethe was greatly sorowed of all his frendes and lovers. The kyng, by that he shewed, toke no great care for his dethe, but sone he was forgotten[2].

And the last sentence is amplified by another at the opening of the following chapter:

Tidynges of the duke of Lancasters dethe came into Fraunce, and kyng Rycharde of Englande in maner of joye wrote therof to the Frenche kyng, and nat to his cosyn therle of Derby[3].

Clearly, these passages provided suggestions for Richard's attitude on the news of Gaunt's sickness at the end of I. 4, and for Gaunt's attitude towards Richard in the death-bed scene.

We must look to Froissart also for the origin of the great speech beginning

Methinks I am a prophet new inspired,

and the speeches that follow to Richard himself, though we must look to an earlier chapter, the same in fact

[1] Berners' *Froissart*, ed. W. P. Ker (Tudor Translations), vi. 335.
[2] *Ibid.* pp. 335–6.
[3] *Ibid.* p. 337.

from which the terms of banishment were drawn. And a remarkable passage it is!

The duke of Lancastre was sore dyspleased in his mynde to se the kynge his nephewe mysse use hymselfe in dyvers thynges as he dyd. He consydred the tyme to come lyke a sage prince, and somtyme sayd to suche as he trusted best: Our nephue the kynge of Englande wyll shame all or he cease: he beleveth to lyghtly yvell counsayle who shall distroy hym; and symply, if he lyve longe, he wyll lese his realme, and that hath been goten with moche coste and travayle by our predecessours and by us; he suffreth to engendre in this realme bytwene the noble men hate and dyscorde, by whom he shulde be served and honoured, and this lande kepte and douted....The Frenchemen are right subtyle; for one myschiefe that falleth amonge us, they wolde it were ten, for otherwyse they canne nat recover their dommages, nor come to their ententes, but by our owne meanes and dyscorde bytwene ourselfe. And we se dayly that all realmes devyded are dystroyed; it hath been sene by the realme of Fraunce, Spayne, Naples...also it hath been sene by the countrey of Flaunders, howe by their owne meanes they are distroyed...in lykewyse amonge ourselfe, without God provyde for us, we shall dystroy our selfe; the apparaunce therof sheweth greatly[1].

'He considered the time to come like a sage prince'! This is a totally different Gaunt from the turbulent and self-seeking baron depicted by Holinshed and other chroniclers[2], indeed by the modern historian as well. But it is the Gaunt of Shakespeare. And though Shakespeare in Gaunt's dying words stresses not national division so much as the farming out of the realm, which he takes over from *Woodstock* almost word for word, as we have seen above[3], that is probably because he had

[1] *Ibid.* p. 311.

[2] But not by Créton, who describes Gaunt as one 'who all his life was gentle and courteous, nor would ever think or act disloyally' (Webb, 108/331).

[3] v. pp. l–li.

already given to the Bastard in *King John* a great speech on the evils of civil strife, here borrowing from *The Troublesome Reign*, which in turn may have been influenced by Froissart. Froissart's words, indeed, which clearly inspired the opening paragraphs of Hall's *Chronicle*, quoted above[1], must have been well known in Shakespeare's day. Written as they were by a contemporary of Gaunt himself, they yet form a remarkable prophecy of the Wars of the Roses, and point the moral of all Tudor political thought, the moral of order and unity. Robert Cecil, as he watched the play in 1595, would consider that Shakespeare had every justification for ranking Lancaster among the prophets.

The play's chief debt to Le Beau or *Traïson* is in the conception of Richard's character after his downfall. I have said above that the germs of that character may all be traced to hints in Holinshed. The despairing speeches and soliloquies in Shakespeare have, however, remarkable parallels in the lengthy lamentations which the French writer places in the King's mouth, so remarkable that it is difficult to believe there is no connexion between them. It is true that there is little similarity in the contents of the two sets of speeches, and it might be contended that both independently spring from the medieval literary fashion of 'lament,' were it not for one striking point in common. The glamour and pathos of Richard's figure owe much, we have seen, to the atmosphere of martyrdom in which Shakespeare succeeds in surrounding him. An important, if not the most important, element in this atmosphere is the suggested comparison of his betrayal and trial with those of Christ. The passages quoted in my notes on 4. 1. 170, 239–42 will show that the comparison was first made by the author of *Traïson*, unless he borrowed it from Créton who draws the same parallel. In a word, the idea of the martyr-king, not found in Holinshed or Hall, in Froissart or even in Daniel, is

[1] v. pp. xxvi–xxvii.

explicit both in the French chroniclers of the early fifteenth century and in Shakespeare, and links them together. In other words, two legends about the character of Richard II have come down to us from the fifteenth century: that of his supporters, which represented him as a saint and a martyr, compared his sufferings and death with those of Christ himself, while they accounted for his capture by an act of base betrayal; and secondly, that of the Lancastrians which depicted him as a weak, cowardly, moody man who surrendered himself and abdicated of his own free will. Shakespeare's genius succeeded in fusing these originally contradictory conceptions and in composing therefrom the figure of a king who seems to us one of the most living of his characters.

Of less dramatic importance but of still greater weight as evidence is the fact that two small points which the commentators have hitherto been at a loss to account for, viz. Carlisle's reference to the banished Mowbray's career as a crusader and his imprisonment in the house of the Abbot of Westminster, are alike traceable to Le Beau or *Traïson* (v. notes 4. 1. 92–100, 152–3), while in the correspondence between striking phrases like 'from sun to sun' (4. 1. 55) and 'entre deux soleilz[1],' or 'the base court' (3. 3. 176) and 'la basse court[2],' the English of Shakespeare seems a direct echo of the French of the old chronicler.

And once the dependence of *Richard II* upon this source is established, it will, I think, be allowed that other features of the play, the origin of which might be sought in Daniel or Froissart, are more likely to be derived directly from *Traïson*. Consider, for example, the problem of the age of Richard's queen. Clearly neither the dramatist nor (at first) Daniel realized that Isabel was a very young girl in 1398, actually only eleven years old. In the Epistle Dedicatorie to the 1609

[1] *Traïson*, p. 15; Le Beau (Buchon, *op. cit.* vol. xv. p. 14).
[2] *Traïson*, p. 59.

edition of *The Civil Wars* Daniel, it is true, makes a belated apology for 'notsuting her passions to her yeares,' but had he been conscious of the truth in 1595 he could hardly have penned stanzas 71 to 93 of Book ii, which I quote on pp. 99–106 below, and so we might have lost the loveliest passage in his poem. Probably both he and the dramatist were led astray, perhaps independently, by *Traïson* which describes a touching farewell between Richard and his consort on his departure for Ireland, when he

took the Queen in his arms, and kissed her more than forty times, saying sorrowfully, 'Adieu, Madame, until we meet again; I commend me to you.' Thus spoke the King to the Queen in the presence of all the people; and the Queen began to weep, saying to the King, 'Alas! my lord, will you leave me here?' Upon which the King's eyes filled with tears on the point of weeping, and he said, 'By no means, Madame; but I will go first, and you, Madame, shall come there afterwards.' Then the King and Queen partook of wine and comfits together at the Deanery, and all who chose did the same. Afterwards the King stooped, and took and lifted the Queen from the ground, and held her a long while in his arms, and kissed her at least ten times, saying ever, 'Adieu, Madame, until we meet again,' and then placed her on the ground and kissed her at least thrice more; and, by our Lady! I never saw so great a lord make so much of, nor shew such great affection to, a lady, as did King Richard to his Queen. Great pity was it that they separated, for never saw they each other more[1].

There is no hint in the chronicle of the Queen being a mere child, and the foregoing might easily have suggested scene 2. 2 in the play, and from that beginning the rest of the scenes in which Isabel appears may have grown.

Another seeming link between the play and contemporary accounts of the persons it deals with is to be found in the stress laid upon Richard's complexion, out of which Shakespeare makes much dramatic capital:

[1] *Traïson*, pp. 166–8 (editor's translation).

Hotspur in retrospect speaks of 'Richard, that sweet lovely rose' (1 *Henry IV*, 1. 3. 175), the Queen calls him 'my fair rose' (5. 1. 8 below), while the references at 2. 1. 118, 3. 2. 75–6, 3. 3. 62–7, 4. 1. 265–88 show that, as Herford has observed, 'high colour, easily yielding to deadly pallor, was part of Shakespeare's conception of Richard.' This, it may be said, is merely a detail of the dramatist's vivid realization of his leading character. Nevertheless, a 'rose-red' Richard is almost certainly a historical fact. Adam of Usk, who knew him by sight, calls him 'cum Absalone pulcher[1]'; Froissart twice refers to his quick change of colour[2], while the following description of his personal appearance, recorded by 'a French Chaplain in the suite of Henry V, but not unfavourable to Richard[3],' a description which should prove of interest to theatrical producers, must surely be connected in some way with the picture in Shakespeare's mind:

> King Richard was of the common stature, his hair yellowish, his face fair and rosy, rather round than long, and sometimes flushed; abrupt and somewhat stammering in his speech, capricious in his manners, and too apt to prefer the recommendations of the young, to the advice of the elder, nobles[3].

Once again Shakespeare seems to be echoing the words of men living in the fifteenth century with personal memories of Richard still fresh in mind. Much reading had undoubtedly gone to the making of this play!

It remains to add a word to what has already been said about the influence of *The Civil Wars* and *Thomas of Woodstock*. From the latter is derived the kindly portrait of Gloucester, 'plain well-meaning soul,' whom

[1] v. p. 43 *Chronicon Adae de Usk*, 1377–1421, ed. E. Maunde Thompson, 1904.

[2] Berners, *op. cit.* vi. pp. 314, 367. Cf. Hardin Craig (note on 2. 1. 118).

[3] v. Appendix F (p. 295) to *Traïson*.

Holinshed, Froissart and Daniel unite in depicting most unfavourably[1], while his Duchess is also a character in the older play, at the end of which she calls down vengeance upon her husband's murderers. Apart from these figures, the influence, though considerable, is mainly verbal in the fashion illustrated above, and more amply in the notes that follow. The relation between *Richard II* and *The Civil Wars* is closer, but more difficult to assess with precision. The numerous verbal echoes prove without any possibility of question, that Shakespeare had been reading the poem while writing the play in 1595. It furnished him too with the framework of his portrait of Bolingbroke, the question of whose guilt Daniel argues at considerable length, concluding that Fortune rather than ambition was the prime mover of his actions. The following stanzas (i. 94–5) seem to sum up his opinion, an opinion which Shakespeare, as we have already seen, almost certainly adopted:

Doubtfull at first, he warie doth proceed,
Seemes not t'affect, that which he did effect,
Or els perhaps seemes as he ment indeed,
Sought but his owne, and did no more expect:
Then fortune thou art guilty of his deed
That didst his state aboue his hopes erect,
And thou must beare some blame of his great sin
That left'st him worse then when he did begin.

Thou didst conspire with pride, and with the time,
To make so easie an assent to wrong,
That he who had no thought so hie to clime,
(With fauouring comfort still allur'd along)

[1] Cf. note 2. 1. 128. Grafton alone of the Tudor chroniclers speaks well of him. He says nothing about his plotting against Richard, and under the heading 'The Duke of Gloucester shamefully murtherd' concludes 'And so was this honorable and good man miserable put to death, which for the honor of the King and wealth of the realme had taken great trauayles' (vol. i. p. 468, 1809 reprint).

Was with occasion thrust into the crime,
Seeing others weakenes and his part so strong:
And ô in such a case who is it will
Do good, and feare that may liue free with ill.

In his *Froissart and the English Chronicle Play*[1], Dr R. M. Smith cites the following 'twelve parallels' between Daniel and Shakespeare, parallels, as he claims, 'differing from the chronicle sources': (1) the reasons given for the banishment of Bolingbroke; (2) the maturity of the Queen; (3) the description of Bolingbroke leading Richard in triumph through the streets of London; (4) the meeting between Richard and Isabel; (5) Bolingbroke's obsequious behaviour to the people; (6) the similarity of the portents before Richard's downfall; (7) the spellings 'Bullingbroke' and 'Herford' found in both versions; (8) Richard's surrender of the crown 'with his own hand'; (9) the conspirators for the restoration of Richard taking 'the Sacrament' together; (10) the use of 'rid' and 'fears' in both accounts of Bolingbroke's speech overheard by Exton; (11) a long soliloquy assigned in both versions to Richard, just before his death, a soliloquy comparing and contrasting the King's estate with that of ordinary men; (12) the disavowal of Exton's deed by Bolingbroke. Some of these are little more than verbal echoes, though none the less important as evidence on that account, and will be dealt with in the notes below. Others, such as 1, 2, 3 and 5, may have been independently derived or inferred from Froissart or *Traïson*. By this I do not mean that Daniel's poem produced no effect upon Shakespeare's shaping imagination in these matters. On the contrary, I think the effect was considerable. All I suggest is that the germs of all or some, how far developed we cannot even guess, may have been present in the 'book' of King Richard the Second before Shakespeare handled it at all. In short, my opinion, arrived at on other grounds, is that his

[1] *Op. cit.* pp. 146–53.

*Richard II* was based, like its predecessor *King John*, on an older play, into which a good deal of the historical and quasi-historical matter we have been considering had already been worked up. Yet, even when the most generous allowance possible has been made for this contingency, the other parallels brought forward by Dr Smith and myself are sufficient to prove that Shakespeare had his head full of the poem while he was engaged upon the play.

## III. The Play in the Making

A student of *King John*, working with *The Troublesome Reign of King John*, its indubitable source, before him, may learn how Shakespeare went to work in the composition of at least one history-play. We found, for example, that he followed the other dramatist 'as closely as his greatly superior dramatic and poetic powers allowed; and he made use of no other source whatsoever[1].' Astonishingly enough, there is not a tittle of evidence that he even consulted Holinshed, though reference to that chronicle, a copy of which editors have assumed generally stood ready on his desk, might have saved him from not a few of the blunders into which he fell through ignorance or carelessness. It is clear, moreover, that while no doubt careful to preserve the general framework of chronicle known and accepted by his contemporaries, he took little or no interest in the accuracy of historical detail, and, provided he could assume ignorance on the part of the audience—he obviously assumed a good deal—was prepared at any moment to sacrifice truth to dramatic convenience. Nor did he trouble his head about small obscurities and inconsistencies in the play so long as they would pass unnoticed on the stage. We found a number of such obscurities and inconsistencies in *King John*, some of them quite in-

[1] *King John* (New Shakespeare), p. xxxiv.

explicable as they stand, which could be at once cleared up, however, by reference to *The Troublesome Reign*, and were often enough seen to be due to hasty misapprehension of historical allusions or names accurately employed by his predecessor. Lastly, we saw that this predecessor, though 'an insipid versifier and an uninspired journeyman playwright[1],' seemed to possess 'a passion for the glorious past of his country[2],' and 'knew how to distil the most excellent dramatic material' from the old chronicles, with which he showed himself exceedingly well acquainted[3].

No similar source-play for *Richard II* has come down to us; yet to suppose that it once existed affords, I think, far the most satisfactory explanation of the otherwise puzzling features of this text. *Richard II* is in the first place, like *King John*, a strange mixture of historical erudition and inaccuracy. The previous section has shown what wide and close reading of the chronicles lies behind it; yet this is combined with such indifference to historical veracity and consistency that Bagot, for instance, is not only confused with the Earl of Wiltshire[4], but, having been sent off to Ireland at 2. 2. 138, is then announced as executed at Bristol at 3. 2. 122, and is finally brought on again, alive and vocal, at the opening of 4. 1! Less glaring is the failure to identify the Lord Marshal at Coventry with the Earl of Surrey of 4. 1, though Holinshed renders it clear enough, and valuable dramatic capital might have been made out of it. Like *King John* again, *Richard II* contains a number of little points, dramatically obscure or unintelligible, which can only be understood, if at all, by reference to one or other of its historical sources.

An interesting example occurs at 2. 1. 167–8, where York, in his outburst after Richard's shameless confiscation of Gaunt's goods, enumerates, among the other

[1] *King John* (New Shakespeare), p. xxxix.
[2] *Ibid.* p. xli. [3] *Ibid.* p. xxxix. [4] v. note 3. 2. 122.

wrongs he and his family had had to endure from his nephew, 'the prevention of poor Bolingbroke about his marriage,' and 'my own disgrace.' There is no reference elsewhere in the play to Bolingbroke's marriage or any prevention of it, and it is only when we turn up Holinshed, or still better, Froissart, that the point becomes clear[1]. Herford supposes 'that Shakespeare credited his audience with sufficient knowledge to understand the allusion,' which seems highly improbable, much as the reign of Richard II was canvassed at that period. Rather, I contend, we have here a loose thread, the presence of which indicates that more was made of the matter in the original play—it was a strong point in favour of Bolingbroke—and that Shakespeare, suppressing the motive in revision, so as to lighten the scales in Richard's favour, overlooked this casual mention of it in York's speech. And this explanation is, I think, corroborated by the reference to 'my own disgrace' which occurs immediately after—another unexplained loose thread, and this time inexplicable, since nothing in the chronicles has been found to throw light upon it, so that it is tempting to regard it as a mere outcrop of an earlier dramatic stratum. Then there is the remarkable charge brought by Bolingbroke against Bushy and Green, in 3. 1. 11–15, which runs:

You have in manner with your sinful hours
Made a divorce betwixt his queen and him,
Broke the possession of a royal bed,
And stained the beauty of a fair queen's cheeks
With tears, drawn from her eyes by your foul wrongs.

It is a charge inconsistent with everything else in the play about the relations between Richard and his Queen, and is described by some editors as an echo of *Edward II*. But may it not be best explained, like the passages quoted above, as a relic of the original play overlooked in revision?

[1] v. note 2. 1. 167–8.

Other obscurities, which belong, I think, to the same category, are the unexpected reference to 'Glendower and his complices' at 3. 1. 43, the equally unexpected and unexplained mention by Bolingbroke at 5. 3. 137 of his 'trusty brother-in-law,' and the strange remark of Richard's at 4. 1. 255 that he had no name:

> No, not that name was given me at the font;

a passage pointless in the play as it stands, but clearly derived from the trumped up tale, referred to in *Traïson* and by Froissart (but not Holinshed), that 'Richard of Bordeaux' was no son of the Black Prince but a bastard whose real name was John. Of like nature and, I do not doubt, of like origin, is the vagueness, not to say inconsistency, which surrounds the question of Gloucester's murder. In the opening scene of the play Bolingbroke accuses Mowbray of being the principal agent in Gloucester's death, an accusation which Mowbray denies. But accusation and denial, indeed the attitude of both men towards Richard in the scene, gain greatly in subtlety and interest directly we realize that the King himself is the real culprit, Gloucester having been put to death at his orders. Yet strangely enough Shakespeare makes no attempt to place the audience in possession of these facts, or even to set forth the circumstances of the murder, until the following scene, when the exposition comes too late for the theatre. Furthermore, while after this we are left under the impression for three acts that Mowbray had done the deed as Richard's agent, at the beginning of act 4 we suddenly find Aumerle, apparently at Bolingbroke's instigation, arraigned as the murderer in parliament, an accusation of which much is made at the time, but nothing afterwards, though some reference to Gloucester's fate would surely have been appropriate in 5. 3, the scene in which Aumerle confesses to Bolingbroke that he had been plotting against his life. The whole business, in short, of Gloucester—

a minor strand in the texture of the play—looks as if it either had been compressed and distorted in the process of revision, or was itself a blend of two or more varying accounts, one of them introduced in the same process.

It owes, as we have seen, much to *Thomas of Woodstock*, a play in which Shakespeare himself may have acted. But *ex hypothesi* the old *Richard II* must have contained some treatment of the Gloucester theme. A fusion of these two elements, the one supplied by the poet's memory, the other by the MS. in front of him, would explain most or all of the oddities just noticed.

Beyond loose ends and inconsistencies like the foregoing we found little in *King John* to link it directly with the parent-play. Shakespeare took over a line here and there, generally on some matter of fact, and obviously carried forward, probably by some trick of memory, a number of phrases or half-lines of small dramatic importance. But he rewrote the play as a whole and left no scene or passage, except the scraps just mentioned, of the original standing. It may seem a bold claim to make; but, unless I am greatly mistaken, *Richard II* contains a good deal more of the old material than this. Indeed, my strong impression, based it is true mainly upon the highly contentious ground of style, is that the revision was rather sketchy in act 5 and that a number of the concluding scenes of the play are for the most part composed of passages of non-Shakespearian verse, cobbled together in some haste at the time of the revision. It will, at any rate, I think be obvious to the most sceptical, once it is pointed out, that there was something odd about the Exton scenes in the manuscript. The play gives no hint of Exton's existence before his sudden entry in 5. 4, and even there he appears as an anonymous knight to whom a name is not assigned in the ears of the audience until just before his entry in the following scene. But the direction for his first entry in the Quarto, which no doubt reproduces that in Shakespeare's manuscript, is stranger still. The brief scene, already quoted for another purpose above, in which Exton repeats Bolingbroke's words, 'Have I no friend will rid me of this living fear?', follows of course immediately upon the scene between Bolingbroke, Aumerle, York and the Duchess. But the two scenes are treated as one in the Quarto, as is clear from the following stage-direction, which it prints as a link between them:

*Exeunt. Manet ſir Pierce Exton, &c.*

In other words, the Quarto gives no 'entry' for Exton; on the contrary, the stage-direction indicates that he has been 'on' during the previous scene. And yet this is quite impossible, for two excellent reasons: (i) After Aumerle's request at 5. 3. 27 'to have some conference with your grace alone,' Bolingbroke clears the chamber, the door of which is then locked by Aumerle, only to be opened later to admit first York and later his Duchess. Even if we assume, then, that Exton made one of the 'nobles' present with Bolingbroke at the opening of the scene, he could not have remained after line 28. (ii) At the beginning of 5. 4, Exton reminds his man of Bolingbroke's words, words which, he clearly implies, have just been spoken in their ears, though they correspond with nothing whatever in the scene just concluded.

There cannot, I infer, be the least doubt that some scene or episode, originally connecting 5. 3 and 5. 4 together, has been cut out in the process of preparing the play for the stage. One may suppose, for instance, that a colloquy between Exton and his man once actually formed the conclusion of 5. 3; that after the exit of York, the Duchess and their son Aumerle, Percy and the nobles who had 'withdrawn' at line 28 returned with Exton, whereupon Bolingbroke informed them of the conspiracy which had just been revealed to him, uttering at the same time the words which Exton quotes later and which are naturally connected with reflections upon the conspiracy; and that in the course of revision Shakespeare deleted this last conversation as dramatically unnecessary but did not delete the old stage-direction which marked its termination. Whatever the manner and purpose of the revision, however, revision of some kind there certainly was.

It may of course have been merely a slight adaptation of his own draft, such as Shakespeare, we can imagine, found desirable at times after rehearsal. I am persuaded, however, that the tell-tale stage-direction points to something more significant; that it is, in short, the relic of a pre-Shakespearian play. And what persuades me is the character of much of the verse, together with other fairly clear signs of adaptation, to be found in these last scenes. Take for instance the following couplets from the last scene of all (5. 6. 7–10):

> The next news is, I have to London sent
> The heads of Salisbury, Spencer, Blunt and Kent.
> The manner of their taking may appear
> At large discoursèd in this paper here.

Is not this the very accent of Quince himself? The immortal lines

> The actors are at hand and by their show
> You shall know all that you are like to know,

go on like rhyming stilts, and to the identical jog-trot in metre. Or consider this (5. 6. 41–4):

> The guilt of conscience take thou for thy labour,
> But neither my good word, nor princely favour:
> With Cain go wander through the shades of night,
> And never show thy head by day nor light.

There are, no doubt, some hardy contemners of the 'disintegration of Shakespeare' who will declare him capable of rhyming 'labour' with 'favour,' but can they, dare they, credit him with the last of these fatuous lines? 'By day nor light' is not merely nonsense; it represents the very bankruptcy of rhyme-tagging. And is the following from the strange 'Duchess' interlude (5. 3. 97–104) any better?

*Aumerle*. Unto my mother's prayers I bend my knee.
*York*. Against them both my true joints bended be.
Ill mayst thou thrive, if thou grant any grace!
*Duchess*. Pleads he in earnest? look upon his face;
His eyes do drop no tears, his prayers are in jest.
His words come from his mouth, ours from our breast.
He prays but faintly, and would be denied,
We pray with heart and soul, and all beside.

For sheer ineptitude 'and all beside' runs 'by day nor light' very close.

Another reason for assigning these couplets to a pre-Shakespearian play, and a reason happily independent of aesthetic considerations, is the fact that the blank verse in earlier acts occasionally reveals fossil-rhymes, which can hardly be explained except on the supposition that Shakespeare was rewriting rhymed verse. A number of such fossils are to be seen in lines 62 to 126 of act 3, scene 3, a passage which happens to be a bibliographical unity inasmuch as it almost certainly covered one side of a leaf in Shakespeare's manuscript[1]. But 1. 3. 183–90 presents a more compact and therefore more quotable example. I italicize the rhymes so that the reader may pick them out at a glance:

You never shall, so help you truth and God,
*Embrace* each other's love in banishment,
Nor never look upon each other's *face*,
Nor never write, *regreet*, nor reconcile
This louring tempest of your home-bred *hate*,
Nor never by advisèd purpose *meet*,
To plot, contrive, or complot any ill,
'Gainst us, our *state*, our subjects, or our land.

Or again, to turn from couplets to blank verse, consider the first nineteen lines of scene 5. 3, lines dealing

[1] v. note 3. 3. 62–126.

with Prince Hal's escapades, and therefore important as links with *Henry IV*. Their metrical flatness, together with their verbal poverty—'they say,' for example, is repeated within two lines, in order to eke out the verse—makes it impossible for me to believe Shakespeare responsible for them at any period. The style is indeed so undistinguished that it might be that of any second-rate dramatist of the time. There is nothing, for instance, to choose between it and the reach-me-down verse of *The Troublesome Reign of King John*, while it is worthy of notice that the posting Duchess of York is own sister to the posting Lady Faulconbridge of that play.

And this, I think, points us to the solution of the whole problem. If any hack poet might have written the blank verse of 5. 3. 1–19, the rhyming couplets above quoted display such a peculiar quality of badness, that it is difficult to imagine a second versifier capable of turning out others quite of that type. When, therefore, *The Troublesome Reign* yields couplets of an exactly similar stamp, may we not legitimately suppose them to have come from the same mint? A good specimen is to be found in the scene between Arthur and Hubert. The young prince warns his gaoler that he is putting his immortal soul in danger in the crime he is about to commit at King John's command, and the dialogue continues:

Advise thee, Hubert, for the case is hard,
To lose salvation for a king's reward.
  *Hubert.* My lord, a subject dwelling in the land
Is tied to execute the king's command.
  *Arthur.* Yet God commands, whose power reacheth further,
That no command should stand in force to murther.
  *Hubert.* But that same Essence hath ordained a law,
A death for guilt, to keep the world in awe.
  *Arthur.* I plead 'not guilty, treasonless and free.'
  *Hubert.* But that appeal, my lord, concerns not me.
  *Arthur.* Why, thou art he that mayst omit the peril.

*Hubert.* Ay, if my sovereign would remit his quarrel.
*Arthur.* His quarrel is unhallowed, false and wrong.
*Hubert.* Then be the blame to whom it doth belong.
*Arthur.* Why, that's to thee, if thou as they proceed;
Conclude their judgement with so vile a deed.
*Hubert.* Why then, no execution can be lawful,
If judges' dooms must be reputed doubtful.
*Arthur.* Yes, where in form of law, in place and time,
The offender is convicted of the crime.

If this passage, with its clumsy manœuvring for rhyme, rhyme sometimes as far-fetched as 'lawful' and 'doubtful,' and with its frequent sacrifice of sense and clarity to metrical considerations, reminds the reader of the couplets in act 5 of *Richard II*, he will perhaps be prepared to admit the possibility that a 'book' of King Richard the Second, by the same author as the learned historian, but very indifferent poet, who wrote the *Troublesome Reign of King John*, formed the basis of Shakespeare's play. And, asking him to admit so much, I need not hesitate to suggest further that the bones of the old play may be seen sticking through in almost every scene of act 5: in the last twenty lines of scene 1, for example, throughout scene 3, in all but the lengthy soliloquy of scene 5, and again throughout scene 6[1]. Reference to the notes will show that I do not imagine that these scenes, or portions of scenes, were taken over by Shakespeare as they stood without any adaptation or rearrangement. On the contrary, there appear to be clear traces of Shakespeare's hand at work here and there. But it is rough cobbling work at best, and I cannot doubt that what he had to do in act 5 he did either in a great hurry or in a mood of lassitude or indifference. Even the undoubtedly Shakespearian soliloquy at the opening of scene 5, interesting as it is in some respects,

[1] My faith here is strengthened by finding myself in close agreement with Mr G. M. Young, who has been good enough to communicate his views on act 5 to me privately.

falls considerably below act 4, in my judgment, as dramatic verse.

'It may be observed,' writes Dr Johnson in a magisterial mood, 'that in many of his plays the latter part is evidently neglected. When he found himself near the end of his work, and in view of his reward, he shortened the labour to snatch the profit.' But lack of artistic conscience may be too simple an explanation. Shakespeare undoubtedly had to work to some kind of time table, a difficult task for a poet, however possible for a novelist like Trollope. Is it not conceivable that he became enthralled in the earlier part of this play, and especially in the parliament scene; spent too long upon it; and when his company came clamouring for the 'book,' for transcription, rehearsal and performance, was found with the last act still hardly begun, so that he had to huddle it through at a few hours' notice and with the help of such scraps of the old play as he could conveniently stitch together? Something of the kind perhaps often happened in the long history of the relations between Shakespeare the poet and Shakespeare the man of the theatre, whose task it was for ever to keep the mill agoing. That the miller knew there was an old play to fall back upon would, no doubt, tend to encourage the poet in his dilatory habits.

But if any of my readers have found it possible to accompany me thus far, let them mark the direction in which the road is taking us. Once again, as in *King John*, we have had to face the question, 'Was Shakespeare a profound historical scholar or merely the reviser of such a scholar's play?' And, as before, we have been compelled to reply that the probabilities are all in favour of the second alternative. That he had read Daniel's *Civil Wars* in the edition of 1595 before he undertook the play is certain. That he had his head full of echoes of *Thomas of Woodstock*, a play in which he may even have acted, is likely enough. But had he consulted any of the chronicles whatever? It is most improbable that he knew anything of *Traïson*, Le Beau or Créton. He may have dipped into the opening paragraphs of Hall or turned up Holinshed, here and there, while it would be pleasant to think of him reading Berners; but there is nothing in the situation analysed above which makes it necessary for him to have done any of these things. His unknown predecessor, soaked in the history of England, had read the chroniclers for him and had digested what they had to say upon the downfall of Richard II into a play-book ready to his revising hand. It was a busy time for the theatre; his company, newly re-formed in 1594, was anxious to recoup themselves as rapidly as possible for the heavy losses of the plague-years, 1591–4, and to hold their own with their rivals, the Admiral's men; and Shakespeare was their chief dramatist, probably at this time their sole dramatist. Moreover, are we not justified in supposing, from everything we know about him, that Shakespeare followed the line of least resistance, whenever he could? I can see no reason for believing that he took the trouble to read Holinshed or any other chronicle for his *Richard II*, any more than he had done for his *King John*. Daniel's poem, an actor's knowledge of *Thomas of Woodstock*, and our hypothetical play-book by the author of *The Troublesome Reign of King John* are together sufficient to account for all the facts.

But if the traditional notion of Shakespeare's dependence upon Holinshed seems to be evaporating, what, it may be asked, about other histories, and in particular the plays we have next to consider in this edition, the two parts of *Henry IV* and *Henry V*? That consideration still lies in the future and must not here be anticipated. But one thing may at least be noted. We have just seen grounds for assigning the opening lines of 5. 3 to the pre-Shakespearian stratum of *Richard II*. And this means, or at any rate strongly suggests, that the original draft of the play was itself, like Shakespeare's version, intended to be introductory to a play, or plays, upon the subject of Henry IV and perhaps Henry V. In other words, the author of *The Troublesome Reign of King John* may have provided Shakespeare not merely with material for his *Richard II*, but for the whole cycle *Richard II* to *Henry V*. Beyond remarking that in a strange publication, entitled *The Famous Victories of Henry the Fifth*, entered in the Stationers' Register on 14 May 1594, we have conclusive proof of the existence a year before Shakespeare began to revise *Richard II* of plays dealing with the reigns of Henry IV and Henry V, in which Sir John Oldcastle appeared as a leading figure, we must leave the matter there for the present.

Links with the Henry VI plays, however, belong to a different category from those just mentioned. The atmosphere of foreboding, for example, referred to at the end of the first section of this introduction, is likely enough to have been due in the main to Shakespeare himself. For when he took up *Richard II* in 1595 he would think of it, and clearly did think of it, primarily in terms of the civil wars that were to spring out of the events with which it dealt, and if he were in any danger of forgetting this, Daniel's poem with its constant reminders on the point would have kept it before his consciousness.

1939 J. D. W.

## Postscript, 1950

Readers should consult an important criticism of the foregoing Introduction entitled *The Sources of Shakespeare's "Richard II"* contributed by Professor M. W. Black to *Joseph Quincy Adams: Memorial Studies*, Washington, The Folger Shakespeare Library, 1948.

# THE STAGE-HISTORY OF *KING RICHARD II*

The first certain mention of Shakespeare's *King Richard II* is in *Palladis Tamia*, 1598, where Meres puts it first among the 'tragedies'; but in his Introduction[1] the editor shows it to have been already seen in 1595. This, then, was the play intended in the official evidence against Essex, compiled in the summer of 1600 in connexion with the trial of John Hayward for writing and Harsnett for publishing the prose history of *The First Part of the Life and Raigne of King Henrie IIII*: 'the Erle himself being so often present at the playing thereof, and with great applause giving countenance and lyking to the same'. In August 1601 Queen Elizabeth told William Lambard, referring to the disaffection of Essex, that this tragedy was played forty times in open streets and houses.[2] It was common at that time to see a likeness between King Richard II and Queen Elizabeth ('I am Richard II. Know ye not that?' said she to Lambard),[3] and there was obvious resemblance between Bolingbroke's courting of the populace, as described by the King (I. iv), and Essex's. The topical interest of the play led to its being raked up again for the strange proceedings of Saturday, February 7, 1601, the day before Essex dared rebellion.[4] The several accounts establish that on the preceding Thursday and Friday some of Essex's adherents went across the river to the Globe playhouse and there asked the Chamberlain's men to act on the Saturday the play of the deposing and killing of King Richard II, and promised 'to gete them xl*s*. more then

[1] v. p. viii. [2] v. Introduction, p. xxxii.
[3] v. Introduction, p. xxx.
[4] v. Introduction, pp. xxxi–xxxii.

their ordynary to play yt'. The players argued that the play was so old and so long out of use that they would have 'small or no Company at yt'; but they were over-persuaded, and the play was acted before a great company of Essex's followers, though he himself was not present. The scandal is thought by some, on slender grounds, to have led to the closing of the Globe for a time, during which the Chamberlain's men went on tour (see *Hamlet* in this edition, pp. 177–8); but the players were clearly held innocent of blame. They acted before the Queen at Whitehall on the 24th of the same month, that is to say on the day after she had signed the warrant for the execution of Essex and the day before he went to the block; and they were at Court at least twice in the following December.

On September 30, 1607, William Keeling, Captain of the East India Company's ship 'Dragon', off Sierra Leone, entered in his diary: 'Captain Hawkins dined with me, when my companions acted King Richard the Second.' On September 5 Keeling's men had acted *Hamlet*. William Hawkins was the Captain of a companion ship, the 'Hector'. There is nothing to prove that this *King Richard II* was Shakespeare's; but if his was the only play of that name in print, the odds are strong in its favour. Next year appeared an edition of the play with the following title: *The Tragedie of King Richard the Second: With new additions of the Parliament Sceane, and the deposing of King Richard. As it hath been lately acted by the Kinges Majesties Servantes, at the Globe. By William Shakespeare...1608.* The word 'lately' indicates a recent performance, at which, perhaps, the copy for the 'new additions' had been procured, 'probably', Dr Pollard thinks, 'by means of shorthand writers'.[1] On June 12, 1631, the King's men acted the play at the Globe before a moderately large

[1] v. Note on the copy, below, p. 112.

audience. Nothing more is known about it before the closing of the playhouses.

*King Richard II* was one of the plays formerly acted at the Blackfriars which were allowed to the King's company in or about January, 1669; but there is no evidence of its having been acted at the Theatre Royal or anywhere else. Nothing more is heard of it until Nahum Tate's alteration of it was produced at the Theatre Royal in the period between 1678 and 1682, when the stage was tempted by the political troubles to revive such Shakespearian tragedies and histories as might illustrate contemporary affairs. Tate's play was unlucky. Exactly what happened is not clear; but in publishing the play in 1681 Tate wrote an introductory letter to George Raynsford, in which he distinctly says that it was suppressed twice, 'first in its own Name, and after in Disguise'. By disguise he means the alterations he had made to his own play in the hope of saving it, the change of the title to *The Sicilian Usurper* and the transference of scenes and characters from Great Britain to Sicily. Probably before he made those alterations he had petitioned to have the play 'perus'd and dealt with as the Contents Deserv'd'; but 'a positive Doom of Suppression without Examination was all that I cou'd procure', and the play was 'Silenc'd on the Third Day'. The only extant order is that of December 14, 1680, in which the Lord Chamberlain commanded the comedians at the Theatre Royal to 'forbeare acting' a play called *Richard II* until further orders. This was probably the suppression 'in its own Name' which induced Tate to put it in its Sicilian 'disguise'. The disguise was then produced (probably early in the year) in 1681. 'For the two days in which it was Acted the Change of the Scene, Names of Persons, etc. was a great Disadvantage.' Then the second blow fell and the play was seen no more. This, it must be remembered, was in the winter of 1680–81, just about the time that the Exclusion Bill was rejected by the Lords; and Tate either did not see or pretended not to see that any play in which a usurper takes the throne would appear dangerous to a dynasty none too firm in the saddle. His disclaimer of the 'unpardonable presumption to form any resemblance between the Times here written of, and the Present' is not supported by his play; and, through the strangest lapse of all, he did not observe that to paint his deposed King as a 'Wise, Active, and Just Prince' was to increase alarm for the safety of the Prince on the throne. In the prefatory letter to Raynsford, Tate merely revealed how he had changed the tenour of Shakespeare's play without relieving it of one jot of its political danger.

His design to 'engage the pitty of the Audience' for Richard in his distresses was by no means badly carried out. At Gaunt's death-bed his Richard laments the 'sallies of my youthful blood', and makes a statement which Tate could indeed claim was 'full of Respect to Majesty and the dignity of Courts':

> Attend him well, and if a Prince's Prayer
> Have more than common interest with Heav'n
> Our Realm shall yet enjoy his honest Council.

And on Gaunt's death Richard does not seize—he borrows his property. Cutting out Bushy, Green and Bagot helps to protect Richard's character. Love-scenes were inevitable at that date. The love-scenes between Richard and his Queen—one before the King goes into Flint Castle, another after his arrival in London, and the last their farewell—may make modern readers laugh or writhe; but they would certainly have raised the King in the estimation of the first hearers. Those hearers, moreover, would see nothing outrageous or ridiculous in a theatrical device at which modern critics have raged—the trick table which sank through the floor just as Richard, in prison, was going to eat off it. To the theatre of Tate this was the natural way of showing 'the most current report at the time', as Hayward puts it, that he was 'princely served with abundance of costly meates, according to the order prescribed by Parliament, but was not suffered to tast or touch any one of them'. Not content with describing Bolingbroke's wooing of the mob, Tate first gives York, at Gaunt's bedside, something like Richard's 'oyster-wench' speech, having cut out the scene of Shakespeare in which it was spoken, and then adds a whole scene, partly for comic relief and partly for characterization, in which Bolingbroke and the people come into visible contact, and Bolingbroke shows himself externally fawning and internally treacherous and violent. York becomes a completely comic character, with the bulk of a Falstaff; and having been boldly on Richard's side through four Acts, he suddenly veers round in the fifth on discovering Aumerle in conspiracy. The language of Shakespeare is trimmed and corrected in the manner usual at that period. Perhaps one instance will be enough:

A little, very little obscure grave.

The play ends on Bolingbroke's wish that he himself were dead and Richard alive and mourning for him. Two songs were written for Richard to sing; one in Act III, 'Love's Delights were past expressing', and one in the prison scene, 'Retir'd from any mortal's sight'.

Nearly thirty years passed before the play was seen again, and then it was staged by the inferior and struggling company at Lincoln's Inn Fields, on December 10, 1719, with 'new scenes and habits'. The version acted was made by Lewis Theobald, who worked on the approved and respectable design to maintain the unity of action and support the dignity of the characters —his play being explicitly a tragedy, not a chronicle play. To secure unity of time, he cut out the first two acts, and he laid all the scenes in or near the Tower of London. To balance Richard and the Queen, he invented a Lady Piercy, daughter of Northumberland, as a lover for Aumerle. Aumerle fails to win pardon for his conspiracy, proof of which he drops during a love-scene with his lady; and after he is led away to execution she stabs herself (off stage). Richard is visited in prison by the Queen, who is ordered away by Northumberland before the King is killed by Exton; and the play ends with a rather ill-judged reflection by Bolingbroke upon the curse which the King's blood, unatoned, must bring upon the land. The company at Lincoln's Inn Fields just then was not in high repute; but with Ryan as Richard, Leigh as Bolingbroke, Smith as Aumerle, Ogden as Northumberland, Mrs Bullock as the Queen, and Mrs Spiller as Lady Piercy, the play caught on well enough to be given seven times in the season of 1719–20. It was revived for three performances in 1721, when Aumerle was acted by Quin, and Lady Piercy by Mrs Bullock.

In February 1738, thanks to the Ladies of the Shakspear Club, whose activity in bringing Shakespeare back to the theatre has been mentioned more than once in these Stage Histories, Shakespeare's *King Richard II* was seen once again. The stage was that of Covent Garden; and the authentic text was presented with proper dignity. The ancient ceremony of the lists was accurately observed; the King sat on a throne of state, and Norfolk and Bolingbroke, in complete armour, sat on two finely adorned chairs, one on either side. The King was acted by Delane, who was good, except that 'he could not exhibit the King's distressful situation in the latter part of the play. His voice was too loudly extended for the despondency of grief' (we shall find Hazlitt saying something of the same sort about Edmund Kean). Bolingbroke was acted by Ryan, Aumerle by Hallam, the Queen by Mrs Horton, the Duchess of York by Mrs Hallam, and the Duchess of Gloucester by Mrs James, who spoke the 'new Prologue addressed to the Ladies by whose desire this play and *King John* were revived'. Ten performances were given in that season, and the play was revived twice in 1738–9 and once in 1739–40.

Then neglect fell upon it. A version by Francis Gentleman, which was acted at Bath in 1754 but never printed, and a version by Goodhall, of Manchester, which was printed in 1772 but never acted, count for nothing. 'The Critics', wrote Steevens, 'may applaud Richard II tho' the successive audiences of more than a century have respectively slumbered over it, as often as it has appeared on the stage.' Garrick, he says, meant to produce the play; and 'his chief expectations would have been founded on scenery displaying the magnificence of our ancient barriers'. Genest replied to Steevens by pointing out that Tate's play was silenced by authority, not sleepiness; and that both Theobald's 'very bad' alteration and Shakespeare's own play in the revival of 1738 had been played several times in their first season and again in later seasons. But Professor Allardyce Nicoll seems to be right in saying that the play was rather admired than acted; and what is recorded of Delane's performance, what Steevens says of Garrick's intentions, and what Hazlitt is shortly to say of Edmund Kean might be read as showing that not until modern times did any leading actor care to take Richard as Shakespeare wrote him, his weakness with his strength.

Edmund Kean staged the play at Drury Lane on March 9, 1815. His version was made by R. Wroughton, who left out the lists and the conspiracy of Aumerle, enlarged the part of the Queen, and patched the play with scraps from other plays by Shakespeare. In the end the Queen, who has obtained leave from a remorseful Bolingbroke to visit her dying husband in the Tower, speaks over his dead body almost exactly King Lear's last words over Cordelia. This might shock a modern audience, but, as Professor Odell has pointed out, the audience of 1815 might well not know where the words came from, as they were never heard upon the stage in *Lear*. In the garden scene, where the Queen sits upon a 'sopha', one of her ladies sings an air. In America, a few years later, it was the regular thing for the lady to sing 'Angels ever bright and fair', and the custom may have been taken from this production by Edmund Kean. Wroughton's version is easily accessible; it went on being printed as Shakespeare's at least as late as Cumberland's edition of 1841; and more important than its borrowings from other plays is its noble and heroic Richard. It was Wroughton who gave Kean the opportunity of making the display on which Hazlitt dropped so heavily. This had been supposed Kean's finest part; but that was a total misrepresentation. There were only one or two electrical shocks in it; in many of his characters he gave a much greater number, and 'the excellence of his acting is in proportion to the number of hits, for he has not equal truth or purity of style'. From something very near sneering Hazlitt then passed to judgment. Kean's 'general outline' of Richard was wrong, because he made it 'a character of *passion*, that is, of feeling combined with energy; whereas it is a character of *pathos*, that is to say, of feeling combined with weakness'. And he instanced his dashing the mirror down with all his might, instead of letting it fall out of his hands, as from an infant's, and his manner of expostulating with Bolingbroke: 'Why on thy knee, thus low, &c.' (he means the kneeling in III. iv. 190–1), which was 'altogether fierce and heroic, instead of being sad, thoughtful, and melancholy'. Hazlitt found Holland 'lamentable' in the Duke of York, Elliston 'indifferent' in Bolingbroke. The Aumerle was J. W. Wallack, who was ere long to play the King in America; the Queen was Mrs Bartley, and the Lady with Song, here named Blanche, was Miss Poole. The play was given thirteen times in that season, and Edmund Kean went on playing it occasionally at Drury Lane until 1828, and gave it in New York in 1820 and 1826.

A few weeks before Edmund Kean first played Richard II at Drury Lane, Macready had acted the part at Bath on January 26, 1815, and on one later date in that season. This was not his first appearance in the part. In his diary on February 26, 1845, he records that he had been reading the play—'I, the first who ever acted it since the time of Shakespeare, produced it here', that is, at Newcastle, under the management of his father, and made it the success of the season of 1812–13. When he wrote, he had forgotten the Covent Garden production of 1738; but it is true that to Macready belongs the credit of first staging the play more or less faithfully since that date. The version that he produced at Bath in 1815 was said to be much nearer Shakespeare than Wroughton's version; it retained, for one thing, the scene of the lists. But though got up at some expense and well acted it failed to please. Macready did not touch the play again till the end of his career. During his last appearances on the stage, at the Haymarket in 1850–51, he gave two performances, 'with singular fidelity to the text'. Of his acting of Richard, G. H. Lewes records merely that it was 'great'.

Professor Allardyce Nicoll has noted a melodrama, *The Life and Death of King Richard II; or, Wat Tyler and Jack Straw*, which he describes as 'partly indebted to Shakespeare', produced at the Royal Amphitheatre (Astley's) in the Westminster Bridge Road under the management of Ducrow in 1834; and in the same year Vandenhoff played Shakespeare's King Richard under the management of Alfred Bunn at Covent Garden. This is all that there is to bridge the gap between Edmund Kean at Drury Lane and Macready at the Haymarket; but after 1851 London had not long to wait for another production of *King Richard II*. Charles Kean, who had already tried it in Philadelphia, staged the play at the Princess's Theatre on March 12, 1857, for a run which lasted for eighty-five nights. The voice of those eighty-five nights may be heard in the preface to Charles Kean's published version of the play. 'When plays, which formerly commanded but occasional repetition, are enabled, by no derogatory means, to attract audiences for successive months, I cannot be wrong in presuming that the course I have adopted is supported by the irresistible force of public opinion, expressed in the suffrages of an overwhelming majority.' The object of this imitation of Mr Vincent Crummles may have been Henry Morley, who had complained, not of the scenic display, but of the cuts made to leave room for it. Between his third and fourth Acts (that is, between the scene at Flint Castle and the scene of the Queen and the Gardeners) Kean 'ventured to introduce the triumphal entry into London' of Bolingbroke with Richard in his train, thus 'embodying in action what Shakespeare has so beautifully described' in the speech of York to his Duchess, which, nevertheless, he retained. He could cite, of course, plenty of authority for every detail in his procession. 'The few sentences intervening amidst the clamorous acclamations of the mob...are selected from the Chronicles which relate to the circumstances of that remarkable event.' The music, like everything else in the production, was as authentically of the period as could be, and F.S.A.'s and Heralds were thick among the authorities whose help Kean acknowledged. This, probably, was his highest achievement in historical accuracy and theatrical splendour. One instance will suffice. John of Gaunt's bedroom is seen but once in the play; but the preliminary drawings for it made by Henry Shaw (now in the Victoria and Albert Museum) include not only very elaborate studies for every piece of furniture but also separate designs, taken from a manuscript in the British Museum, for the fifteen pictures painted on the walls.

The whole production being on this scale, cutting of the text was inevitable. Needless to say, Charles Kean did not cut out the scene of the lists. His major cuts were Act I, sc. iv, Act II, sc. iv, and Act III, sc. i. From Act IV, sc. i he dropped the quarrel between the nobles in Parliament, all the Bishop of Carlisle's protest and King Richard's references to Christ; from Act V, scc. ii and iii, the whole of Aumerle's conspiracy and its end, and from the prison scene most of Richard's lines about thoughts and all his lines about music. It is surprising, indeed, that he should have troubled to keep the names of Bushy, Green, Bagot and the Bishop of Carlisle in his Dramatis Personae, because the last two never speak and Bushy and Green have only a few of their lines in Act II, sc. ii; but it is characteristic of Charles Kean that, although Carlisle never speaks, the printed version has a note giving his personal name and some particulars of his career. The educational value of Shakespeare is thus put beyond doubt. The remaining cuts are of the elementary kind, but in making them Kean robbed John of Gaunt of most of his speech about England and York of his protest against the confiscation. Henry Morley did well to point out that by leaving out the talk between Richard and his friends about Ireland and the announcement of Gaunt's illness (I. iv), by making Gaunt die on the stage and lie a corpse under Richard's eyes, and by showing nothing of the evil nature of the King's friends or of their extermination by Bolingbroke, Kean robbed Richard of much of the sympathy which it is the purpose of the play to excite.

For all that, this must have been one of Charles Kean's best things.[1] Ellen Terry, who 'climbed up a pole in the street scene' of the procession, recalled her childish memory that King Richard II was one of

[1] v. Introduction, pp. xv–xvi.

Charles Kean's two best parts (the other being Wolsey), and told how in this play the magical charm of his voice was alone enough to keep the house spell-bound. Mrs Kean acted the Queen (she must have looked rather old for the part); Ellen Terry's father had six lines as Ross; and her sister Marion Terry had a line to speak as a boy in the 'Episode' of the procession. That line was not Shakespeare's; it was: 'Behold King Richard, who has done so much harm to the Kingdom of England!' [*Murmurs from the Mob*]. Ryder's Bolingbroke was commended by Morley, and no doubt Cooper as York and Walter Lacy as Gaunt were up to the mark. So little was left of Aumerle that Mr Brazier's performance can hardly have mattered.

The next to take up the play was Sir Frank Benson. He staged it early in his career as manager, and acted it on tour, at the Shakespeare Festivals at Stratford-on-Avon (first in 1896) and in his London seasons of 1900 and 1901. The part of Richard was one in which he himself excelled. He realized the force of the poet-king's imagination, and gave him, in his weakness and his strength, a flower-like beauty which appealed irresistibly for sympathy. In Frank Rodney he had an ideal Bolingbroke, and now and then George R. Weir would play the part of the First Gardener with grave and pathetic beauty. Throughout Sir Frank Benson's management this play was one in which his successive companies showed their best. He cut it very slightly, only omitting the scene of Salisbury and the Welsh Captain (II. iv) and the condemnation of Bushy, Green and Bagot.

On August 21, 1899, on the five-hundredth anniversary of King Richard's surrender there to Bolingbroke, the play was acted by Benson and his company at Flint Castle. The stage was set up out of doors in front of one of the towers of the castle.

It was in September 1903 that this play was put on by Beerbohm Tree at His Majesty's Theatre. The production was one of his most splendid; and it included not only a new version of Kean's 'Episode' of the entry into London but also a coronation for King Henry IV. The play was shortened by the omission of the conspiracy of Aumerle, and neatly divided into three Acts. Tree was happy in the part of Richard. Although he made him, it is true, less the poet-king than the actor-king, obviously pleased with the 'fat' part that he has to play he brought out clearly the sacramental quality of the agony and death of the sacrificial victim.[1] For Bolingbroke and the Queen he had Oscar Asche and Miss Lily Brayton, who had played these parts with Benson. At the revival in 1905 Lyn Harding played Bolingbroke and Miss Viola Tree the Queen; and in both productions the part of the Gardener was taken by Lionel Brough, and the Bishop of Carlisle by Mr Fisher White.

Some four years before Tree staged the play with all realism and splendour at His Majesty's Theatre, a very different sort of performance was given in a very different sort of theatre. On the afternoon of Saturday, November 11, 1899, the Elizabethan Stage Society presented *King Richard II* in the lecture theatre of the University of London in Burlington Gardens.[2] There was no scenery. Tapestry hung at the back of the 'stage'; sage-green screens stood at each side, and the only furniture was a raised seat for the King in the middle in front of the tapestry, two or three oak chairs and a couple of tables. Nothing in the whole production was so sumptuous as the cloak worn by King Richard in the first Act, which was copied from that in his portrait in Westminster Abbey. In Act III the King appeared 'in accordance with History in the disguise of a Friar'; and the

[1] v. Introduction, p. xvi.

[2] For some of the particulars of this production I am indebted to Mr Granville Barker, and to Mr Vincent Nello, who acted Northumberland.

Duchess of Gloucester was dressed as a nun of Barking, 'as represented on her monumental brass in Westminster Abbey'. The groupings and stage movements, continues the programme, were taken 'from descriptions in the contemporary Chronicles and from contemporary illustrations'—matters with which it is rather surprising to find William Poel concerning himself, since his fundamental purpose was always to present a play as nearly as possible as it would have been presented on the stage in Shakespeare's time. Partly through the nature of the building and partly through his own conscientious wilfulness, his audience found their acquiescence tried rather high now and then. Most of the exits and entrances had to be made over the footlights, the departing actors going up the steep steps to the dressing-rooms at the back of the auditorium. That John of Gaunt should be carried on and carried off in the arms of his retainers need have troubled no one; but for the scene 'on the walls' of Flint Castle (III. iii) Poel put the King, Aumerle and the others in the gallery (corresponding to the dress circle in a theatre) among the audience, with Northumberland on the floor of the 'stalls' below; and the spectators, according to one account, 'stretched their necks in vain' to see what was going on. Another of Poel's peculiar convictions was that York must be a comic character, not in the vein of Tate's York but ridiculously fussy as a contrast to the firmness of Gaunt. The acting was said by one critic to be as slow as it would have been at the Lyceum or Her Majesty's; and another recorded that the performance lasted for four hours.

Yet, with all its oddity, this performance of *King Richard II* made no small stir at the time, and certainly helped to forward the revolt against the current method of adapting and decorating Shakespeare. The cast was mainly composed of amateurs; but it included a young player named Granville Barker, whose acting of the

King is remembered by those who saw it and can be imagined by those who did not to have been of exceeding beauty. And in spite of all that was wilful and deliberately difficult in Poel's production, one or two of the critics welcomed it. For some reason William Archer, in the *World*, lost his temper over it. 'Mr Poel's genius, being unaccompanied by common sense' is a fair hit; but Archer cursed the exits and entrances through the audience, cursed the King's monkish dress, cursed (and was not alone in cursing) the special, incidental, and apparently very doleful music, and even declared that the text had been 'considerably curtailed', which was both untrue and a deadly hit at one of Poel's dearest purposes. On the other hand, Joseph Knight in the *Athenaeum* (though he was uncomfortable with no room for his long legs) growled a little (he made the queer objection that 'it was, of course, impossible for the fight between Mowbray and Hereford to take place'—as if it ever did) and then turned to praise. 'The exponents of the various characters neither mouthed, strutted, nor ranted. From the chief iniquities of most performances of Shakespearean tragedy the representation was accordingly free, and one was able to enjoy undisturbed the poetry of a play much of which is divinely inspired.' The critic of *The Times* was even better pleased. He had high praise for the actor of King Richard. He found that the simple arrangement of the stage worked well, and that the grouping was picturesque and effective against the tapestry background; and he concluded that 'Those who love poetry and drama better than spectacle find their minds well attuned to such a play as *Richard II* by the plain surroundings which the Society offers.'

*The Times* spoke to much the same effect of the performances given by the Marlowe Society of Cambridge University in the Victoria Assembly Rooms in February 1910. Here, again, the play was acted before hangings, 'severe and simple', and with elaborate costume and effective grouping. The music was taken from Purcell. The performers (whose names were not given in the programme) brought out the beauty of the poetry, 'which they interpret with a quiet gravity that is a refreshing contrast to the familiar theatrical declamation'. The whole was 'a quiet and intelligent attempt to let Shakespeare speak for himself'.

In September 1937 Mr John Gielgud, who had played the part of *King Richard II* some years before in one of the productions at the Old Vic (not to mention Richard of Bordeaux in the long run of Gordon Daviot's play of that name) staged Shakespeare's play and acted the part of the King with his own company at the Queen's Theatre, choosing it for the first production of his management there. The setting was not hangings but scenery; but it was not allowed to come between the audience and the play; and the omission of scenes ii and iii of Act v—the conspiracy of Aumerle and its sequel—is now generally accepted as the best way of shortening, without injuring the tragedy. Bolingbroke was acted by Mr Michael Redgrave, Gaunt by Mr Leon Quartermaine, York by Mr George Howe, Northumberland by Mr Frederick Lloyd, the Bishop of Carlisle by Mr Harcourt Williams, the Queen by Miss Peggy Ashcroft, and the Duchess of Gloucester by Miss Dorothy Green.

HAROLD CHILD

# TO THE READER

The following is a brief description of the punctuation and other typographical devices employed in the text, which have been more fully explained in the *Note on Punctuation* and the *Textual Introduction* to be found in *The Tempest* volume:

An obelisk (†) implies corruption or emendation, and suggests a reference to the Notes.

A single bracket at the beginning of a speech signifies an 'aside.'

Four dots represent a *full-stop* in the original, except when it occurs at the end of a speech, and they mark a long pause. Original *colons* or *semicolons*, which denote a somewhat shorter pause, are retained, or represented as three dots when they appear to possess special dramatic significance. Similarly, significant *commas* have been given as dashes.

Round brackets are taken from the original, and mark a significant change of voice; when the original brackets seem to imply little more than the drop in tone accompanying parenthesis, they are conveyed by commas or dashes.

Single inverted commas (' ') are editorial; double ones (" ") derive from the original, where they are used to draw attention to maxims, quotations, etc.

The reference number for the first line is given at the head of each page. Numerals in square brackets are placed at the beginning of the traditional acts and scenes.

# THE Tragedie of King Ri-chard the ſe-cond.

*As it hath beene publikely acted by the right Honourable the Lorde Chamberlaine his Ser-uants.*

LONDON

Printed by Valentine Simmes for Androw Wiſe, and are to be ſold at his ſhop in Paules church yard at the ſigne of the Angel.

1597.

The scene: England and Wales

## CHARACTERS IN THE PLAY

KING RICHARD THE SECOND

JOHN OF GAUNT, *Duke of Lancaster* } *uncles to the king*

EDMUND, *Duke of York* }

HENRY BOLINGBROKE, *Duke of Hereford, son to John of Gaunt; afterwards King* HENRY IV

DUKE OF AUMERLE, *son to the Duke of York*

THOMAS MOWBRAY, *Duke of Norfolk*

DUKE OF SURREY

EARL OF SALISBURY

LORD BERKELEY

BUSHY }

BAGOT } *servants to King Richard*

GREEN }

EARL OF NORTHUMBERLAND

HENRY PERCY, *his son*

LORD ROSS

LORD WILLOUGHBY

LORD FITZWATER

BISHOP OF CARLISLE

ABBOT OF WESTMINSTER

SIR STEPHEN SCROOP

SIR PIERCE OF EXTON

*Lord Marshal*

*Captain of a band of Welshmen*

QUEEN *to King Richard*

DUCHESS OF YORK

DUCHESS OF GLOUCESTER

*Lady attending on the Queen*

*Lords, Heralds, Officers, Soldiers, two Gardeners, Keeper, Messenger, Groom, and other Attendants*

# KING RICHARD II

[I. I.] *A great scaffold within the castle at Windsor, with seats thereon, and a space of ground before it*

*'Enter* KING RICHARD, JOHN OF GAUNT, *with the* DUKE OF SURREY, *other nobles and attendants.' They ascend the scaffold and sit in their places, the King in a chair of justice in the midst*

*K. Richard.* Old John of Gaunt, time-honoured Lancaster,
Hast thou according to thy oath and band
Brought hither Henry Hereford thy bold son,
Here to make good the boist'rous late appeal,
Which then our leisure would not let us hear,
Against the Duke of Norfolk, Thomas Mowbray?
*Gaunt.* I have, my liege.
*K. Richard.* Tell me, moreover, hast thou sounded him,
If he appeal the duke on ancient malice,
Or worthily as a good subject should
On some known ground of treachery in him?
*Gaunt.* As near as I could sift him on that argument,
On some apparent danger seen in him
Aimed at your highness, no inveterate malice.
*K. Richard.* Then call them to our presence—face to face,
And frowning brow to brow, ourselves will hear
The accuser and the accused freely speak:
High-stomached are they both and full of ire,
In rage, deaf as the sea, hasty as fire.

*'Enter* BOLINGBROKE *and* MOWBRAY*'*

*Bolingbroke.* Many years of happy days befal
My gracious sovereign, my most loving liege!
*Mowbray.* Each day still better other's happiness,
Until the heavens, envying earth's good hap,
Add an immortal title to your crown!
*K. Richard.* We thank you both, yet one but flatters us,
As well appeareth by the cause you come,
Namely, to appeal each other of high treason:
Cousin of Hereford, what dost thou object
Against the Duke of Norfolk, Thomas Mowbray?
*Bolingbroke.* First—heaven be the record to my speech
In the devotion of a subject's love,
Tend'ring the precious safety of my prince,
And free from other misbegotten hate,
Come I appellant to this princely presence....
Now Thomas Mowbray do I turn to thee,
And mark my greeting well: for what I speak
My body shall make good upon this earth,
Or my divine soul answer it in heaven:
Thou art a traitor and a miscreant,
Too good to be so, and too bad to live,
Since the more fair and crystal is the sky,
The uglier seem the clouds that in it fly:
Once more, the more to aggravate the note,
With a foul traitor's name stuff I thy throat,
And wish (so please my sovereign) ere I move,
What my tongue speaks my right drawn sword may prove.
*Mowbray.* Let not my cold words here accuse my zeal.
'Tis not the trial of a woman's war,

The bitter clamour of two eager tongues,
Can arbitrate this cause betwixt us twain.
The blood is hot that must be cooled for this.
Yet can I not of such tame patience boast
As to be hushed and nought at all to say....
First the fair reverence of your highness curbs me
From giving reins and spurs to my free speech,
Which else would post until it had returned
These terms of treason doubled down his throat:
Setting aside his high blood's royalty,
And let him be no kinsman to my liege,
I do defy him, and I spit at him,
Call him a slanderous coward, and a villain,
Which to maintain I would allow him odds,
And meet him were I tied to run afoot,
Even to the frozen ridges of the Alps,
Or any other ground inhabitable,
Where ever Englishman durst set his foot.
Mean time, let this defend my loyalty—
By all my hopes most falsely doth he lie.
*Bolingbroke.* Pale trembling coward there I throw my gage, [*he casts it at Mowbray's feet*
Disclaiming here the kindred of the king,
And lay aside my high blood's royalty,
Which fear, not reverence, makes thee to except....
If guilty dread have left thee so much strength,
As to take up mine honour's pawn, then stoop.
By that, and all the rites of knighthood else,
Will I make good against thee, arm to arm,
What I have spoke, or thou canst worse devise.
*Mowbray.* I take it up, and by that sword I swear,
Which gently laid my knighthood on my shoulder,
I'll answer thee in any fair degree,
Or chivalrous design of knightly trial:

And when I mount, alive may I not light,
If I be traitor or unjustly fight!

*K. Richard.* What doth our cousin lay to Mowbray's charge?
It must be great that can inherit us
So much as of a thought of ill in him.

*Bolingbroke.* Look what I speak, my life shall prove it true,
That Mowbray hath received eight thousand nobles
In name of 'lendings' for your highness' soldiers,
The which he hath detained for lewd employments,
Like a false traitor, and injurious villain:
Besides I say, and will in battle prove,
Or here, or elsewhere to the furthest verge
That ever was surveyed by English eye,
That all the treasons for these eighteen years,
Complotted and contrived in this land...
Fetch from false Mowbray their first head and spring!
Further I say, and further will maintain
Upon his bad life to make all this good,
That he did plot the Duke of Gloucester's death,
Suggest his soon-believing adversaries,
And consequently like a traitor coward,
Sluiced out his innocent soul through streams of blood,
Which blood, like sacrificing Abel's, cries,
Even from the tongueless caverns of the earth,
To me for justice and rough chastisement:
And by the glorious worth of my descent,
This arm shall do it, or this life be spent.

*K. Richard.* How high a pitch his resolution soars!
Thomas of Norfolk, what say'st thou to this?

*Mowbray.* O, let my sovereign turn away his face,
And bid his ears a little while be deaf,
Till I have told this slander of his blood,

How God and good men hate so foul a liar.
*K. Richard.* Mowbray, impartial are our eyes and ears,
Were he my brother, nay, my kingdom's heir,
As he is but my father's brother's son,
Now by my sceptre's awe I make a vow,
Such neighbour nearness to our sacred blood
Should nothing privilege him nor partialize
The unstooping firmness of my upright soul.
He is our subject, Mowbray, so art thou,
Free speech and fearless I to thee allow.
*Mowbray.* Then Bolingbroke as low as to thy heart
Through the false passage of thy throat thou liest!
Three parts of that receipt I had for Calais
Disbursed I duly to his highness' soldiers,
The other part reserved I by consent,
For that my sovereign liege was in my debt,
Upon remainder of a dear account,
Since last I went to France to fetch his queen:
Now swallow down that lie....For Gloucester's death,
I slew him not, but to my own disgrace
Neglected my sworn duty in that case:
For you, my noble lord of Lancaster,
The honourable father to my foe,
Once did I lay an ambush for your life,
A trespass that doth vex my grievéd soul:
But ere I last received the sacrament,
I did confess it, and exactly begged
Your grace's pardon, and I hope I had it....
This is my fault—as for the rest appealed
It issues from the rancour of a villain,
A recreant and most degenerate traitor,
Which in myself I boldly will defend,
And interchangeably hurl down my gage

Upon this overweening traitor's foot,
To prove myself a loyal gentleman,
Even in the best blood chambered in his bosom,
In haste whereof most heartily I pray
Your highness to assign our trial day.

*K. Richard.* Wrath-kindled gentlemen, be ruled by me,
Let's purge this choler without letting blood.
This we prescribe, though no physician—
Deep malice makes too deep incision—
Forget, forgive, conclude and be agreed.
Our doctors say this is no month to bleed...
Good uncle, let this end where it begun,
We'll calm the Duke of Norfolk, you your son.

*Gaunt.* To be a make-peace shall become my age,
Throw down, my son, the Duke of Norfolk's gage.

*K. Richard.* And, Norfolk, throw down his.

*Gaunt.* When, Harry? when?
Obedience bids I should not bid again.

*K. Richard.* Norfolk, throw down we bid, there is no boot.

*Mowbray.* Myself I throw, dread sovereign, at thy foot,
My life thou shalt command, but not my shame,
The one my duty owes, but my fair name,
Despite of death that lives upon my grave,
To dark dishonour's use thou shalt not have:
I am disgraced, impeached, and baffled here,
Pierced to the soul with slander's venomed spear,
The which no balm can cure but his heart-blood
Which breathed this poison.

*K. Richard.* Rage must be withstood.
Give me his gage; lions make leopards tame.

*Mowbray.* Yea, but not change his spots: take but my shame,

And I resign my gage. My dear dear lord,
The purest treasure mortal times afford,
Is spotless reputation—that away
Men are but gilded loam, or painted clay.
A jewel in a ten-times-barred-up chest
Is a bold spirit in a loyal breast:
Mine honour is my life, both grow in one,
Take honour from me, and my life is done:
Then, dear my liege, mine honour let me try—
In that I live, and for that will I die.

*K. Richard.* Cousin, throw up your gage, do you begin.

*Bolingbroke.* O God defend my soul from such deep sin!
Shall I seem crest-fallen in my father's sight?
Or with pale beggar-fear impeach my height
Before this out-dared dastard? ere my tongue
Shall wound my honour with such feeble wrong,
Or sound so base a parle, my teeth shall tear
The slavish motive of recanting fear,
And spit it bleeding in his high disgrace,
Where shame doth harbour, even in Mowbray's face.

*K. Richard.* We were not born to sue, but to command,
Which since we cannot do, to make you friends,
Be ready, as your lives shall answer it,
At Coventry upon Saint Lambert's day.
There shall your swords and lances arbitrate
The swelling difference of your settled hate.
Since we can not atone you, we shall see
Justice design the victor's chivalry.
Lord marshal, command our officers at arms
Be ready to direct these home alarms. [*they go*

[1. 2.] *A room in the Duke of Lancaster's house*

*'Enter* JOHN OF GAUNT *with the* DUCHESS OF GLOUCESTER'

*Gaunt.* Alas, the part I had in Woodstock's blood
Doth more solicit me than your exclaims
To stir against the butchers of his life,
But since correction lieth in those hands,
Which made the fault that we cannot correct...
Put we our quarrel to the will of heaven,
Who, when they see the hours ripe on earth,
Will rain hot vengeance on offenders' heads.

*Duchess.* Finds brotherhood in thee no sharper spur?
Hath love in thy old blood no living fire?
Edward's seven sons, whereof thyself art one,
Were as seven vials of his sacred blood,
Or seven fair branches springing from one root:
Some of those seven are dried by nature's course,
Some of those branches by the Destinies cut:
But Thomas, my dear lord, my life, my Gloucester,
One vial full of Edward's sacred blood,
One flourishing branch of his most royal root,
Is cracked, and all the precious liquor spilt,
Is hacked down, and his summer leaves all faded,
By envy's hand, and murder's bloody axe.... [*she weeps*
Ah, Gaunt, his blood was thine! that bed, that womb,
That mettle, that self mould, that fashioned thee
Made him a man; and though thou livest and breathest,
Yet art thou slain in him. Thou dost consent
In some large measure to thy father's death,

In that thou seest thy wretched brother die,
Who was the model of thy father's life...
Call it not patience, Gaunt, it is despair.
In suff'ring thus thy brother to be slaught'red,
Thou showest the naked pathway to thy life,
Teaching stern murder how to butcher thee:
That which in mean men we intitle patience,
Is pale cold cowardice in noble breasts....
What shall I say? to safeguard thine own life,
The best way is to venge my Gloucester's death.
*Gaunt.* God's is the quarrel—for God's substitute,
His deputy anointed in His sight,
Hath caused his death, the which if wrongfully,
Let heaven revenge, for I may never lift
An angry arm against His minister.
*Duchess.* Where then, alas, may I complain myself?
*Gaunt.* To God, the widow's champion and defence.
*Duchess.* Why then, I will...Farewell, old Gaunt.
Thou goest to Coventry, there to behold
Our cousin Hereford and fell Mowbray fight.
O, sit my husband's wrongs on Hereford's spear,
That it may enter butcher Mowbray's breast!
Or if misfortune miss the first career,
Be Mowbray's sins so heavy in his bosom,
That they may break his foaming courser's back,
And throw the rider headlong in the lists,
A caitiff recreant to my cousin Hereford!
Farewell old Gaunt, thy sometimes brother's wife
With her companion Grief must end her life.
*Gaunt.* Sister farewell, I must to Coventry,
As much good stay with thee, as go with me!
*Duchess.* Yet one word more—Grief boundeth where it falls,
Not with the empty hollowness, but weight:

I take my leave before I have begun,
For sorrow ends not when it seemeth done:
Commend me to thy brother, Edmund York.
Lo, this is all...nay, yet depart not so,
Though this be all, do not so quickly go...
I shall remember more...Bid him—ah, what?—
With all good speed at Plashy visit me.
Alack and what shall good old York there see
But empty lodgings and unfurnished walls,
Unpeopled offices, untrodden stones?
And what hear there for welcome but my groans?
Therefore commend me, let him not come there,
To seek out sorrow that dwells every where.
Desolate, desolate, will I hence and die:
The last leave of thee takes my weeping eye. [*they go*

[1. 3.] *The lists at Coventry; to the side a platform, with a throne (richly hanged and adorned) for the king, and seats for his court; at either end of the lists chairs for the combatants; a great throng of spectators. Heralds, &c. attending*

'*Enter the Lord Marshal and the* DUKE AUMERLE'

*Marshal.* My Lord Aumerle, is Harry Hereford armed?
*Aumerle.* Yea, at all points, and longs to enter in.
*Marshal.* The Duke of Norfolk, sprightfully and bold,
Stays but the summons of the appellant's trumpet.
*Aumerle.* Why then, the champions are prepared and stay
For nothing but his majesty's approach.

*The trumpets sound and the* KING, *bearing a truncheon, enters with his nobles* (GAUNT *among them*): *when they are set, enter the* DUKE OF NORFOLK *in arms defendant*

*K. Richard.* Marshal, demand of yonder champion
The cause of his arrival here in arms,
Ask him his name, and orderly proceed
To swear him in the justice of his cause.
*Marshal.* In God's name and the king's say who thou art,
And why thou comest thus knightly clad in arms,
Against what man thou com'st, and what thy quarrel.
Speak truly, on thy knighthood, and thy oath,
And so defend thee heaven and thy valour!
*Mowbray.* My name is Thomas Mowbray, Duke of Norfolk,
Who hither come engagéd by my oath
(Which God defend a knight should violate!)
Both to defend my loyalty and truth,
To God, my king, and my succeeding issue,
Against the Duke of Hereford that appeals me,
And by the grace of God, and this mine arm,
To prove him, in defending of myself,
A traitor to my God, my king, and me—
And as I truly fight, defend me heaven!
[*he takes his seat*

*The trumpets sound. Enter the* DUKE OF HEREFORD *appellant in armour*

*K. Richard.* Marshal, ask yonder knight in arms,
Both who he is, and why he cometh hither,
Thus plated in habiliments of war,
And formally, according to our law,
Depose him in the justice of his cause.

*Marshal.* What is thy name? and wherefore com'st thou hither,
Before King Richard in his royal lists?
Against whom comest thou? and what's thy quarrel?
Speak like a true knight, so defend thee heaven!
*Bolingbroke.* Harry of Hereford, Lancaster and Derby
Am I, who ready here do stand in arms
To prove by God's grace, and my body's valour
In lists, on Thomas Mowbray Duke of Norfolk,
That he is a traitor foul and dangerous,
To God of heaven, King Richard and to me:
And as I truly fight, defend me heaven!
*Marshal.* On pain of death, no person be so bold,
Or daring-hardy, as to touch the lists,
Except the marshal and such officers
Appointed to direct these fair designs.
*Bolingbroke.* Lord marshal, let me kiss my sovereign's hand,
And bow my knee before his majesty,
For Mowbray and myself are like two men
That vow a long and weary pilgrimage,
Then let us take a ceremonious leave,
And loving farewell of our several friends.
*Marshal.* The appellant in all duty greets your highness,
And craves to kiss your hand, and take his leave.
*K. Richard.* [*rises*] We will descend and fold him in our arms.
Cousin of Hereford, as thy cause is right,
So be thy fortune in this royal fight...
[*he descends with Gaunt and other nobles into the lists and embraces Bolingbroke*
Farewell, my blood, which if to-day thou shed,
Lament we may, but not revenge thee dead.

*Bolingbroke.* O, let no noble eye profane a tear
For me, if I be gored with Mowbray's spear:
As confident as is the falcon's flight
Against a bird, do I with Mowbray fight....
My loving lord, [*to the Marshal*] I take my leave of you:
Of you, my noble cousin, Lord Aumerle—
Not sick, although I have to do with death,
But lusty, young, and cheerly drawing breath:
Lo, as at English feasts, so I regreet
The daintiest last, to make the end most sweet....
[*to Gaunt*
O thou, the earthly author of my blood,
Whose youthful spirit in me regenerate
Doth with a twofold vigour lift me up
To reach at victory above my head...
Add proof unto mine armour with thy prayers,
And with thy blessings steel my lance's point,
That it may enter Mowbray's waxen coat,
And furbish new the name of John a Gaunt,
Even in the lusty haviour of his son.
*Gaunt.* God in thy good cause make thee prosperous,
Be swift like lightning in the execution,
And let thy blows, doubly redoubled,
Fall like amazing thunder on the casque
Of thy adverse pernicious enemy!
Rouse up thy youthful blood, be valiant and live.
*Bolingbroke.* —Mine innocency and Saint George to thrive! [*he takes his seat*
*Mowbray.* [*rising*] However God or fortune cast my lot,
There lives or dies true to King Richard's throne,
A loyal, just, and upright gentleman:
Never did captive with a freer heart

Cast off his chains of bondage, and embrace
His golden uncontrolled enfranchisement,
More than my dancing soul doth celebrate
This feast of battle with mine adversary.
Most mighty liege, and my companion peers,
Take from my mouth the wish of happy years:
As gentle and as jocund as to jest
Go I to fight—truth hath a quiet breast.
*K. Richard.* Farewell, my lord, securely I espy
Virtue with valour couchéd in thine eye.
Order the trial, marshal, and begin.
[*the King and his lords return to their seats; Bolingbroke and Mowbray don their helmets and lower the visors*
*Marshal.* Harry of Hereford, Lancaster and Derby,
Receive thy lance, and God defend the right!
*Bolingbroke.* Strong as a tower in hope I cry 'amen'.
*Marshal.* [*to a knight*] Go bear this lance to Thomas, Duke of Norfolk.
*1 Herald.* Harry of Hereford, Lancaster, and Derby,
Stands here, for God, his sovereign, and himself,
On pain to be found false and recreant,
To prove the Duke of Norfolk, Thomas Mowbray,
A traitor to his God, his king, and him,
And dares him to set forward to the fight.
*2 Herald.* Here standeth Thomas Mowbray, Duke of Norfolk,
On pain to be found false and recreant,
Both to defend himself, and to approve
Henry of Hereford, Lancaster, and Derby,
To God, his sovereign, and to him disloyal,
Courageously, and with a free desire,
Attending but the signal to begin.

*Marshal.* Sound, trumpets, and set forward, combatants...

'*A charge sounded.*' *The champions are about to join battle, when the* KING *rises and casts his truncheon into the lists*

Stay, the king hath thrown his warder down.

*K. Richard.* Let them lay by their helmets and their spears,
And both return back to their chairs again.
Withdraw with us [*to the councillors about him*], and let the trumpets sound,
While we return these dukes what we decree....

*The trumpets sound a long flourish, as the* KING *and his council retire to a room at the back of the platform; the combatants remove their helmets and return to their chairs, and the spectators murmur in astonishment. After some moments, the* KING *returns and summons the combatants to him*

Draw near
And list what with our council we have done...
For that our kingdom's earth should not be soiled
With that dear blood which it hath fosteréd;
And for our eyes do hate the dire aspect
Of civil wounds ploughed up with neighbours' sword,
And for we think the eagle-wingéd pride
Of sky-aspiring and ambitious thoughts,
With rival-hating envy, set on you
To wake our peace, which in our country's cradle
Draws the sweet infant breath of gentle sleep;
†Which so roused up with boist'rous untuned drums,
With harsh-resounding trumpets' dreadful bray,
And grating shock of wrathful iron arms,

Might from our quiet confines fright fair peace,
And make us wade even in our kindred's blood;
Therefore we banish you our territories:
You, cousin Hereford, upon pain of life,
Till twice five summers have enriched our fields,
Shall not regreet our fair dominions,
But tread the stranger paths of banishment.

*Bolingbroke*. Your will be done; this must my comfort be,
That sun that warms you here, shall shine on me,
And those his golden beams to you here lent,
Shall point on me, and gild my banishment.

*K. Richard*. Norfolk, for thee remains a heavier doom,
Which I with some unwillingness pronounce.
The sly slow hours shall not determinate
The dateless limit of thy dear exile.
The hopeless word of 'never to return'
Breathe I against thee, upon pain of life.

*Mowbray*. A heavy sentence, my most sovereign liege,
And all unlooked for from your highness' mouth.
A dearer merit, not so deep a maim
As to be cast forth in the common air,
Have I deservéd at your highness' hands...
The language I have learnt these forty years,
My native English, now I must forego,
And now my tongue's use is to me no more
Than an unstringéd viol or a harp,
Or like a cunning instrument cased up—
Or being open, put into his hands
That knows no touch to tune the harmony:
Within my mouth you have engaoled my tongue,
Doubly portcullised with my teeth and lips,
And dull unfeeling barren ignorance
Is made my gaoler to attend on me:

I am too old to fawn upon a nurse,
Too far in years to be a pupil now,
What is thy sentence then but speechless death,
Which robs my tongue from breathing native breath?
*K. Richard.* It boots thee not to be compassionate,
After our sentence plaining comes too late.
*Mowbray.* Then thus I turn me from my country's light,
To dwell in solemn shades of endless night.
[*he moves away*
*K. Richard.* Return again, and take an oath with thee.
Lay on our royal sword your banished hands,
Swear by the duty that you owe to God
(Our part therein we banish with yourselves,)
To keep the oath that we administer:
You never shall, so help you truth and God,
Embrace each other's love in banishment,
Nor never look upon each other's face,
Nor never write, regreet, nor reconcile
This louring tempest of your home-bred hate,
Nor never by advisèd purpose meet,
To plot, contrive, or complot any ill,
'Gainst us, our state, our subjects, or our land.
*Bolingbroke.* I swear.
*Mowbray.* And I, to keep all this.
*Bolingbroke.* Norfolk, so fare as to mine enemy...
By this time, had the king permitted us,
One of our souls had wand'red in the air,
Banished this frail sepulchre of our flesh,
As now our flesh is banished from this land.
Confess thy treasons ere thou fly the realm—
Since thou hast far to go, bear not along
The clogging burthen of a guilty soul.
*Mowbray.* No, Bolingbroke, if ever I were traitor,
My name be blotted from the book of life,

And I from heaven banished as from hence:
But what thou art, God, thou, and I do know,
And all too soon, I fear, the king shall rue:
Farewell, my liege. Now no way can I stray—
Save back to England all the world's my way. [*he goes*
*K. Richard.* Uncle, even in the glasses of thine eyes
I see thy grievéd heart: thy sad aspect
Hath from the number of his banished years
Plucked four away. [*to Bolingbroke*] Six frozen winters spent,
Return with welcome home from banishment.
*Bolingbroke.* How long a time lies in one little word!
Four lagging winters and four wanton springs
End in a word—such is the breath of kings.
*Gaunt.* I thank my liege that, in regard of me,
He shortens four years of my son's exile,
But little vantage shall I reap thereby:
For, ere the six years that he hath to spend
Can change their moons, and bring their times about,
My oil-dried lamp and time-bewasted light
Shall be extinct with age and endless night,
My inch of taper will be burnt and done,
And blindfold Death not let me see my son.
*K. Richard.* Why, uncle, thou hast many years to live.
*Gaunt.* But not a minute, king, that thou canst give,
Shorten my days thou canst with sullen sorrow,
And pluck nights from me, but not lend a morrow:
Thou canst help time to furrow me with age,
But stop no wrinkle in his pilgrimage:
Thy word is current with him for my death,
But dead, thy kingdom cannot buy my breath.
*K. Richard.* Thy son is banished upon good advice,
Whereto thy tongue a party-verdict gave,
Why at our justice seem'st thou then to lour?

*Gaunt.* Things sweet to taste, prove in digestion sour....
You urged me as a judge, but I had rather,
You would have bid me argue like a father:
O, had it been a stranger, not my child,
To smooth his fault I should have been more mild:
A partial slander sought I to avoid,
And in the sentence my own life destroyed:
Alas, I looked when some of you should say,
I was too strict to make mine own away:
But you gave leave to my unwilling tongue,
Against my will to do myself this wrong.

*K. Richard.* Cousin, farewell—and uncle, bid him so,
Six years we banish him and he shall go.

['*Flourish.*' *K. Richard departs with his train*

*Aumerle.* [*following*] Cousin, farewell, what presence must not know,
From where you do remain let paper show.

*Marshal.* My lord, no leave take I, for I will ride
As far as land will let me by your side.

*Gaunt.* O, to what purpose dost thou hoard thy words,
That thou returnest no greeting to thy friends?

*Bolingbroke.* I have too few to take my leave of you,
When the tongue's office should be prodigal
To breathe the abundant dolour of the heart.

*Gaunt.* Thy grief is but thy absence for a time.

*Bolingbroke.* Joy absent, grief is present for that time.

*Gaunt.* What is six winters? they are quickly gone—

*Bolingbroke.* To men in joy, but grief makes one hour ten.

*Gaunt.* Call it a travel that thou tak'st for pleasure.

*Bolingbroke.* My heart will sigh when I miscall it so,
Which finds it an inforcéd pilgrimage.

*Gaunt.* The sullen passage of thy weary steps

Esteem as foil wherein thou art to set
The precious jewel of thy home return.
*Bolingbroke.* Nay, rather, every tedious stride I make
Will but remember me what a deal of world
I wander from the jewels that I love....
Must I not serve a long apprenticehood
To foreign passages, and in the end,
Having my freedom, boast of nothing else,
But that I was a journeyman to grief?
*Gaunt.* All places that the eye of heaven visits
Are to a wise man ports and happy havens:
Teach thy necessity to reason thus—
There is no virtue like necessity.
Think not the king did banish thee,
But thou the king....Woe doth the heavier sit,
Where it perceives it is but faintly borne:
Go, say I sent thee forth to purchase honour,
And not the king exiled thee; or suppose
Devouring pestilence hangs in our air,
And thou art flying to a fresher clime:
Look, what thy soul holds dear, imagine it
To lie that way thou goest, not whence thou com'st:
Suppose the singing birds musicians,
The grass whereon thou tread'st the presence strewed,
The flowers fair ladies, and thy steps no more
Than a delightful measure or a dance,
For gnarling sorrow hath less power to bite
The man that mocks at it and sets it light.
*Bolingbroke.* O, who can hold a fire in his hand
By thinking on the frosty Caucasus?
Or cloy the hungry edge of appetite
By bare imagination of a feast?
Or wallow naked in December snow
By thinking on fantastic summer's heat?

O no, the apprehension of the good
Gives but the greater feeling to the worse:
Fell sorrow's tooth doth never rankle more
Than when he bites, but lanceth not the sore.

*Gaunt.* Come, come, my son, I'll bring thee on thy way,
Had I thy youth and cause, I would not stay.

*Bolingbroke.* Then England's ground farewell, sweet soil adieu,
My mother and my nurse that bears me yet!
Where'er I wander boast of this I can,
Though banished, yet a trueborn Englishman.

[*they go*

[1. 4.] *The court*

'*Enter the* KING' *with* BAGOT *and* GREEN '*at one door, and the* LORD AUMERLE *at another*'

*K. Richard.* We did observe....Cousin Aumerle,
How far brought you high Hereford on his way?

*Aumerle.* I brought high Hereford, if you call him so,
But to the next highway, and there I left him.

*K. Richard.* And say, what store of parting tears were shed?

*Aumerle.* Faith, none for me, except the north-east wind
Which then blew bitterly against our faces,
Awaked the sleeping rheum, and so by chance
Did grace our hollow parting with a tear.

*K. Richard.* What said our cousin when you parted with him?

*Aumerle.* 'Farewell'—
And for my heart disdainèd that my tongue
Should so profane the word, that taught me craft
To counterfeit oppression of such grief

That words seemed buried in my sorrow's grave:
Marry, would the word 'farewell' have length'ned hours,
And added years to his short banishment,
He should have had a volume of farewells:
But since it would not, he had none of me.
*K. Richard.* He is our cousin's cousin, but 'tis doubt,
When time shall call him home from banishment,
Whether our kinsman come to see his friends....
Ourself and Bushy
Observed his courtship to the common people,
How he did seem to dive into their hearts,
With humble and familiar courtesy,
What reverence he did throw away on slaves,
Wooing poor craftsmen with the craft of smiles
And patient underbearing of his fortune,
As 'twere to banish their affects with him.
Off goes his bonnet to an oyster-wench,
A brace of draymen bid God speed him well,
And had the tribute of his supple knee,
With 'Thanks, my countrymen, my loving friends'—
As were our England in reversion his,
And he our subjects' next degree in hope.
*Green.* Well, he is gone; and with him go these thoughts.
Now for the rebels which stand out in Ireland,
Expedient manage must be made, my liege,
Ere further leisure yield them further means
For their advantage and your highness' loss.
*K. Richard.* We will ourself in person to this war,
And for our coffers with too great a court
And liberal largess are grown somewhat light,
We are inforced to farm our royal realm,
The revenue whereof shall furnish us
For our affairs in hand—if that come short,

Our substitutes at home shall have blank charters,
Whereto, when they shall know what men are rich,
They shall subscribe them for large sums of gold,
And send them after to supply our wants,
For we will make for Ireland presently....

*BUSHY enters*

What news?
*Bushy*. Old John of Gaunt is grievous sick, my lord,
Suddenly taken, and hath sent post haste
To entreat your majesty to visit him.
*K. Richard*. Where lies he?
*Bushy*. At Ely House.[1]
*K. Richard*. Now put it, God, in the physician's mind,
To help him to his grave immediately!
The lining of his coffers shall make coats
To deck our soldiers for these Irish wars....
Come, gentlemen, let's all go visit him,
Pray God we may make haste and come too late!
*All*. Amen. [*they go out*

[2. 1.] *Ely House*

'*Enter JOHN OF GAUNT sick' borne in a chair,*
'*with the DUKE OF YORK, &c.*'

*Gaunt*. Will the king come that I may breathe my last
In wholesome counsel to his unstaid youth?
*York*. Vex not yourself, nor strive not with your breath,
For all in vain comes counsel to his ear.
*Gaunt*. O, but they say the tongues of dying men
Enforce attention like deep harmony:
Where words are scarce they are seldom spent in vain,
For they breathe truth that breathe their words in pain:

He that no more must say is listened more
Than they whom youth and ease have taught to glose,
More are men's ends marked than their lives before:
The setting sun, and music at the close,
As the last taste of sweets, is sweetest last,
Writ in remembrance more than things long past.
Though Richard my life's counsel would not hear,
My death's sad tale may yet undeaf his ear.
*York.* No, it is stopped with other flattering sounds,
†As praises, of whose taste the wise are fond,
Lascivious metres, to whose venom sound
The open ear of youth doth always listen,
Report of fashions in proud Italy,
Whose manners still our tardy apish nation
Limps after in base imitation:
Where doth the world thrust forth a vanity—
So it be new, there's no respect how vile—
That is not quickly buzzed into his ears?
Then all too late comes counsel to be heard,
Where will doth mutiny with wit's regard:
Direct not him whose way himself will choose,
'Tis breath thou lack'st, and that breath wilt thou lose.
*Gaunt.* Methinks I am a prophet new inspired—
And thus expiring do foretell of him—
His rash fierce blaze of riot cannot last;
For violent fires soon burn out themselves,
Small showers last long, but sudden storms are short:
He tires betimes that spurs too fast betimes:
With eager feeding food doth choke the feeder:
Light vanity, insatiate cormorant,
Consuming means, soon preys upon itself:
This royal throne of kings, this sceptered isle,
This earth of majesty, this seat of Mars,
This other Eden, demi-paradise,

This fortress built by nature for herself
Against infection and the hand of war,
This happy breed of men, this little world,
This precious stone set in the silver sea,
Which serves it in the office of a wall,
Or as a moat defensive to a house,
Against the envy of less happier lands....
This blessed plot, this earth, this realm, this England,
This nurse, this teeming womb of royal kings,
Feared by their breed, and famous by their birth,
Renownéd for their deeds as far from home,
For Christian service and true chivalry,
As is the sepulchre in stubborn Jewry
Of the world's ransom, blessed Mary's Son:
This land of such dear souls, this dear dear land,
Dear for her reputation through the world,
Is now leased out—I die pronouncing it—
Like to a tenement or pelting farm....
England, bound in with the triumphant sea,
Whose rocky shore beats back the envious siege
Of wat'ry Neptune, is now bound in with shame,
With inky blots, and rotten parchment bonds:
That England, that was wont to conquer others,
Hath made a shameful conquest of itself:
Ah, would the scandal vanish with my life,
How happy then were my ensuing death!

'*Enter* KING, QUEEN, AUMERLE, BUSHY, GREEN, BAGOT, ROSS, *and* WILLOUGHBY'

*York.* The king is come, deal mildly with his youth,
†For young hot colts, being ragged, do rage the more.
*Queen.* How fares our noble uncle, Lancaster?
*K. Richard.* What comfort, man? how is't with aged Gaunt?

*Gaunt.* O, how that name befits my composition!
Old Gaunt indeed, and gaunt in being old:
Within me grief hath kept a tedious fast,
And who abstains from meat that is not gaunt?
For sleeping England long time have I watched,
Watching breeds leanness, leanness is all gaunt:
The pleasure that some fathers feed upon
Is my strict fast; I mean my children's looks,
And therein fasting hast thou made me gaunt:
Gaunt am I for the grave, gaunt as a grave,
Whose hollow womb inherits nought but bones.
*K. Richard.* Can sick men play so nicely with their names?
*Gaunt.* No, misery makes sport to mock itself—
Since thou dost seek to kill my name in me,
I mock my name, great king, to flatter thee.
*K. Richard.* Should dying men flatter with those that live?
*Gaunt.* No, no, men living flatter those that die.
*K. Richard.* Thou now a-dying sayest thou flatterest me.
*Gaunt.* Oh no, thou diest, though I the sicker be.
*K. Richard.* I am in health, I breathe, and see thee ill.
*Gaunt.* Now He that made me knows I see thee ill,
Ill in myself to see, and in thee, seeing ill.
Thy death-bed is no lesser than thy land,
Wherein thou liest in reputation sick,
And thou too careless patient as thou art
Commit'st thy anointed body to the cure
Of those physicians that first wounded thee.
A thousand flatterers sit within thy crown,
Whose compass is no bigger than thy head,
And yet incagéd in so small a verge,
The waste is no whit lesser than thy land:

O, had thy grandsire with a prophet's eye
Seen how his son's son should destroy his sons,
From forth thy reach he would have laid thy shame,
Deposing thee before thou wert possessed,
Which art possessed now to depose thyself:
Why, cousin, wert thou regent of the world,
It were a shame to let this land by lease:
But for thy world enjoying but this land,
Is it not more than shame to shame it so?
Landlord of England art thou now, not king,
Thy state of law is bondslave to the law,
And thou—
*K. Richard.* A lunatic lean-witted fool,
Presuming on an ague's privilege,
Darest with thy frozen admonition
Make pale our cheek, chasing the royal blood
With fury from his native residence....
Now by my seat's right royal majesty,
Wert thou not brother to great Edward's son,
This tongue that runs so roundly in thy head
Should run thy head from thy unreverent shoulders.
*Gaunt.* O, spare me not, my brother Edward's son,
For that I was his father Edward's son,
That blood already, like the pelican,
Hast thou tapped out and drunkenly caroused.
My brother Gloucester, plain well-meaning soul,
Whom fair befal in heaven 'mongst happy souls,
May be a precedent and witness good...
That thou respect'st not spilling Edward's blood!
Join with the present sickness that I have,
And thy unkindness be like crooked age,
To crop at once a too long withered flower.
Live in thy shame, but die not shame with thee!
These words hereafter thy tormentors be!

Convey me to my bed, then to my grave—
Love they to live that love and honour have.
[*he is borne out by attendants*

*K. Richard.* And let them die that age and sullens have,
For both hast thou, and both become the grave.

*York.* I do beseech your majesty, impute his words
To wayward sickliness and age in him.
He loves you, on my life, and holds you dear
As Harry Duke of Hereford, were he here.

*K. Richard.* Right, you say true—as Hereford's love, so his,
As theirs, so mine, and all be as it is.

*NORTHUMBERLAND enters*

*Northumberland.* My liege, old Gaunt commends him to your majesty.

*K. Richard.* What says he?

*Northumberland.* Nay nothing, all is said:
His tongue is now a stringless instrument,
Words, life, and all, old Lancaster hath spent.

*York.* Be York the next that must be bankrupt so!
Though death be poor, it ends a mortal woe.

*K. Richard.* The ripest fruit first falls, and so doth he,
His time is spent, our pilgrimage must be;
So much for that....Now for our Irish wars—
We must supplant those rough rug-headed kerns,
Which live like venom, where no venom else
But only they have privilege to live.
And for these great affairs do ask some charge,
Towards our assistance we do seize to us...
The plate, coin, revenues, and moveables,
Whereof our uncle Gaunt did stand possessed.
[*he goes about the room, rating the costly objects therein*

*York.* How long shall I be patient? ah, how long

Shall tender duty make me suffer wrong?
Not Gloucester's death, nor Hereford's banishment,
Not Gaunt's rebukes, nor England's private wrongs,
Nor the prevention of poor Bolingbroke
About his marriage, nor my own disgrace,
Have ever made me sour my patient cheek,
Or bend one wrinkle on my sovereign's face:
I am the last of noble Edward's sons,
Of whom thy father, Prince of Wales, was first.
In war was never lion raged more fierce,
In peace was never gentle lamb more mild,
Than was that young and princely gentleman:
His face thou hast, for even so looked he,
Accomplished with the number of thy hours;
But when he frowned it was against the French,
And not against his friends; his noble hand
Did win what he did spend, and spent not that
Which his triumphant father's hand had won:
His hands were guilty of no kindred blood,
But bloody with the enemies of his kin:
O, Richard...York is too far gone with grief,
Or else he never would compare between....
[*he sobs aloud*

*K. Richard.* [*turns*] Why, uncle, what's the matter?
*York.* O, my liege,
Pardon me, if you please—if not, I pleased
Not to be pardoned, am content withal.
Seek you to seize and gripe into your hands
The royalties and rights of banished Hereford?
Is not Gaunt dead? and doth not Hereford live?
Was not Gaunt just? and is not Harry true?
Did not the one deserve to have an heir?
Is not his heir a well-deserving son?
Take Hereford's rights away, and take from Time

His charters and his customary rights;
Let not to-morrow then ensue to-day;
Be not thyself....for how art thou a king
But by fair sequence and succession?
Now, afore God—God forbid I say true!—
If you do wrongfully seize Hereford's rights,
Call in the letters-patents that he hath
By his attorneys-general to sue
His livery, and deny his off'red homage,
You pluck a thousand dangers on your head,
You lose a thousand well-disposéd hearts,
And prick my tender patience to those thoughts
Which honour and allegiance cannot think.

*K. Richard.* Think what you will, we seize into our hands
His plate, his goods, his money and his lands.

*York.* I'll not be by the while—my liege, farewell—
What will ensue hereof there's none can tell:
But by bad courses may be understood,
That their events can never fall out good. [*he goes*

*K. Richard.* Go, Bushy, to the Earl of Wiltshire straight,
Bid him repair to us to Ely House,
To see this business: to-morrow next
We will for Ireland, and 'tis time, I trow.
And we create, in absence of ourself,
Our uncle York lord governor of England;
For he is just, and always loved us well...
Come on, our queen, to-morrow must we part,
Be merry, for our time of stay is short.

[*he leads out the Queen, followed by Bushy, Aumerle, Green, and Bagot*

*Northumberland.* Well, lords, the Duke of Lancaster is dead.

*Ross.* And living too, for now his son is duke.

*Willoughby.* Barely in title, not in revenues.
*Northumberland.* Richly in both, if justice had her right.
*Ross.* My heart is great, but it must break with silence,
Ere't be disburdened with a liberal tongue.
*Northumberland.* Nay, speak thy mind, and let him ne'er speak more
That speaks thy words again to do thee harm.
*Willoughby.* Tends that thou wouldst speak to the Duke of Hereford?
If it be so, out with it boldly, man.
Quick is mine ear to hear of good towards him.
*Ross.* No good at all that I can do for him,
Unless you call it good to pity him,
Bereft, and gelded of his patrimony.
*Northumberland.* Now afore God 'tis shame such wrongs are borne
In him, a royal prince, and many moe
Of noble blood in this declining land.
The king is not himself, but basely led
By flatterers, and what they will inform,
Merely in hate, 'gainst any of us all,
That will the king severely prosecute
'Gainst us, our lives, our children, and our heirs.
*Ross.* The commons hath he pilled with grievous taxes,
†And quite lost their hearts. The nobles hath he fined
For ancient quarrels, and quite lost their hearts.
*Willoughby.* And daily new exactions are devised,
As blanks, benevolences, and I wot not what:
But what a God's name doth become of this?
*Northumberland.* Wars hath not wasted it, for warred he hath not,
But basely yielded upon compromise
That which his noble ancestors achieved with blows.

More hath he spent in peace than they in wars.
*Ross.* The Earl of Wiltshire hath the realm in farm.
*Willoughby.* The king's grown bankrupt like a broken man.
*Northumberland.* Reproach and dissolution hangeth over him.
*Ross.* He hath not money for these Irish wars,
His burthenous taxations notwithstanding,
But by the robbing of the banished duke.
*Northumberland.* His noble kinsman—most degenerate king!
But, lords, we hear this fearful tempest sing,
Yet seek no shelter to avoid the storm:
We see the wind sit sore upon our sails,
And yet we strike not, but securely perish.
*Ross.* We see the very wrack that we must suffer,
And unavoided is the danger now,
For suffering so the causes of our wrack.
*Northumberland.* Not so, even through the hollow eyes of death
I spy life peering, but I dare not say
How near the tidings of our comfort is.
*Willoughby.* Nay, let us share thy thoughts as thou dost ours.
*Ross.* Be confident to speak, Northumberland,
We three are but thyself, and speaking so
Thy words are but as thoughts, therefore be bold.
*Northumberland.* Then thus—I have from le Port Blanc,
A bay in Britain, received intelligence
That Harry Duke of Hereford, Rainold Lord Cobham,
[The son of Richard Earl of Arundel,]
That late broke from the Duke of Exeter,
His brother, Archbishop late of Canterbury,

Sir Thomas Erpingham, Sir John Ramston,
Sir John Norbery, Sir Robert Waterton and
Francis Coint;
All these, well furnished by the Duke of Britain,
With eight tall ships, three thousand men of war,
Are making hither with all due expedience,
And shortly mean to touch our northern shore:
Perhaps they had ere this, but that they stay
The first departing of the king for Ireland....
If then we shall shake off our slavish yoke,
Imp out our drooping country's broken wing,
Redeem from broking pawn the blemished crown,
Wipe off the dust that hides our sceptre's gilt,
And make high majesty look like itself,
Away with me in post to Ravenspurgh:
But if you faint, as fearing to do so,
Stay, and be secret, and myself will go.
*Ross.* To horse, to horse! urge doubts to them that fear.
*Willoughby.* Hold out my horse, and I will first be there. [*they hurry forth*

[2. 2.] *Windsor Castle*

'*Enter the* QUEEN, BUSHY, *and* BAGOT'

*Bushy.* Madam, your majesty is too much sad.
You promised, when you parted with the king,
To lay aside life-harming heaviness,
And entertain a cheerful disposition.
*Queen.* To please the king I did—to please myself
I cannot do it; yet I know no cause
Why I should welcome such a guest as grief,
Save bidding farewell to so sweet a guest
As my sweet Richard: yet again methinks

Some unborn sorrow ripe in Fortune's womb
Is coming towards me, and my inward soul
†With nothing trembles, yet at something grieves,
More than with parting from my lord the king.

*Bushy.* Each substance of a grief hath twenty shadows,
Which shows like grief itself, but is not so:
For Sorrow's eye glazéd with blinding tears,
Divides one thing entire to many objects,
Like perspectives, which rightly gazed upon
Show nothing but confusion; eyed awry,
Distinguish form: so your sweet majesty,
Looking awry upon your lord's departure,
Find shapes of grief more than himself to wail,
Which looked on as it is, is nought but shadows
Of what it is not; then, thrice-gracious queen,
More than your lord's departure weep not—more is not seen,
Or if it be, 'tis with false Sorrow's eye,
Which, for things true, weeps things imaginary.

*Queen.* It may be so; but yet my inward soul
Persuades me it is otherwise: howe'er it be,
I cannot but be sad; so heavy sad,
As, though on thinking on no thought I think,
Makes me with heavy nothing faint and shrink.

*Bushy.* 'Tis nothing but conceit, my gracious lady.

*Queen.* 'Tis nothing less: conceit is still derived
From some forefather grief. Mine is not so,
For nothing hath begot my something grief,
Or something hath the nothing that I grieve—
'Tis in reversion that I do possess—
But what it is that is not yet known, what
I cannot name, 'tis nameless woe I wot.

*GREEN enters*

*Green.* God save your majesty! and well met, gentlemen.
I hope the king is not yet shipped for Ireland.
*Queen.* Why hopest thou so? 'tis better hope he is,
For his designs crave haste, his haste good hope:
Then wherefore dost thou hope he is not shipped?
*Green.* That he, our hope, might have retired his power,
And driven into despair an enemy's hope,
Who strongly hath set footing in this land.
The banished Bolingbroke repeals himself,
And with uplifted arms is safe arrived
At Ravenspurgh.
*Queen.* Now God in heaven forbid!
*Green.* Ah madam, 'tis too true, and that is worse...
The Lord Northumberland, his son young Henry Percy,
The Lords of Ross, Beaumond, and Willoughby,
With all their powerful friends, are fled to him.
*Bushy.* Why have you not proclaimed Northumberland
And all the rest revolted faction traitors?
*Green.* We have, whereupon the Earl of Worcester
Hath broken his staff, resigned his stewardship,
And all the household servants fled with him
To Bolingbroke.
*Queen.* So, Green, thou art the midwife to my woe,
And Bolingbroke my sorrow's dismal heir.
Now hath my soul brought forth her prodigy,
And I, a gasping new-delivered mother,
Have woe to woe, sorrow to sorrow joined.
*Bushy.* Despair not, madam.
*Queen.* Who shall hinder me?
I will despair, and be at enmity

With cozening Hope—he is a flatterer,
A parasite, a keeper back of Death,
Who gently would dissolve the bands of life,
Which false Hope lingers in extremity.

*YORK enters with his gorget on*

*Green.* Here comes the Duke of York.
*Queen.* With signs of war about his aged neck.
O, full of careful business are his looks!
Uncle, for God's sake, speak comfortable words.
*York.* Should I do so, I should belie my thoughts.
Comfort's in heaven, and we are on the earth,
Where nothing lives but crosses, cares, and grief:
Your husband he is gone to save far off,
Whilst others come to make him lose at home:
Here am I left to underprop his land,
Who weak with age cannot support myself.
Now comes the sick hour that his surfeit made,
Now shall he try his friends that flattered him.

*A servingman enters*

*Servingman.* My lord, your son was gone before I came.
*York.* He was? Why, so! go all which way it will!
†The nobles they are fled, the commons cold,
And will, I fear, revolt on Hereford's side....
Sirrah,
Get thee to Plashy, to my sister Gloucester,
Bid her send me presently a thousand pound.
Hold, take my ring.
*Servingman.* My lord, I had forgot to tell your lordship:
To-day as I came by I callèd there—
But I shall grieve you to report the rest.

*York.* What is't, knave?
*Servingman.* An hour before I came the duchess died.
*York.* God for his mercy, what a tide of woes
Comes rushing on this woeful land at once!
I know not what to do: I would to God
(So my untruth had not provoked him to it)
The king had cut off my head with my brother's....
What, are there no posts dispatched for Ireland?
How shall we do for money for these wars?
Come, sister—cousin, I would say, pray pardon me:
Go, fellow, get thee home, provide some carts,
And bring away the armour that is there....
[*the servingman goes*
Gentlemen, will you go muster men?
If I know
How or which way to order these affairs,
Thus thrust disorderly into my hands,
Never believe me...Both are my kinsmen—
Th'one is my sovereign, whom both my oath
And duty bids defend; th'other again
Is my kinsman, whom the king hath wronged,
Whom conscience and my kindred bids to right....
Well, somewhat we must do....Come, cousin, I'll
Dispose of you:
Gentlemen, go, muster up your men,
And meet me presently at Berkeley:
I should to Plashy too,
But time will not permit: all is uneven,
And every thing is left at six and seven.
[*he leads the Queen forth*
*Bushy.* The wind sits fair for news to go to Ireland,
But none returns. For us to levy power
Proportionable to the enemy
Is all unpossible.

*Green.* Besides, our nearness to the king in love
Is near the hate of those love not the king.
*Bagot.* And that is the wavering commons, for their love
Lies in their purses, and whoso empties them,
By so much fills their hearts with deadly hate.
*Bushy.* Wherein the king stands generally condemned.
*Bagot.* If judgement lie in them, then so do we,
Because we ever have been near the king.
*Green.* Well, I will for refuge straight to Bristol Castle—
The Earl of Wiltshire is already there.
*Bushy.* Thither will I with you, for little office
The hateful commons will perform for us,
Except like curs to tear us all to pieces:
Will you go along with us?
*Bagot.* No, I will to Ireland to his majesty.
Farewell—if heart's presages be not vain,
We three here part that ne'er shall meet again.
*Bushy.* That's as York thrives to beat back Bolingbroke.
*Green.* Alas, poor duke! the task he undertakes
Is numb'ring sands, and drinking oceans dry—
Where one on his side fights, thousands will fly:
Farewell at once, for once, for all, and ever.
*Bushy.* Well, we may meet again.
*Bagot.* I fear me, never.
[*they go*

[2. 3.] *Near Berkeley Castle*

*BOLINGBROKE and NORTHUMBERLAND, marching with forces up a hill*

*Bolingbroke.* How far is it, my lord, to Berkeley now?
*Northumberland.* Believe me, noble lord,
I am a stranger here in Gloucestershire.

These high wild hills and rough uneven ways
Draws out our miles and makes them wearisome,
And yet your fair discourse hath been as sugar,
Making the hard way sweet and delectable.
But I bethink me what a weary way
From Ravenspurgh to Cotswold will be found
In Ross and Willoughby, wanting your company,
Which I protest hath very much beguiled
The tediousness and process of my travel:
But theirs is sweet'ned with the hope to have
The present benefit which I possess,
And hope to joy is little less in joy
Than hope enjoyed: by this the weary lords
Shall make their way seem short, as mine hath done
By sight of what I have, your noble company.

*Bolingbroke.* Of much less value is my company
Than your good words....But who comes here?

*HARRY PERCY comes over the crest of the hill*

*Northumberland.* It is my son, young Harry Percy,
Sent from my brother Worcester, whencesoever....
Harry, how fares your uncle?

*Percy.* I had thought, my lord, to have learned his health of you.

*Northumberland.* Why, is he not with the queen?

*Percy.* No, my good lord, he hath forsook the court,
Broken his staff of office, and dispersed
The household of the king.

*Northumberland.* What was his reason?
He was not so resolved, when last we spake together.

*Percy.* Because your lordship was proclaiméd traitor.
But he, my lord, is gone to Ravenspurgh,
To offer service to the Duke of Hereford,
And sent me over by Berkeley to discover

What power the Duke of York had levied there,
Then with directions to repair to Ravenspurgh.
*Northumberland.* Have you forgot the Duke of Hereford, boy?
*Percy.* No, my good lord, for that is not forgot
Which ne'er I did remember—to my knowledge
I never in my life did look on him.
*Northumberland.* Then learn to know him now. This is the duke.
*Percy.* My gracious lord, I tender you my service,
Such as it is, being tender, raw, and young,
Which elder days shall ripen and confirm
To more approvéd service and desert.
*Bolingbroke.* I thank thee, gentle Percy, and be sure
I count myself in nothing else so happy
As in a soul rememb'ring my good friends,
And as my fortune ripens with thy love,
It shall be still thy true love's recompense.
My heart this covenant makes, my hand thus seals it.
*Northumberland.* How far is it to Berkeley? And what stir
Keeps good old York there with his men of war?
*Percy.* There stands the castle, by yon tuft of trees,
Manned with three hundred men, as I have heard,
And in it are the Lords of York, Berkeley, and Seymour—
None else of name and noble estimate.

*Ross and Willoughby come up*

*Northumberland.* Here come the Lords of Ross and Willoughby,
Bloody with spurring, fiery-red with haste.
*Bolingbroke.* Welcome, my lords. I wot your love pursues
A banished traitor: all my treasury

Is yet but unfelt thanks, which more enriched
Shall be your love and labour's recompense.
*Ross.* Your presence makes us rich, most noble lord.
*Willoughby.* And far surmounts our labour to attain it.
*Bolingbroke.* Evermore thank's the exchequer of the poor,
Which till my infant fortune comes to years,
Stands for my bounty: but who comes here?

*BERKELEY approaches*

*Northumberland.* It is my Lord of Berkeley, as I guess.
*Berkeley.* My Lord of Hereford, my message is to you.
*Bolingbroke.* My lord, my answer is to 'Lancaster',
And I am come to seek that name in England,
And I must find that title in your tongue,
Before I make reply to aught you say.
*Berkeley.* Mistake me not, my lord, 'tis not my meaning
To raze one title of your honour out:
To you, my lord, I come, what lord you will,
From the most gracious regent of this land,
The Duke of York; to know what pricks you on
To take advantage of the absent time,
And fright our native peace with self-borne arms.

*YORK with a retinue draws near*

*Bolingbroke.* I shall not need transport my words by you,
Here comes his grace in person.
My noble uncle! [*he kneels*
*York.* Show me thy humble heart, and not thy knee,
Whose duty is deceivable and false.
*Bolingbroke.* My gracious uncle!
*York.* Tut, tut!

Grace me no grace, nor uncle me no uncle,
I am no traitor's uncle, and that word 'grace'
In an ungracious mouth is but profane:
Why have those banished and forbidden legs
Dared once to touch a dust of England's ground?
But then more 'why?' why have they dared to march
So many miles upon her peaceful bosom,
Frighting her pale-faced villages with war,
And ostentation of despiséd arms?
Com'st thou because the anointed king is hence?
Why, foolish boy, the king is left behind,
And in my loyal bosom lies his power.
Were I but now the lord of such hot youth,
As when brave Gaunt, thy father, and myself,
Rescued the Black Prince, that young Mars of men,
From forth the ranks of many thousand French,
O, then how quickly should this arm of mine,
Now prisoner to the palsy, chastise thee,
And minister correction to thy fault!
*Bolingbroke.* My gracious uncle, let me know my fault,
On what condition stands it and wherein?
*York.* Even in condition of the worst degree—
In gross rebellion and detested treason.
Thou art a banished man, and here art come,
Before the expiration of thy time,
In braving arms against thy sovereign.
*Bolingbroke.* As I was banished, I was banished Hereford,
But as I come, I come for Lancaster....
And, noble uncle, I beseech your grace
Look on my wrongs with an indifferent eye:
You are my father, for methinks in you
I see old Gaunt alive....O then my father,
Will you permit that I shall stand condemned

A wandering vagabond, my rights and royalties
Plucked from my arms perforce...and given away
To upstart unthrifts? Wherefore was I born?
If that my cousin king be king in England,
It must be granted I am Duke of Lancaster:
You have a son, Aumerle, my noble cousin,
Had you first died, and he been thus trod down,
He should have found his uncle Gaunt a father,
To rouse his wrongs and chase them to the bay....
I am denied to sue my livery here,
And yet my letters-patents give me leave....
My father's goods are all distrained and sold,
And these and all are all amiss employed....
What would you have me do? I am a subject;
And I challenge law. Attorneys are denied me,
And therefore personally I lay my claim
To my inheritance of free descent.

*Northumberland.* The noble duke hath been too much abused.

*Ross.* It stands your grace upon to do him right.

*Willoughby.* Base men by his endowments are made great.

*York.* My lords of England, let me tell you this:
I have had feeling of my cousin's wrongs,
And laboured all I could to do him right:
But in this kind to come, in braving arms,
Be his own carver and cut out his way,
To find out right with wrong, it may not be:
And you that do abet him in this kind
Cherish rebellion, and are rebels all.

*Northumberland.* The noble duke hath sworn his coming is
But for his own; and for the right of that
We all have strongly sworn to give him aid:

And let him never see joy that breaks that oath.
*York.* Well, well, I see the issue of these arms.
I cannot mend it, I must needs confess,
Because my power is weak and all ill left:
But if I could, by Him that gave me life,
I would attach you all, and make you stoop
Unto the sovereign mercy of the king;
But, since I cannot, be it known unto you,
I do remain as neuter. So, fare you well,
Unless you please to enter in the castle,
And there repose you for this night.
*Bolingbroke.* An offer, uncle, that we will accept.
But we must win your grace to go with us
To Bristow castle, which, they say, is held
By Bushy, Bagot, and their complices,
The caterpillars of the commonwealth,
Which I have sworn to weed and pluck away.
*York.* It may be I will go with you—but yet I'll pause,
For I am loath to break our country's laws.
Nor friends nor foes, to me welcome you are:
Things past redress are now with me past care.
[*they go forward*

[2. 4.] *A camp in Wales*

*SALISBURY, and a Welsh Captain*

*Captain.* My Lord of Salisbury, we have stayed ten days,
And hardly kept our countrymen together,
And yet we hear no tidings from the king,
Therefore we will disperse ourselves. Farewell.
*Salisbury.* Stay yet another day, thou trusty Welshman.
The king reposeth all his confidence in thee.

*Captain.* 'Tis thought the king is dead; we will not stay.
The bay-trees in our country are all withered,
And meteors fright the fixéd stars of heaven,
The pale-faced moon looks bloody on the earth,
And lean-looked prophets whisper fearful change,
Rich men look sad, and ruffians dance and leap—
The one in fear to lose what they enjoy,
The other to enjoy by rage and war:
These signs forerun the death or fall of kings....
Farewell. Our countrymen are gone and fled,
As well assured Richard their king is dead. [*he goes*

*Salisbury.* Ah, Richard! with the eyes of heavy mind
I see thy glory like a shooting star
Fall to the base earth from the firmament.
Thy sun sets weeping in the lowly west,
Witnessing storms to come, woe, and unrest.
Thy friends are fled to wait upon thy foes,
And crossly to thy good all fortune goes. [*he goes*

[3. 1.] *Bristol. Before the castle*

*Enter* BOLINGBROKE, YORK, NORTHUMBERLAND, *with* BUSHY *and* GREEN, *prisoners*

*Bolingbroke.* Bring forth these men....
Bushy and Green, I will not vex your souls,
Since presently your souls must part your bodies,
With too much urging your pernicious lives,
For 'twere no charity; yet to wash your blood
From off my hands, here in the view of men,
I will unfold some causes of your deaths:
You have misled a prince, a royal king,

A happy gentleman in blood and lineaments,
By you unhappied and disfigured clean.
You have in manner with your sinful hours
Made a divorce betwixt his queen and him,
Broke the possession of a royal bed,
And stained the beauty of a fair queen's cheeks
With tears, drawn from her eyes by your foul wrongs.
Myself, a prince by fortune of my birth,
Near to the king in blood, and near in love,
Till you did make him misinterpret me,
Have stooped my neck under your injuries,
And sighed my English breath in foreign clouds,
Eating the bitter bread of banishment,
Whilst you have fed upon my signories,
Disparked my parks, and felled my forest woods;
From my own windows torn my household coat,
Razed out my imprese, leaving me no sign,
Save men's opinions and my living blood,
To show the world I am a gentleman....
This and much more, much more than twice all this,
Condemns you to the death...See them delivered over
To execution and the hand of death.

*Bushy.* More welcome is the stroke of death to me
Than Bolingbroke to England. Lords, farewell.

*Green.* My comfort is, that heaven will take our souls,
And plague injustice with the pains of hell.

*Bolingbroke.* My Lord Northumberland, see
them dispatched...

[*Northumberland and others depart with the prisoners*

Uncle, you say, the queen is at your house,
For God's sake fairly let her be entreated,
Tell her I send to her my kind commends;
Take special care my greetings be delivered.

*York.* A gentleman of mine I have dispatched

With letters of your love to her at large.
*Bolingbroke.* Thanks, gentle uncle...Come, lords, away,
To fight with Glendower and his complices.
Awhile to work, and after holiday. [*they go*

[3. 2.] *Near the coast of Wales*

*King Richard, the Bishop of Carlisle, Aumerle, and Soldiers, newly disembarked*

*K. Richard.* Barkloughly castle call they this at hand?
*Aumerle.* Yea, my lord. How brooks your grace the air,
After your late tossing on the breaking seas?
*K. Richard.* Needs must I like it well. I weep for joy
To stand upon my kingdom once again:
[*he sits upon a bank, caressing the grass with his hand*
Dear earth, I do salute thee with my hand,
Though rebels wound thee with their horses' hoofs:
As a long-parted mother with her child
Plays fondly with her tears and smiles in meeting;
So, weeping, smiling, greet I thee, my earth,
And do thee favours with my royal hands;
Feed not thy sovereign's foe, my gentle earth,
Nor with thy sweets comfort his ravenous sense,
But let thy spiders that suck up thy venom
And heavy-gaited toads lie in their way,
Doing annoyance to the treacherous feet,
Which with usurping steps do trample thee.
Yield stinging nettles to mine enemies:
And when they from thy bosom pluck a flower,
Guard it, I pray thee, with a lurking adder,
Whose double tongue may with a mortal touch

Throw death upon thy sovereign's enemies....
Mock not my senseless conjuration, lords,
This earth shall have a feeling, and these stones
Prove armèd soldiers, ere her native king
Shall falter under foul rebellion's arms. [*he rises*

*Carlisle*. Fear not, my lord. That Power that made you king,
Hath power to keep you king in spite of all.
The means that heaven yields must be embraced,
And not neglected; else, if heaven would,
And we will not, heaven's offer we refuse,
The proffered means of succour and redress.

*Aumerle*. He means, my lord, that we are too remiss,
Whilst Bolingbroke, through our security,
Grows strong and great in substance and in power.

*K. Richard*. Discomfortable cousin! know'st thou not
That when the searching eye of heaven is hid,
Behind the globe, that lights the lower world,
Then thieves and robbers range abroad unseen,
In murders and in outrage, boldly here,
But when from under this terrestrial ball
He fires the proud tops of the eastern pines,
And darts his light through every guilty hole,
Then murders, treasons, and detested sins,
The cloak of night being plucked from off their backs,
Stand bare and naked, trembling at themselves?
So when this thief, this traitor, Bolingbroke,
Who all this while hath revelled in the night,
Whilst we were wand'ring with the antipodes,
Shall see us rising in our throne the east,
His treasons will sit blushing in his face,
Not able to endure the sight of day,
But self-affrighted tremble at his sin.
Not all the water in the rough rude sea

Can wash the balm off from an anointed king.
The breath of worldly men cannot depose
The deputy elected by the Lord,
For every man that Bolingbroke hath pressed
To lift shrewd steel against our golden crown,
God for his Richard hath in heavenly pay
A glorious angel; then, if angels fight,
Weak men must fall, for heaven still guards the right.

*SALISBURY comes up*

Welcome, my lord: how far off lies your power?
*Salisbury.* Nor near nor farther off, my gracious lord,
Than this weak arm; discomfort guides my tongue,
And bids me speak of nothing but despair.
One day too late, I fear me, noble lord,
Hath clouded all thy happy days on earth:
O, call back yesterday, bid time return,
And thou shalt have twelve thousand fighting men!
To-day, to-day, unhappy day too late,
O'erthrows thy joys, friends, fortune and thy state,
For all the Welshmen, hearing thou wert dead,
Are gone to Bolingbroke, dispersed and fled.
*Aumerle.* Comfort, my liege, why looks your grace so pale?
*K. Richard.* But now the blood of twenty thousand men
Did triumph in my face, and they are fled:
And till so much blood thither come again,
Have I not reason to look pale and dead?
All souls that will be safe, fly from my side,
For time hath set a blot upon my pride.
*Aumerle.* Comfort, my liege, remember who you are.
*K. Richard.* I had forgot myself, am I not king?
Awake thou coward majesty! thou sleepest.

Is not the king's name twenty thousand names?
Arm, arm, my name! a puny subject strikes
At thy great glory. Look not to the ground,
Ye favourites of a king, are we not high?
High be our thoughts. I know my uncle York
Hath power enough to serve our turn: but who
comes here?

*SCROOP is seen approaching*

*Scroop.* More health and happiness betide my liege
Than can my care-tuned tongue deliver him.
*K. Richard.* Mine ear is open, and my heart prepared,
The worst is worldly loss thou canst unfold.
Say, is my kingdom lost? why, 'twas my care,
And what loss is it to be rid of care?
Strives Bolingbroke to be as great as we?
Greater he shall not be. If he serve God,
We'll serve him too, and be his fellow so:
Revolt our subjects? that we cannot mend,
They break their faith to God as well as us:
Cry, woe, destruction, ruin, and decay,
The worst is death, and death will have his day.
*Scroop.* Glad am I, that your highness is so armed
To bear the tidings of calamity.
Like an unseasonable stormy day,
Which makes the silver rivers drown their shores,
As if the world were all dissolved to tears;
So high above his limits swells the rage
Of Bolingbroke, covering your fearful land
With hard bright steel, and hearts harder than steel.
White-beards have armed their thin and hairless scalps
Against thy majesty: boys, with women's voices,
Strive to speak big and clap their female joints
In stiff unwieldy arms against thy crown,

Thy very beadsmen learn to bend their bows
Of double-fatal yew against thy state,
Yea, distaff-women manage rusty bills
Against thy seat. Both young and old rebel,
And all goes worse than I have power to tell.

*K. Richard.* Too well, too well thou tell'st a tale so ill.
Where is the Earl of Wiltshire? where is Bagot?
What is become of Bushy? where is Green?
That they have let the dangerous enemy
Measure our confines with such peaceful steps?
If we prevail, their heads shall pay for it:
I warrant they have made peace with Bolingbroke.

*Scroop.* Peace have they made with him, indeed, my lord.

*K. Richard.* O villains, vipers, damned without redemption!
Dogs, easily won to fawn on any man!
Snakes, in my heart-blood warmed, that sting my heart!
Three Judases, each one thrice worse than Judas!
Would they make peace? terrible hell
Make war upon their spotted souls for this!

*Scroop.* Sweet love, I see, changing his property,
Turns to the sourest and most deadly hate.
Again uncurse their souls, their peace is made
With heads and not with hands, those whom you curse
Have felt the worst of death's destroying wound,
And lie full low graved in the hollow ground.

*Aumerle.* Is Bushy, Green, and the Earl of Wiltshire dead?

*Scroop.* Ay, all of them at Bristow lost their heads.

*Aumerle.* Where is the duke my father with his power?

*K. Richard.* No matter where, of comfort no man speak:
Let's talk of graves, of worms, and epitaphs,

Make dust our paper, and with rainy eyes
Write sorrow on the bosom of the earth....
Let's choose executors and talk of wills:
And yet not so, for what can we bequeath,
Save our deposéd bodies to the ground?
Our lands, our lives, and all are Bolingbroke's,
And nothing can we call our own, but death;
And that small model of the barren earth,
Which serves as paste and cover to our bones.
For God's sake let us sit upon the ground,
And tell sad stories of the death of kings—
How some have been deposed, some slain in war,
Some haunted by the ghosts they have deposed,
Some poisoned by their wives, some sleeping killed;
All murdered—for within the hollow crown
That rounds the mortal temples of a king,
Keeps Death his court, and there the antic sits,
Scoffing his state and grinning at his pomp,
Allowing him a breath, a little scene,
To monarchize, be feared, and kill with looks,
Infusing him with self and vain conceit,
As if this flesh which walls about our life,
Were brass impregnable: and humoured thus,
Comes at the last, and with a little pin
Bores through his castle wall, and farewell king!
Cover your heads, and mock not flesh and blood
With solemn reverence, throw away respect,
Tradition, form, and ceremonious duty,
For you have but mistook me all this while:
I live with bread like you, feel want,
Taste grief, need friends—subjected thus,
How can you say to me, I am a king?

*Carlisle*. My lord, wise men ne'er sit and wail their woes,

But presently prevent the ways to wail.
To fear the foe, since fear oppresseth strength,
Gives in your weakness strength unto your foe,
And so your follies fight against yourself:
Fear and be slain, no worse can come to fight,
And fight and die is death destroying death,
Where fearing dying pays death servile breath.
*Aumerle.* My father hath a power, inquire of him,
And learn to make a body of a limb.
*K. Richard.* Thou chid'st me well—proud Bolingbroke, I come
To change blows with thee for our day of doom:
This ague fit of fear is over-blown.
An easy task it is to win our own....
Say, Scroop, where lies our uncle with his power?
Speak sweetly, man, although thy looks be sour.
*Scroop.* Men judge by the complexion of the sky
The state and inclination of the day;
So may you by my dull and heavy eye,
My tongue hath but a heavier tale to say.
I play the torturer by small and small
To lengthen out the worst that must be spoken:
Your uncle York is joined with Bolingbroke,
And all your northern castles yielded up,
And all your southern gentlemen in arms
Upon his party.
*K. Richard.* Thou hast said enough:
[*to Aumerle*
Beshrew thee, cousin, which didst lead me forth
Of that sweet way I was in to despair!
What say you now? what comfort have we now?
By heaven I'll hate him everlastingly
That bids me be of comfort any more....
Go to Flint castle, there I'll pine away—

A king, woe's slave, shall kingly woe obey:
That power I have, discharge, and let them go
To ear the land that hath some hope to grow,
For I have none. Let no man speak again,
To alter this, for counsel is but vain.

*Aumerle.* My liege, one word.

*K. Richard.* He does me double wrong,
That wounds me with the flatteries of his tongue....
Discharge my followers, let them hence away,
From Richard's night, to Bolingbroke's fair day.
[*they go*

[3. 3.] *Wales. Before Flint Castle*

*Enter marching with drum and colours,* BOLINGBROKE, YORK, NORTHUMBERLAND, *and their forces*

*Bolingbroke.* So that by this intelligence we learn
The Welshmen are dispersed, and Salisbury
Is gone to meet the king, who lately landed
With some few private friends upon this coast.

*Northumberland.* The news is very fair and good, my lord,
Richard, not far from hence, hath hid his head.

*York.* It would beseem the Lord Northumberland,
To say 'King Richard': alack the heavy day,
When such a sacred king should hide his head.

*Northumberland.* Your grace mistakes; only to be brief
Left I his title out.

*York.* The time hath been,
Would you have been so brief with him, he would
Have been so brief with you, to shorten you,
For taking so the head, your whole head's length.

*Bolingbroke.* Mistake not, uncle, further than you should.

*York.* Take not, good cousin, further than you should,
Lest you mis-take: the heavens are o'er our heads.
*Bolingbroke.* I know it, uncle, and oppose not myself
Against their will....But who comes here?

*Enter* PERCY

Welcome, Harry; what, will not this castle yield?
*Percy.* The castle royally is manned, my lord,
Against thy entrance.
*Bolingbroke.* Royally!
Why, it contains no king?
*Percy.* Yes, my good lord,
It doth contain a king. King Richard lies
Within the limits of yon lime and stone,
And with him are the Lord Aumerle, Lord Salisbury,
Sir Stephen Scroop, besides a clergyman
Of holy reverence, who I cannot learn.
*Northumberland.* O belike it is the Bishop of Carlisle.
*Bolingbroke.* Noble lord, [*to Northumberland*
Go to the rude ribs of that ancient castle,
Through brazen trumpet send the breath of parley
Into his ruined ears, and thus deliver....
Henry Bolingbroke
On both his knees doth kiss King Richard's hand,
And sends allegiance and true faith of heart
To his most royal person: hither come
Even at his feet to lay my arms and power;
Provided that my banishment repealed
And lands restored again be freely granted;
If not, I'll use the advantage of my power,
And lay the summer's dust with showers of blood,
Rained from the wounds of slaughtered Englishmen,
The which, how far off from the mind of Bolingbroke
It is such crimson tempest should bedrench

The fresh green lap of fair King Richard's land,
My stooping duty tenderly shall show:
Go, signify as much, while here we march
Upon the grassy carpet of this plain...
[*Northumberland advances to the castle, with a trumpeter*
Let's march without the noise of threat'ning drum,
That from this castle's tattered battlements
Our fair appointments may be well perused....
Methinks, King Richard and myself should meet
With no less terror than the elements
Of fire and water, when their thund'ring shock
At meeting tears the cloudy cheeks of heaven.
Be he the fire, I'll be the yielding water;
The rage be his, whilst on the earth I rain
My waters—on the earth, and not on him....
March on, and mark King Richard how he looks.

*NORTHUMBERLAND sounds a parle without, and is answered by another trumpet within: then a flourish. Enter on the walls* KING RICHARD, *the* BISHOP OF CARLISLE, AUMERLE, SCROOP, *and* SALISBURY

See, see, King Richard doth himself appear,
As doth the blushing discontented sun
From out the fiery portal of the east,
When he perceives the envious clouds are bent
To dim his glory, and to stain the track
Of his bright passage to the occident.
*York.* Yet looks he like a king! behold his eye,
As bright as is the eagle's, lightens forth
Controlling majesty; alack, alack, for woe,
That any harm should stain so fair a show!
*K. Richard* [*to Northumberland*]. We are amazed, and thus long have we stood
To watch the fearful bending of thy knee,

Because we thought ourself thy lawful king:
And if we be, how dare thy joints forget
To pay their awful duty to our presence?
If we be not, show us the hand of God
That hath dismissed us from our stewardship,
For well we know no hand of blood and bone
Can gripe the sacred handle of our sceptre,
Unless he do profane, steal, or usurp.
And though you think that all, as you have done,
Have torn their souls, by turning them from us,
And we are barren and bereft of friends...
Yet know, my master, God omnipotent,
Is mustering in his clouds, on our behalf,
Armies of pestilence, and they shall strike
Your children yet unborn, and unbegot,
That lift your vassal hands against my head,
And threat the glory of my precious crown....
Tell Bolingbroke—for yon methinks he stands—
That every stride he makes upon my land,
Is dangerous treason: he is come to open
The purple testament of bleeding war:
But ere the crown he looks for live in peace,
Ten thousand bloody crowns of mothers' sons
Shall ill become the flower of England's face,
Change the complexion of her maid-pale peace
To scarlet indignation and bedew
Her pasture's grass with faithful English blood.

*Northumberland.* The king of heaven forbid our lord the king
Should so with civil and uncivil arms
Be rushed upon! Thy thrice noble cousin,
Harry Bolingbroke, doth humbly kiss thy hand,
And by the honourable tomb he swears,
That stands upon your royal grandsire's bones,

And by the royalties of both your bloods,
Currents that spring from one most gracious head,
And by the buried hand of warlike Gaunt,
And by the worth and honour of himself,
Comprising all that may be sworn or said,
His coming hither hath no further scope
Than for his lineal royalties, and to beg
Enfranchisement immediate on his knees,
Which on thy royal party granted once,
His glittering arms he will commend to rust,
His barbéd steeds to stables, and his heart
To faithful service of your majesty....
This swears he, as he is a prince, is just;
And, as I am a gentleman, I credit him.

*K. Richard.* Northumberland, say thus the king returns—
His noble cousin is right welcome hither,
And all the number of his fair demands
Shall be accomplished without contradiction.
With all the gracious utterance thou hast,
Speak to his gentle hearing kind commends....

[*Northumberland retires to Bolingbroke; Richard turns to Aumerle*

We do debase ourselves, cousin, do we not,
To look so poorly, and to speak so fair?
Shall we call back Northumberland and send
Defiance to the traitor, and so die?

*Aumerle.* No, good my lord; let's fight with gentle words,
Till time lend friends, and friends their helpful swords.

*K. Richard.* O God! O God! that e'er this tongue of mine,
That laid the sentence of dread banishment
On yon proud man, should take it off again

With words of sooth! O, that I were as great
As is my grief, or lesser than my name!
Or that I could forget what I have been!
Or not remember what I must be now!
Swell'st thou, proud heart? I'll give thee scope to beat,
Since foes have scope to beat both thee and me.

*Aumerle.* Northumberland comes back from Bolingbroke.

*K. Richard.* What must the king do now? must he submit?
The king shall do it: must he be deposed?
The king shall be contented: must he lose
The name of king? a God's name let it go:
I'll give my jewels for a set of beads:
My gorgeous palace for a hermitage:
My gay apparel for an almsman's gown:
My figured goblets for a dish of wood:
My sceptre for a palmer's walking-staff:
My subjects for a pair of carvéd saints,
And my large kingdom for a little grave,
A little little grave, an obscure grave,
Or I'll be buried in the king's highway,
Some way of common trade, where subjects' feet
May hourly trample on their sovereign's head;
For on my heart they tread now whilst I live:
And buried once, why not upon my head?
Aumerle, thou weep'st (my tender-hearted cousin!),
We'll make foul weather with despiséd tears;
Our sighs and they shall lodge the summer corn,
And make a dearth in this revolting land:
Or shall we play the wantons with our woes,
And make some pretty match with shedding tears?
As thus to drop them still upon one place,
Till they have fretted us a pair of graves

Within the earth, and therein laid...there lies
Two kinsmen digged their graves with weeping eyes!
Would not this ill do well? Well, well, I see
I talk but idly, and you laugh at me....
Most mighty prince, my Lord Northumberland,
What says King Bolingbroke? will his majesty
Give Richard leave to live till Richard die?
You make a leg, and Bolingbroke says 'ay'.

*Northumberland.* My lord, in the base court he doth attend,
To speak with you, may it please you to come down?

*K. Richard.* Down, down I come, like glist'ring Phaethon:
Wanting the manage of unruly jades....
In the base court? Base court, where kings grow base,
To come at traitors' calls, and do them grace.
In the base court? Come down? Down court! down king!
For night-owls shriek where mounting larks should sing.
[*he goes down from the battlements*

*Bolingbroke.* [*coming forward*] What says his majesty?

*Northumberland.* Sorrow and grief of heart
Makes him speak fondly like a frantic man,
Yet he is come.

*KING RICHARD, the DUKE OF YORK and attendants come forth*

*Bolingbroke.* Stand all apart,
And show fair duty to his majesty...
My gracious lord. ['*he kneels down*'

*K. Richard.* Fair cousin, you debase your princely knee,
To make the base earth proud with kissing it:
Me rather had my heart might feel your love,

Than my unpleased eye see your courtesy:
Up, cousin, up—your heart is up, I know,
Thus high [*touching his own head*] at least, although your knee be low.
*Bolingbroke*. My gracious lord, I come but for mine own.
*K. Richard*. Your own is yours, and I am yours and all.
*Bolingbroke*. So far be mine, my most redoubted lord,
As my true service shall deserve your love.
*K. Richard*. Well you deserve: they well deserve to have,
That know the strong'st and surest way to get.
Uncle, give me your hands, nay, dry your eyes,
Tears show their love, but want their remedies....
Cousin, I am too young to be your father,
Though you are old enough to be my heir.
What you will have, I'll give, and willing too,
For do we must, what force will have us do...
Set on towards London, cousin, is it so?
*Bolingbroke*. Yea, my good lord.
*K. Richard*. Then I must not say no.
[*they go*

[3. 4.] *The* DUKE OF YORK'*s garden*

*Enter the* QUEEN *and two Ladies*

*Queen*. What sport shall we devise here in this garden,
To drive away the heavy thought of care?
*Lady*. Madam, we'll play at bowls.
*Queen*. 'Twill make me think the world is full of rubs,

And that my fortune runs against the bias.
*Lady.* Madam, we'll dance.
*Queen.* My legs can keep no measure in delight,
When my poor heart no measure keeps in grief:
Therefore, no dancing, girl—some other sport.
*Lady.* Madam, we'll tell tales.
*Queen.* Of sorrow or of joy?
*Lady.* Of either, madam.
*Queen.* Of neither, girl:
For if of joy, being altogether wanting,
It doth remember me the more of sorrow;
Or if of grief, being altogether had,
It adds more sorrow to my want of joy:
For what I have I need not to repeat,
And what I want it boots not to complain.
*Lady.* Madam, I'll sing.
*Queen.* 'Tis well that thou hast cause,
But thou shouldst please me better, wouldst thou weep.
*Lady.* I could weep, madam, would it do you good.
*Queen.* And I could sing, would weeping do me good,
And never borrow any tear of thee....

*'Enter Gardeners' with spades &c.*

But stay, here come the gardeners.
Let's step into the shadow of these trees.
My wretchedness unto a row of pins,
They will talk of state, for every one doth so
Against a change: woe is forerun with woe.
[*Queen and her ladies retire*
*Gardener.* [*to one of his men*] Go, bind thou up yon dangling apricocks,
Which like unruly children make their sire

Stoop with oppression of their prodigal weight,
Give some supportance to the bending twigs.
[*to the other*] Go thou, and like an executioner
Cut off the heads of too fast growing sprays,
That look too lofty in our commonwealth—
All must be even in our government....
You thus employed, I will go root away
The noisome weeds which without profit suck
The soil's fertility from wholesome flowers.
*Man.* Why should we, in the compass of a pale,
Keep law and form and due proportion,
Showing as in a model our firm estate,
When our sea-wallèd garden, the whole land,
Is full of weeds, her fairest flowers choked up,
Her fruit-trees all unpruned, her hedges ruined,
Her knots disordered, and her wholesome herbs
Swarming with caterpillars?
*Gardener.* Hold thy peace—
He that hath suffered this disordered spring
Hath now himself met with the fall of leaf:
The weeds which his broad-spreading leaves did shelter,
That seemed in eating him to hold him up,
Are plucked up root and all by Bolingbroke—
I mean the Earl of Wiltshire, Bushy, Green.
*Man.* What, are they dead?
*Gardener.* They are, and Bolingbroke
Hath seized the wasteful king. O! what pity is it
That he had not so trimmed and dressed his land,
As we this garden! We at time of year
Do wound the bark, the skin of our fruit-trees,
Lest being over-proud in sap and blood,
With too much riches it confound itself.
Had he done so to great and growing men,

They might have lived to bear, and he to taste,
Their fruits of duty: superfluous branches
We lop away, that bearing boughs may live:
Had he done so, himself had borne the crown,
Which waste of idle hours hath quite thrown down.
*Man.* What, think you then the king shall be deposed?
*Gardener.* Depressed he is already, and deposed
'Tis doubt he will be....Letters came last night
To a dear friend of the good Duke of York's,
That tell black tidings.
*Queen.* O, I am pressed to death through want of speaking! [*comes forth*
Thou, old Adam's likeness, set to dress this garden,
How dares thy harsh rude tongue sound this unpleasing news?
What Eve, what serpent, hath suggested thee
To make a second fall of curséd man?
Why dost thou say King Richard is deposed?
Dar'st thou, thou little better thing than earth,
Divine his downfal? Say, where, when, and how,
Cam'st thou by these ill tidings? speak, thou wretch!
*Gardener.* Pardon me, madam. Little joy have I
To breathe this news, yet what I say is true:
King Richard, he is in the mighty hold
Of Bolingbroke: their fortunes both are weighed:
In your lord's scale is nothing but himself,
And some few vanities that make him light;
But in the balance of great Bolingbroke,
Besides himself, are all the English peers,
And with that odds he weighs King Richard down;
Post you to London, and you will find it so,
I speak no more than every one doth know.
*Queen.* Nimble mischance, that art so light of foot,

Doth not thy embassage belong to me,
And am I last that knows it? O, thou thinkest
To serve me last, that I may longest keep
Thy sorrow in my breast...Come, ladies, go,
To meet at London London's king in woe....
What, was I born to this, that my sad look
Should grace the triumph of great Bolingbroke?
Gardener, for telling me these news of woe,
Pray God the plants thou graft'st may never grow.
[*she leaves the garden with her ladies*

*Gardener.* Poor queen! so that thy state might be no worse,
I would my skill were subject to thy curse:
Here did she fall a tear, here in this place
I'll set a bank of rue, sour herb of grace.
Rue, even for ruth, here shortly shall be seen,
In the remembrance of a weeping queen. [*they go*

[4. 1.] *Westminster Hall, with the king's throne*

*Enter as to the Parliament* BOLINGBROKE, AUMERLE, SURREY, NORTHUMBERLAND, PERCY, FITZWATER, *and other lords, the* BISHOP OF CARLISLE, *and the* ABBOT OF WESTMINSTER. *Herald and Officers with* BAGOT

*Bolingbroke.* Call forth Bagot....
[*he is brought forward*
Now, Bagot, freely speak thy mind,
What thou dost know of noble Gloucester's death,
Who wrought it with the king, and who performed
The bloody office of his timeless end.

*Bagot.* Then set before my face the Lord Aumerle.

*Bolingbroke*. Cousin, stand forth, and look upon that man.

*Bagot*. My Lord Aumerle, I know your daring tongue
Scorns to unsay what once it hath delivered.
In that dead time when Gloucester's death was plotted,
I heard you say, 'Is not my arm of length,
That reacheth from the restful English court
As far as Calais, to my uncle's head?'
Amongst much other talk that very time
I heard you say that you had rather refuse
The offer of an hundred thousand crowns
Than Bolingbroke's return to England—
Adding withal, how blest this land would be,
In this your cousin's death.

*Aumerle*. Princes and noble lords,
What answer shall I make to this base man?
Shall I so much dishonour my fair stars,
On equal terms to give him chastisement?
Either I must, or have mine honour soiled
With the attainder of his slanderous lips.
There is my gage, the manual seal of death,
That marks thee out for hell! I say thou liest,
And will maintain what thou hast said is false
In thy heart-blood, though being all too base
To stain the temper of my knightly sword.

*Bolingbroke*. Bagot, forbear, thou shalt not take it up.

*Aumerle*. Excepting one, I would he were the best
In all this presence that hath moved me so.

*Fitzwater*. If that thy valour stand on sympathy,
There is my gage, Aumerle, in gage to thine:
By that fair sun which shows me where thou stand'st,
I heard thee say, and vauntingly thou spak'st it,
That thou wert cause of noble Gloucester's death.
If thou deny'st it twenty times, thou liest,

And I will turn thy falsehood to thy heart,
Where it was forgéd, with my rapier's point.
*Aumerle.* Thou dar'st not, coward, live to see that day.
*Fitzwater.* Now, by my soul, I would it were this hour.
*Aumerle.* Fitzwater, thou art damned to hell for this.
*Percy.* Aumerle, thou liest, his honour is as true
In this appeal as thou art all unjust,
And that thou art so, there I throw my gage,
To prove it on thee to the extremest point
Of mortal breathing—seize it if thou dar'st.
*Aumerle.* An if I do not, may my hands rot off,
And never brandish more revengeful steel
Over the glittering helmet of my foe!
*Another Lord.* I task the earth to the like, forsworn Aumerle,
And spur thee on with full as many lies
As may be holloaed in thy treacherous ear
From sun to sun: there is my honour's pawn—
Engage it to the trial if thou darest.
*Aumerle.* Who sets me else? by heaven, I'll throw at all!
I have a thousand spirits in one breast,
To answer twenty thousand such as you.
*Surrey.* My Lord Fitzwater, I do remember well
The very time Aumerle and you did talk.
*Fitzwater.* 'Tis very true, you were in presence then,
And you can witness with me this is true.
*Surrey.* As false, by heaven, as heaven itself is true.
*Fitzwater.* Surrey, thou liest.
*Surrey.* Dishonourable boy!
That lie shall lie so heavy on my sword,
That it shall render vengeance and revenge,
Till thou the lie-giver, and that lie, do lie
In earth as quiet as thy father's skull....

In proof whereof, there is my honour's pawn—
Engage it to the trial if thou dar'st.
*Fitzwater.* How fondly dost thou spur a forward horse!
If I dare eat, or drink, or breathe, or live,
I dare meet Surrey in a wilderness,
And spit upon him, whilst I say he lies,
And lies, and lies: there is my bond of faith,
To tie thee to my strong correction:
As I intend to thrive in this new world,
Aumerle is guilty of my true appeal:
Besides, I heard the banished Norfolk say,
That thou, Aumerle, didst send two of thy men
To execute the noble duke at Calais.
*Aumerle.* Some honest Christian trust me with a gage,
That Norfolk lies—here do I throw down this,
If he may be repealed to try his honour.
*Bolingbroke.* These differences shall all rest under gage,
Till Norfolk be repealed. Repealed he shall be,
And, though mine enemy, restored again
To all his lands and signories: when he's returned,
Against Aumerle we will enforce his trial.
*Carlisle.* That honourable day shall ne'er be seen.
Many a time hath banished Norfolk fought
For Jesu Christ in glorious Christian field,
Streaming the ensign of the Christian cross
Against black pagans, Turks, and Saracens,
And toiled with works of war, retired himself
To Italy, and there at Venice gave
His body to that pleasant country's earth,
And his pure soul unto his captain Christ
Under whose colours he had fought so long.
*Bolingbroke.* Why, bishop, is Norfolk dead?
*Carlisle.* As surely as I live, my lord.

*Bolingbroke*. Sweet peace conduct his sweet soul to the bosom
Of good old Abraham! Lords appellants,
Your differences shall all rest under gage,
Till we assign you to your days of trial.

*YORK enters the hall*

*York*. Great Duke of Lancaster, I come to thee
From plume-plucked Richard, who with willing soul
Adopts thee heir, and his high sceptre yields
To the possession of thy royal hand:
Ascend his throne, descending now from him,
And long live Henry, of that name the fourth!
*Bolingbroke*. In God's name, I'll ascend the regal throne.
*Carlisle*. Marry, God forbid!
Worst in this royal presence may I speak,
Yet best beseeming me to speak the truth.
Would God that any in this noble presence
Were enough noble to be upright judge
Of noble Richard....Then true noblesse would
Learn him forbearance from so foul a wrong.
What subject can give sentence on his king?
And who sits here that is not Richard's subject?
Thieves are not judged but they are by to hear,
Although apparent guilt be seen in them,
And shall the figure of God's majesty,
His captain, steward, deputy-elect,
Anointed, crowned, planted many years,
Be judged by subject and inferior breath,
And he himself not present? O, forfend it, God,
That in a Christian climate souls refined
Should show so heinous, black, obscene a deed!
I speak to subjects, and a subject speaks,

Stirred up by God thus boldly for his king.
My Lord of Hereford here, whom you call king,
Is a foul traitor to proud Hereford's king,
And if you crown him, let me prophesy,
The blood of English shall manure the ground,
And future ages groan for this foul act,
Peace shall go sleep with Turks and infidels,
And, in this seat of peace, tumultuous wars
Shall kin with kin, and kind with kind confound;
Disorder, horror, fear, and mutiny
Shall here inhabit, and this land be called
The field of Golgotha and dead men's skulls.
O, if you raise this house against this house,
It will the woefullest division prove
That ever fell upon this cursèd earth:
Prevent 't, resist it, let it not be so,
Lest child, child's children, cry against you 'woe!'

*Northumberland.* Well have you argued, sir, and, for your pains,
Of capital treason we arrest you here:
My Lord of Westminster, be it your charge
To keep him safely till his day of trial....
May it please you, lords, to grant the commons' suit?

*Bolingbroke.* Fetch hither Richard, that in common view
He may surrender; so we shall proceed
Without suspicion.

*York.* I will be his conduct. [*he goes*

*Bolingbroke.* Lords, you that here are under our arrest,
Procure your sureties for your days of answer:
Little are we beholding to your love,
And little looked for at your helping hands.

*York returns with King Richard, guarded and stripped of his royal robes; Officers follow bearing the Crown, &c.*

*K. Richard.* Alack, why am I sent for to a king,
Before I have shook off the regal thoughts
Wherewith I reigned? I hardly yet have learned
To insinuate, flatter, bow, and bend my knee:
Give sorrow leave awhile to tutor me
To this submission....Yet I well remember
The favours of these men: were they not mine?
Did they not sometime cry 'all hail!' to me?
So Judas did to Christ: but he, in twelve,
Found truth in all, but one; I, in twelve thousand, none....
God save the king! Will no man say amen?
Am I both priest and clerk? well then, amen.
God save the king! although I be not he;
And yet, amen, if heaven do think him me....
To do what service am I sent for hither?
*York.* To do that office of thine own good will,
Which tired majesty did make thee offer:
The resignation of thy state and crown
To Henry Bolingbroke.
*K. Richard.* Give me the crown....Here, cousin, seize the crown:
Here, cousin,
On this side, my hand, and on that side, thine....
Now is this golden crown like a deep well
That owes two buckets, filling one another,
The emptier ever dancing in the air,
The other down, unseen, and full of water:
That bucket down, and full of tears, am I,
Drinking my griefs, whilst you mount up on high.
*Bolingbroke.* I thought you had been willing to resign.

*K. Richard.* My crown I am, but still my griefs are mine:
You may my glories and my state depose,
But not my griefs; still am I king of those.

*Bolingbroke.* Part of your cares you give me with your crown.

*K. Richard.* Your cares set up do not pluck my cares down.
My care is loss of care, by old care done,
Your care is gain of care, by new care won:
The cares I give, I have, though given away,
They tend the crown, yet still with me they stay.

*Bolingbroke.* Are you contented to resign the crown?

*K. Richard.* Ay, no; no, ay; for I must nothing be:
Therefore no 'no', for I resign to thee....
Now mark me how I will undo myself:
I give this heavy weight from off my head,
And this unwieldy sceptre from my hand,
The pride of kingly sway from out my heart;
With mine own tears I wash away my balm,
With mine own hands I give away my crown,
With mine own tongue deny my sacred state,
With mine own breath release all duteous oaths:
All pomp and majesty I do forswear;
My manors, rents, revenues, I forgo;
My acts, decrees, and statutes, I deny:
God pardon all oaths that are broke to me!
God keep all vows unbroke are made to thee!
Make me, that nothing have, with nothing grieved,
And thou with all pleased, that hast all achieved!
Long mayst thou live in Richard's seat to sit,
And soon lie Richard in an earthy pit....
God save King Henry, unkinged Richard says,
And send him many years of sunshine days....

What more remains?

*Northumberland.* No more, but that you read
These accusations and these grievous crimes,
Committed by your person and your followers
Against the state and profit of this land;
That, by confessing them, the souls of men
May deem that you are worthily deposed.

*K. Richard.* Must I do so? and must I ravel out
My weaved-up follies? Gentle Northumberland,
If thy offences were upon record,
Would it not shame thee, in so fair a troop,
To read a lecture of them? If thou wouldst,
There shouldst thou find one heinous article,
Containing the deposing of a king,
And cracking the strong warrant of an oath,
Marked with a blot, damned in the book of heaven....
Nay, all of you, that stand and look upon me,
Whilst that my wretchedness doth bait myself,
Though some of you, with Pilate, wash your hands,
Showing an outward pity; yet you Pilates
Have here delivered me to my sour cross,
And water cannot wash away your sin.

*Northumberland.* My lord, dispatch, read o'er these articles.

*K. Richard.* Mine eyes are full of tears, I cannot see:
And yet salt water blinds them not so much,
But they can see a sort of traitors here.
Nay, if I turn mine eyes upon myself,
I find myself a traitor with the rest:
For I have given here my soul's consent
T' undeck the pompous body of a king;
Made glory base; and sovereignty, a slave;
Proud majesty, a subject; state, a peasant.

*Northumberland.* My lord—

*K. Richard.* No lord of thine, thou haught, insulting man;
Nor no man's lord; I have no name, no title;
No, not that name was given me at the font,
But 'tis usurped: alack the heavy day,
That I have worn so many winters out,
And know not now what name to call myself!
O, that I were a mockery king of snow,
Standing before the sun of Bolingbroke,
To melt myself away in water-drops!
Good king, great king, and yet not greatly good,
An if my word be sterling yet in England,
Let it command a mirror hither straight,
That it may show me what a face I have,
Since it is bankrupt of his majesty.

*Bolingbroke.* Go some of you, and fetch a looking-glass.
[*an attendant goes out*

*Northumberland.* Read o'er this paper, while the glass doth come.

*K. Richard.* Fiend, thou torments me ere I come to hell.

*Bolingbroke.* Urge it no more, my Lord Northumberland.

*Northumberland.* The commons will not then be satisfied.

*K. Richard.* They shall be satisfied; I'll read enough,
When I do see the very book indeed
Where all my sins are writ, and that's myself.

*The attendant returns with a glass*

Give me that glass, and therein will I read....
No deeper wrinkles yet? hath sorrow struck
So many blows upon this face of mine,
And made no deeper wounds? O, flatt'ring glass,

Like to my followers in prosperity,
Thou dost beguile me! Was this face the face
That every day under his household roof
Did keep ten thousand men? Was this the face,
That, like the sun, did make beholders wink?
Was this the face, that faced so many follies,
And was at last out-faced by Bolingbroke?
A brittle glory shineth in this face,
As brittle as the glory is the face,
[*he dashes the glass to the ground*
For there it is, cracked in a hundred shivers....
Mark, silent king, the moral of this sport,
How soon my sorrow hath destroyed my face.
*Bolingbroke*. The shadow of your sorrow hath destroyed
The shadow of your face.
*K. Richard*. Say that again.
The shadow of my sorrow...ha! let's see—
'Tis very true, my grief lies all within,
And these external manners of lament
Are merely shadows to the unseen grief,
That swells with silence in the tortured soul....
There lies the substance: and I thank thee, king,
For thy great bounty, that not only giv'st
Me cause to wail, but teachest me the way
How to lament the cause....I'll beg one boon,
And then be gone, and trouble you no more.
Shall I obtain it?
*Bolingbroke*. Name it, fair cousin.
*K. Richard*. 'Fair cousin'? I am greater than a king:
For when I was a king, my flatterers
Were then but subjects; being now a subject,
I have a king here to my flatterer:
Being so great, I have no need to beg.

*Bolingbroke.* Yet ask.
*K. Richard.* And shall I have?
*Bolingbroke.* You shall.
*K. Richard.* Then give me leave to go.
*Bolingbroke.* Whither?
*K. Richard.* Whither you will, so I were from your sights.
*Bolingbroke.* Go, some of you, convey him to the Tower.
*K. Richard.* O, good! convey? conveyers are you all,
That rise thus nimbly by a true king's fall.
[*certain lords conduct Richard guarded from the hall*
*Bolingbroke.* On Wednesday next we solemnly set down
Our coronation: lords, prepare yourselves.

BOLINGBROKE *and the Lords depart in procession: the* ABBOT OF WESTMINSTER, *the* BISHOP OF CARLISLE *and* AUMERLE *linger behind*

*Abbot.* A woeful pageant have we here beheld.
*Carlisle.* The woe's to come—the children yet unborn
Shall feel this day as sharp to them as thorn.
*Aumerle.* You holy clergymen, is there no plot
To rid the realm of this pernicious blot?
*Abbot.* My lord,
Before I freely speak my mind herein,
You shall not only take the sacrament
To bury mine intents, but also to effect
Whatever I shall happen to devise:
I see your brows are full of discontent,
Your hearts of sorrow, and your eyes of tears:
Come home with me to supper; I will lay
A plot shall show us all a merry day. [*they go*

[5. 1.] *London. A street leading to the Tower*

*'Enter the* QUEEN *with her attendants'*

*Queen.* This way the king will come, this is the way
To Julius Cæsar's ill-erected tower,
To whose flint bosom my condemnéd lord
Is doomed a prisoner by proud Bolingbroke....
Here let us rest, if this rebellious earth
Have any resting for her true king's queen.

RICHARD *with guards comes into the street*

But soft, but see, or rather do not see,
My fair rose wither—yet look up, behold,
That you in pity may dissolve to dew,
And wash him fresh again with true-love tears...
Ah, thou, the model where old Troy did stand!
Thou map of honour, thou King Richard's tomb,
And not King Richard; thou most beauteous inn,
Why should hard-favoured grief be lodged in thee,
When triumph is become an alehouse guest?
*Richard.* Join not with grief, fair woman, do not so,
To make my end too sudden. Learn, good soul,
To think our former state a happy dream,
From which awaked, the truth of what we are
Shows us but this: I am sworn brother, sweet,
To grim Necessity, and he and I
Will keep a league till death....Hie thee to France,
And cloister thee in some religious house.
Our holy lives must win a new world's crown,
Which our profane hours here have throwen down.
*Queen.* What, is my Richard both in shape and mind
Transformed and weak'ned? hath Bolingbroke deposed
Thine intellect? hath he been in thy heart?

The lion dying thrusteth forth his paw,
And wounds the earth, if nothing else, with rage
To be o'erpowered, and wilt thou pupil-like
Take the correction, mildly kiss the rod,
And fawn on rage with base humility,
Which art a lion and the king of beasts?

*Richard.* A king of beasts, indeed! if aught but beasts,
I had been still a happy king of men....
Good sometimes queen, prepare thee hence for France.
Think I am dead, and that even here thou takest
As from my death-bed thy last living leave;
In winter's tedious nights sit by the fire
With good old folks, and let them tell thee tales
Of woeful ages long ago betid;
And ere thou bid good night, to quit their griefs,
Tell thou the lamentable fall of me,
And send the hearers weeping to their beds:
For why, the senseless brands will sympathize
The heavy accent of thy moving tongue,
And in compassion weep the fire out,
And some will mourn in ashes, some coal-black,
For the deposing of a rightful king.

*NORTHUMBERLAND comes up*

*Northumberland.* My lord, the mind of Bolingbroke is changed,
You must to Pomfret, not unto the Tower....
And, madam, there is order ta'en for you,
With all swift speed you must away to France.

*Richard.* Northumberland, thou ladder wherewithal
The mounting Bolingbroke ascends my throne,
The time shall not be many hours of age
More than it is, ere foul sin gathering head
Shall break into corruption. Thou shalt think,

Though he divide the realm and give thee half,
It is too little, helping him to all....
And he shall think that thou, which knowest the way
To plant unrightful kings, wilt know again,
Being ne'er so little urged another way
To pluck him headlong from the usurped throne:
The love of wicked men converts to fear,
That fear to hate, and hate turns one or both
To worthy danger and deservéd death.

*Northumberland.* My guilt be on my head, and there an end:
Take leave and part, for you must part forthwith.

*Richard.* Doubly divorced! Bad men, you violate
A twofold marriage—'twixt my crown and me,
And then betwixt me and my married wife....
Let me unkiss the oath 'twixt thee and me;
And yet not so, for with a kiss 'twas made....
Part us, Northumberland—I towards the north,
Where shivering cold and sickness pines the clime;
My wife to France, from whence set forth in pomp
She came adornéd hither like sweet May,
Sent back like Hallowmas or short'st of day.

*Queen.* And must we be divided? must we part?

*Richard.* Ay, hand from hand, my love, and heart from heart.

*Queen.* Banish us both, and send the king with me.

*Northumberland.* That were some love, but little policy.

*Queen.* Then whither he goes, thither let me go.

*Richard.* So two, together weeping, make one woe.
Weep thou for me in France, I for thee here;
Better far off than near, be ne'er the near.
Go, count thy way with sighs, I mine with groans.

*Queen.* So longest way shall have the longest moans.

*Richard.* Twice for one step I'll groan, the way being short,
And piece the way out with a heavy heart....
Come, come, in wooing sorrow let's be brief,
Since, wedding it, there is such length in grief:
One kiss shall stop our mouths, and dumbly part—
Thus give I mine, and thus take I thy heart. [*they kiss*
*Queen.* Give me mine own again, 'twere no good part
To take on me to keep and kill thy heart:
[*they kiss again*
So, now I have mine own again, be gone,
That I may strive to kill it with a groan.
*Richard.* We make woe wanton with this fond delay,
Once more, adieu, the rest let sorrow say. [*they go*

[5. 2.] *The Duke of York's palace*

*The* DUKE OF YORK *and the* DUCHESS

*Duchess.* My lord, you told me you would tell the rest,
When weeping made you break the story off
Of our two cousins coming into London.
*York.* Where did I leave?
*Duchess.* At that sad stop, my lord,
Where rude misgoverned hands, from windows' tops,
Threw dust and rubbish on King Richard's head.
*York.* Then, as I said, the duke, great Bolingbroke,
Mounted upon a hot and fiery steed,
Which his aspiring rider seemed to know,
With slow but stately pace kept on his course,
Whilst all tongues cried 'God save thee, Bolingbroke!'
You would have thought the very windows spake,
So many greedy looks of young and old
Through casements darted their desiring eyes

Upon his visage, and that all the walls
With painted imagery had said at once
'Jesu preserve thee! welcome, Bolingbroke!'
Whilst he from one side to the other turning
Bareheaded, lower than his proud steed's neck,
Bespake them thus: 'I thank you, countrymen':
And thus still doing, thus he passed along.
*Duchess.* Alack poor Richard! where rode he the whilst?
*York.* As in a theatre the eyes of men,
After a well-graced actor leaves the stage,
Are idly bent on him that enters next,
Thinking his prattle to be tedious;
Even so, or with much more contempt, men's eyes
Did scowl on Richard; no man cried, 'God save him!'
No joyful tongue gave him his welcome home,
But dust was thrown upon his sacred head;
Which with such gentle sorrow he shook off,
His face still combating with tears and smiles,
The badges of his grief and patience,
That had not God for some strong purpose steeled
The hearts of men, they must perforce have melted,
And barbarism itself have pitied him:
But heaven hath a hand in these events,
To whose high will we bound our calm contents....
To Bolingbroke are we sworn subjects now,
Whose state and honour I for aye allow.

*AUMERLE comes to the door*

*Duchess.* Here comes my son Aumerle.
*York.* Aumerle that was,
But that is lost for being Richard's friend:
And, madam, you must call him Rutland now:

I am in parliament pledge for his truth
And lasting fealty to the new made king.
*Duchess.* Welcome, my son. Who are the violets now,
That strew the green lap of the new come spring?
*Aumerle.* Madam, I know not, nor I greatly care not.
God knows I had as lief be none as one.
*York.* Well, bear you well in this new spring of time,
Lest you be cropped before you come to prime.
What news from Oxford? do these justs and
triumphs hold?
*Aumerle.* For aught I know, my lord, they do.
*York.* You will be there, I know.
*Aumerle.* If God prevent not, I purpose so.
*York.* What seal is that, that hangs without thy bosom?
Yea, look'st thou pale? let me see the writing.
*Aumerle.* My lord, 'tis nothing.
*York.* No matter then who see it.
I will be satisfied, let me see the writing.
*Aumerle.* I do beseech your grace to pardon me;
It is a matter of small consequence,
Which for some reasons I would not have seen.
*York.* Which for some reasons, sir, I mean to see....
I fear, I fear—
*Duchess.* What should you fear?
'Tis nothing but some bond that he is ent'red into
For gay apparel 'gainst the triumph day.
*York.* Bound to himself! what doth he with a bond,
That he is bound to? Wife, thou art a fool...
Boy, let me see the writing.
*Aumerle.* I do beseech you, pardon me, I may not
show it.
*York.* I will be satisfied, let me see it, I say.
[*'he plucks it out of his bosom and reads it'*
Treason! foul treason! villain! traitor! slave!

*Duchess.* What is the matter, my lord?
*York.* [*shouts*] Ho! who is within there? saddle my horse. [*he reads again*
God for his mercy! what treachery is here!
*Duchess.* Why, what is it, my lord?
*York.* [*shouts louder*] Give me my boots I say, saddle my horse. [*he reads again*
Now by mine honour, by my life, by my troth,
I will appeach the villain.
*Duchess.* What is the matter?
*York.* Peace, foolish woman.
*Duchess.* I will not peace. What is the matter, Aumerle?
*Aumerle.* Good mother, be content—it is no more
Than my poor life must answer.
*Duchess.* Thy life answer!
*York.* Bring me my boots, I will unto the king.

'*His man enters with his boots*'

*Duchess.* Strike him, Aumerle. Poor boy, thou art amazed.
Hence, villain! never more come in my sight.
*York.* [*to the man*] Give me my boots, I say.
[*the man helps him into them*
*Duchess.* Why, York, what wilt thou do?
Wilt thou not hide the trespass of thine own?
Have we more sons? or are we like to have?
Is not my teeming date drunk up with time?
And wilt thou pluck my fair son from mine age,
And rob me of a happy mother's name?
Is he not like thee? is he not thine own?
*York.* Thou fond mad woman,
Wilt thou conceal this dark conspiracy?
A dozen of them here have ta'en the sacrament,
And interchangeably set down their hands,

To kill the king at Oxford.
*Duchess.* He shall be none.
We'll keep him here, then what is that to him?
*York.* Away, fond woman! were he twenty times my son,
I would appeach him.
*Duchess.* Hadst thou groaned for him
As I have done, thou wouldst be more pitiful.
But now I know thy mind, thou dost suspect
That I have been disloyal to thy bed,
And that he is a bastard, not thy son:
Sweet York, sweet husband, be not of that mind,
He is as like thee as a man may be,
Not like to me, or any of my kin,
And yet I love him.
*York.* Make way, unruly woman.
[*he stalks forth*
*Duchess.* After, Aumerle; mount thee upon his horse,
Spur post, and get before him to the king,
And beg thy pardon ere he do accuse thee.
I'll not be long behind—though I be old,
I doubt not but to ride as fast as York,
And never will I rise up from the ground,
Till Bolingbroke have pardoned thee: away, be gone!
[*they hurry out*

[5. 3.] *Windsor Castle*

*Enter* BOLINGBROKE, PERCY *and other nobles*

*Bolingbroke.* Can no man tell me of my unthrifty son?
'Tis full three months since I did see him last,
If any plague hang over us, 'tis he:
I would to God, my lords, he might be found:

Inquire at London, 'mongst the taverns there,
For there, they say, he daily doth frequent,
With unrestrainéd loose companions,
Even such, they say, as stand in narrow lanes,
And beat our watch, and rob our passengers,
While he, young wanton and effeminate boy,
Takes on the point of honour to support
So dissolute a crew.

*Percy*. My lord, some two days since I saw the prince,
And told him of those triumphs held at Oxford.

*Bolingbroke*. And what said the gallant?

*Percy*. His answer was, he would unto the stews,
And from the common'st creature pluck a glove,
And wear it as a favour, and with that
He would unhorse the lustiest challenger.

*Bolingbroke*. As dissolute as desperate—yet through both
I see some sparks of better hope, which elder years
May happily bring forth....But who comes here?

*'Enter* AUMERLE *amazed'*

*Aumerle*. Where is the king?

*Bolingbroke*. What means our cousin, that he stares and looks
So wildly?

*Aumerle*. God save your grace, I do beseech your majesty,
To have some conference with your grace alone.

*Bolingbroke*. Withdraw yourselves, and leave us here alone.... [*Percy and the rest withdraw*
What is the matter with our cousin now?

*Aumerle*. [*kneels*] For ever may my knees grow to the earth,
My tongue cleave to my roof within my mouth,
Unless a pardon ere I rise or speak.

*Bolingbroke.* Intended, or committed, was this fault?
If on the first, how heinous e'er it be,
To win thy after-love, I pardon thee.
*Aumerle.* Then give me leave that I may turn the key,
That no man enter till my tale be done.
*Bolingbroke.* Have thy desire. [*the key is turned*

'*The* Duke of York *knocks at the door and crieth*'

*York.* [*without*] My liege, beware, look to thyself,
Thou hast a traitor in thy presence there.
*Bolingbroke.* Villain, I'll make thee safe. [*he draws*
*Aumerle.* [*kneels again*] Stay thy revengeful hand, thou hast no cause to fear.
*York.* [*without*] Open the door, secure, foolhardy king,
Shall I for love speak treason to thy face?
Open the door, or I will break it open.

Bolingbroke *opens, admits* York *and locks the door again*

*Bolingbroke.* What is the matter, uncle? speak, recover breath,
Tell us how near is danger,
That we may arm us to encounter it.
*York.* Peruse this writing here, and thou shalt know [*he delivers the indenture*
The treason that my haste forbids me show.
*Aumerle.* Remember, as thou read'st, thy promise passed.
I do repent me, read not my name there,
My heart is not confederate with my hand.
*York.* It was, villain, ere thy hand did set it down....
I tore it from the traitor's bosom, king.
Fear, and not love, begets his penitence:

Forget to pity him, lest thy pity prove
A serpent that will sting thee to the heart.
*Bolingbroke.* O heinous, strong, and bold conspiracy!
O loyal father of a treacherous son!
Thou sheer, immaculate and silver fountain,
From whence this stream, through muddy passages,
Hath held his current, and defiled himself!
Thy overflow of good converts to bad;
And thy abundant goodness shall excuse
This deadly blot in thy digressing son.
*York.* So shall my virtue be his vice's bawd,
And he shall spend mine honour with his shame,
As thriftless sons their scraping fathers' gold:
Mine honour lives when his dishonour dies,
Or my shamed life in his dishonour lies.
Thou kill'st me in his life—giving him breath,
The traitor lives, the true man's put to death.
*Duchess.* [*without*] What ho, my liege! for God's sake, let me in.
*Bolingbroke.* What shrill-voiced suppliant makes this eager cry?
*Duchess.* A woman, and thy aunt, great king—'tis I.
Speak with me, pity me, open the door,
A beggar begs that never begged before.
*Bolingbroke.* Our scene is altered from a serious thing,
And now changed to 'The Beggar and the King':
My dangerous cousin, let your mother in,
I know she is come to pray for your foul sin.
*York.* If thou do pardon, whosoever pray,
More sins for this forgiveness prosper may:
This fest'red joint cut off, the rest rest sound,
This let alone will all the rest confound.

*Aumerle admits the Duchess*

*Duchess.* O king, believe not this hard-hearted man!
Love loving not itself none other can.
*York.* Thou frantic woman, what dost thou make here?
Shall thy old dugs once more a traitor rear?
*Duchess.* Sweet York, be patient. Hear me, gentle liege. [*she kneels*
*Bolingbroke.* Rise up, good aunt.
*Duchess.* Not yet, I thee beseech.
For ever will I walk upon my knees,
And never see day that the happy sees,
Till thou give joy—until thou bid me joy,
By pardoning Rutland, my transgressing boy.
*Aumerle.* Unto my mother's prayers I bend my knee. [*kneels*
*York.* Against them both my true joints bended be. [*kneels*
Ill mayst thou thrive, if thou grant any grace!
*Duchess.* Pleads he in earnest? look upon his face;
His eyes do drop no tears, his prayers are in jest.
His words come from his mouth, ours from our breast.
He prays but faintly, and would be denied,
We pray with heart and soul, and all beside.
His weary joints would gladly rise, I know,
Our knees shall kneel till to the ground they grow.
His prayers are full of false hypocrisy,
Ours of true zeal and deep integrity.
Our prayers do out-pray his—then let them have
That mercy which true prayer ought to have.
*Bolingbroke.* Good aunt, stand up.
*Duchess.* Nay, do not say 'stand up';
Say 'pardon' first, and afterwards 'stand up'.

An if I were thy nurse, thy tongue to teach,
'Pardon' should be the first word of thy speech:
I never longed to hear a word till now,
Say 'pardon', king, let pity teach thee how.
The word is short, but not so short as sweet,
No word like 'pardon' for kings' mouths so meet.
*York.* Speak it in French, king, say 'pardonne moy'.
*Duchess.* Dost thou teach pardon pardon to destroy?
Ah, my sour husband, my hard-hearted lord,
That sets the word itself against the word!
Speak 'pardon' as 'tis current in our land—
The chopping French we do not understand.
Thine eye begins to speak, set thy tongue there:
Or in thy piteous heart plant thou thine ear,
That hearing how our plaints and prayers do pierce,
Pity may move thee 'pardon' to rehearse.
*Bolingbroke.* Good aunt, stand up.
*Duchess.* I do not sue to stand.
Pardon is all the suit I have in hand.
*Bolingbroke.* I pardon him, as God shall pardon me.
*Duchess.* O happy vantage of a kneeling knee!
Yet am I sick for fear, speak it again,
Twice saying 'pardon' doth not pardon twain,
But makes one pardon strong.
*Bolingbroke.* With all my heart
I pardon him.
*Duchess.* A god on earth thou art.
*Bolingbroke.* But for our trusty brother-in-law, and the abbot,
With all the rest of that consorted crew,
Destruction straight shall dog them at the heels.
Good uncle, help to order several powers
To Oxford, or where'er these traitors are.
They shall not live within this world, I swear,

But I will have them, if I once know where....
Uncle, farewell, and cousin too, adieu—
Your mother well hath prayed, and prove you true!
*Duchess.* Come, my old son—I pray God make thee new. [*they go*

[5.4.] *SIR PIERCE OF EXTON enters with his manservant*

*Exton.* Didst thou not mark the king, what words he spake?
'Have I no friend will rid me of this living fear?'
Was it not so?
*Servant.* These were his very words.
*Exton.* 'Have I no friend?' quoth he—he spake it twice,
And urged it twice together, did he not?
*Servant.* He did.
*Exton.* And, speaking it, he wishtly looked on me,
As who should say, 'I would thou wert the man
That would divorce this terror from my heart',
Meaning the king at Pomfret....Come, let's go,
I am the king's friend, and will rid his foe. [*they go*

[5.5.] *Pomfret Castle*
*'RICHARD alone'*

*Richard.* I have been studying how I may compare
This prison where I live unto the world:
And for because the world is populous,
And here is not a creature but myself,
I cannot do it; yet I'll hammer it out.

My brain I'll prove the female to my soul,
My soul the father, and these two beget
A generation of still-breeding thoughts:
And these same thoughts people this little world,
In humours like the people of this world:
For no thought is contented: the better sort,
As thoughts of things divine, are intermixed
With scruples, and do set the word itself
Against the word,
As thus: 'Come, little ones', and then again,
'It is as hard to come, as for a camel
To thread the postern of a small needle's eye'...
Thoughts tending to ambition, they do plot
Unlikely wonders: how these vain weak nails
May tear a passage through the flinty ribs
Of this hard world, my ragged prison walls;
And, for they cannot, die in their own pride.
Thoughts tending to content flatter themselves
That they are not the first of fortune's slaves,
Nor shall not be the last—like silly beggars
Who sitting in the stocks refuge their shame,
That many have and others must sit there:
And in this thought they find a kind of ease,
Bearing their own misfortunes on the back
Of such as have before endured the like....
Thus play I in one person many people,
And none contented: sometimes am I king,
Then treasons make me wish myself a beggar,
And so I am: then crushing penury
Persuades me I was better when a king;
Then am I kinged again, and by and by
Think that I am unkinged by Bolingbroke,
And straight am nothing....But whate'er I be,
Nor I, nor any man that but man is,

With nothing shall be pleased, till he be eased
With being nothing....Music do I hear? ['*music plays*'
Ha, ha! keep time—how sour sweet music is,
When time is broke and no proportion kept!
So is it in the music of men's lives:
And here have I the daintiness of ear
To check time broke in a disordered string;
But for the concord of my state and time
Had not an ear to hear my true time broke.
I wasted time, and now doth time waste me:
For now hath time made me his numb'ring clock;
My thoughts are minutes, and with sighs they jar
Their watches on unto mine eyes, the outward watch,
Whereto my finger, like a dial's point,
Is pointing still, in cleansing them from tears.
Now, sir, the sound that tells what hour it is
Are clamorous groans which strike upon my heart,
Which is the bell—so sighs, and tears, and groans,
Show minutes, times, and hours: but my time
Runs posting on in Bolingbroke's proud joy,
While I stand fooling here, his Jack of the clock....
This music mads me, let it sound no more,
For though it have holp madmen to their wits,
In me it seems it will make wise men mad:
Yet blessing on his heart that gives it me!
For 'tis a sign of love; and love to Richard
Is a strange brooch in this all-hating world.

'*Enter a Groom of the stable*'

*Groom*. Hail, royal prince!
*Richard*. Thanks, noble peer;
The cheapest of us is ten groats too dear.
What art thou? and how comest thou hither,
Where no man never comes, but that sad dog

That brings me food to make misfortune live?
*Groom.* I was a poor groom of thy stable, king,
When thou wert king; who, travelling towards York,
With much ado at length have gotten leave
To look upon my sometimes royal master's face:
O, how it erned my heart when I beheld,
In London streets that coronation day,
When Bolingbroke rode on roan Barbary!
That horse that thou so often hast bestrid,
That horse that I so carefully have dressed!
*Richard.* Rode he on Barbary? tell me, gentle friend,
How went he under him?
*Groom.* So proudly as if he disdained the ground.
*Richard.* So proud that Bolingbroke was on his back...
That jade hath eat bread from my royal hand,
This hand hath made him proud with clapping him:
Would he not stumble? would he not fall down,
Since pride must have a fall, and break the neck
Of that proud man that did usurp his back?
Forgiveness, horse! why do I rail on thee,
Since thou, created to be awed by man,
Wast born to bear? I was not made a horse,
And yet I bear a burthen like an ass,
Spurred, galled, and tired by jauncing Bolingbroke.

*'Enter one to Richard with meat'*

*Keeper.* [*to the Groom*] Fellow, give place, here is no longer stay.
*Richard.* If thou love me, 'tis time thou wert away.
*Groom.* What my tongue dares not, that my heart shall say. [*he goes*
*Keeper.* [*placing the dish upon the table*] My lord, will't please you to fall to?
*Richard.* Taste of it first, as thou art wont to do.

*Keeper*. My lord, I dare not, Sir Pierce of Exton, who lately came from the king, commands the contrary.

*Richard*. The devil take Henry of Lancaster and thee!
Patience is stale, and I am weary of it.

[*he beats the Keeper*

*Keeper*. Help, help, help!

*EXTON and the other murderers rush in*

*Richard*. How now! what means death in this
rude assault?
Villain, thy own hand yields thy death's instrument....

[*he snatches an axe from one and kills him*

Go thou, and fill another room in hell.

[*he kills another, but* '*here Exton strikes him down*'

That hand shall burn in never-quenching fire
That staggers thus my person: Exton, thy fierce hand
Hath with the king's blood stained the king's own land....
Mount, mount, my soul! thy seat is up on high,
Whilst my gross flesh sinks downward, here to die.

[*he dies*

*Exton*. As full of valour as of royal blood:
Both have I spilled. O, would the deed were good!
For now the devil that told me I did well
Says that this deed is chronicled in hell:
This dead king to the living king I'll bear....
Take hence the rest, and give them burial here.

[*they carry out the bodies*

[5. 6.] *Windsor Castle*

*BOLINGBROKE and the DUKE OF YORK*

*Bolingbroke*. Kind uncle York, the latest news we hear,
Is that the rebels have consumed with fire

Our town of Cicester in Gloucestershire,
But whether they be ta'en or slain we hear not.

*NORTHUMBERLAND enters*

Welcome, my lord, what is the news?
*Northumberland.* First, to thy sacred state wish I all happiness.
The next news is, I have to London sent
The heads of Salisbury, Spencer, Blunt and Kent.
The manner of their taking may appear
At large discoursèd in this paper here. [*he presents it*
*Bolingbroke.* We thank thee, gentle Percy, for thy pains,
And to thy worth will add right worthy gains.

*FITZWATER enters*

*Fitzwater.* My lord, I have from Oxford sent to London
The heads of Brocas and Sir Bennet Seely,
Two of the dangerous consorted traitors,
That sought at Oxford thy dire overthrow.
*Bolingbroke.* Thy pains, Fitzwater, shall not be forgot,
Right noble is thy merit, well I wot.

*PERCY enters, with the BISHOP OF CARLISLE guarded*

*Percy.* The grand conspirator, Abbot of Westminster,
With clog of conscience and sour melancholy
Hath yielded up his body to the grave.
But here is Carlisle living, to abide
Thy kingly doom and sentence of his pride.
*Bolingbroke.* Carlisle, this is your doom:
Choose out some secret place, some reverend room,
More than thou hast, and with it joy thy life;
So as thou liv'st in peace, die free from strife,

For though mine enemy thou hast ever been,
High sparks of honour in thee have I seen.

*Enter* EXTON, *with persons bearing a coffin*

*Exton.* Great king, within this coffin I present
Thy buried fear: herein all breathless lies
The mightiest of thy greatest enemies,
Richard of Bordeaux, by me hither brought.

*Bolingbroke.* Exton, I thank thee not, for thou hast wrought
A deed of slander with thy fatal hand
Upon my head and all this famous land.

*Exton.* From your own mouth, my lord, did I this deed.

*Bolingbroke.* They love not poison that do poison need,
Nor do I thee; though I did wish him dead,
I hate the murderer, love him murderéd:
The guilt of conscience take thou for thy labour,
But neither my good word, nor princely favour:
With Cain go wander through the shades of night,
And never show thy head by day nor light....
Lords, I protest, my soul is full of woe,
That blood should sprinkle me to make me grow:
Come, mourn with me for what I do lament,
And put on sullen black incontinent.
I'll make a voyage to the Holy Land,
To wash this blood off from my guilty hand:
March sadly after, grace my mournings here,
In weeping after this untimely bier.

[*The coffin is borne slowly out, Bolingbroke and the rest following*

# THE MEETING OF RICHARD AND ISABEL

Daniel's *Civil Wars* (1595), Bk ii. stanzas 71 to 98

Now *Isabell* the young afflicted Queene,
Whose yeares had neuer shew'd her but delights,
Nor louely eies before had euer seene
Other then smiling ioies and ioyfull sights:
Borne great, matcht great, liu'd great and euer beene
Partaker of the worlds best benefits,
Had plac'd her selfe, hearing her Lord should passe
That way where shee vnseene in secret was.

Sicke of delay and longing to behold
Her long mist loue in fearfull ieoperdies,
To whom although it had in sort beene told
Of their proceeding, and of his surprize,
Yet thinking they would neuer be so bold
To lead their Lord in any shamefull wise,
But rather would conduct him as their king,
As seeking but the states reordering.

And foorth shee looks: and notes the formost traine
And grieues to view some there she wisht not there,
Seeing the chiefe not come, staies, lookes againe,
And yet she sees not him that should appeare:
Then backe she stands, and then desires as[1] faine
Againe to looke to see if hee were nere,
At length a glittring troupe farre off she spies,
Perceiues the thronge and heares the shoots & cries.

[1] 'was' (1595) corr. 1609.

Lo yonder now at length he comes (saith shee)
Looke my good women where he is in sight:
Do you not see him? yonder that is hee
Mounted on that white courser all in white,
There where the thronging troupes of people bee,
I know him by his seate, he sits s'vpright:
Lo, now he bows: deare Lord with what sweet grace:
How long haue I longd to behold that face?

O what delight my hart takes by mine eie?
I doubt me when he comes but something neere
I shall set wide the window: what care I
Who doth see me, so him I may see cleare?
Thus doth false ioy delude her wrongfully
Sweete lady in the thing she held so deare;
For nearer come, shee findes shee had mistooke,
And him she markt was *Henrie Bullingbrooke.*

Then *Enuie* takes the place in her sweet eies,
Where sorrow had prepard her selfe a seat,
And words of wrath from whẽce complaints should rise,
Proceed from egar lookes, and browes that threat;
Traytor saith she; i'st thou that in this wise
To braue thy Lord and king art made so great?
And haue mine eies done vnto me this wrong
To looke on thee? for this staid I so long?

O haue they grac'd a periur'd rebell so?
Well for their error I will weepe them out,
And hate the tongue defilde that praisde my fo,
And loath the minde that gaue me not to doubt:
O haue I added shame vnto my woe?
Ile looke no more; *Ladies* looke you about,
And tell me if my Lord bee in this traine,
Least my betraying eies should erre againe.

And in this passion turnes her selfe away:
The rest looke all, and carefull note each wight;
Whilst she impatient of the least delay
Demaunds againe, and what not yet in sight?
Where is my Lord? what gone some other way?
I muse at this, O God graunt all go right.
Then to the window goes againe at last
And sees the chiefest traine of all was past.

And sees not him her soule desir'd to see,
And yet hope spent makes her not leaue to looke,
At last her loue-quicke eies which ready be,
Fastens on one whom though she neuer tooke
Could be her Lord: yet that sad cheere which he
Then shew'd, his habit and his wofull looke,
The grace he doth in base attire retaine,
Causd her she could not from his sight refraine.

What might he be she said that thus alone
Rides pensiue in this vniuersall ioy:
Some I perceiue as well as we do mone,
All are not pleasd with euery thing this day,
It maie be he laments the wronge is done
Vnto my Lord, and grieues as well he may,
Then he is some of ours, and we of right
Must pitty him, that pitties our sad plight.

But stay, ist not my Lord himselfe I see?
In truth if twere not for his base araie,
I verily should thinke that it were he;
And yet his basenes doth a grace bewray:
Yet God forbid, let me deceiued be;
O be it not my Lord although it may:
And let desire make vowes against desire,
And let my sight approue my sight a liar.

Let me not see him, but himselfe, a king;
For so he left me, so he did remoue:
This is not he, this feeles some other thing,
A passion of dislike or els of loue:
O yes tis he, that princely face doth bring
The euidence of maiestie to proue:
That face I haue conferr'd which now I see
With that within my hart, and they agree.

Thus as shee stoode assur'd and yet in doubt,
Wishing to see, what seene she grieud to see,
Hauing beliefe, yet faine would be without;
Knowing, yet striuing not to know twas he:
Her heart relenting, yet her heart so stout
As would not yeeld to thinke what was, could be:
Till quite condemnd by open proofe of sight
Shee must confesse or else denie the light.

For whether loue in him did sympathize
Or chance so wrought to manifest her doubt,
Euen iust before, where she thus secret pries[1],
He staies and with cleare face lookes all about:
When she: tis ô too true, I know his eies
Alas it is my owne deare Lord, cries out:
And with that crie sinkes downe vpon the flore,
Abundant griefe lackt words to vtter more.

Sorrow keepes full possession in her soule,
Lockes him within, laies vp the key of breath,
Raignes all alone a *Lord* without controule
So long till greater horror threatneth:
And euen in daunger brought, to loose the whole
H'is forst come forth or else to stay with death,
Opens a sigh and lets in sence againe,
And sence at lẽgth giues words leaue to complaine.

[1] 'prize' (1595) corr. 1609.

Then like a torrent had beene stopt before,
Teares, sighes, and words, doubled togither flow,
Confusdly striuing whether should do more,
The true intelligence of griefe to show:
Sighes hindred words, words perisht in their store,
Both intermixt in one together grow:
One would do all, the other more then's part
Being both sent equall agents from the hart.

At length when past the first of sorrowes worst,
When calm'd confusion better forme affords
Her heart commands her words should passe[1] out first,
And then her sighes should interpoint her words;
The whiles her eies out into teares should burst,
This order with her sorrow she accords,
Which orderles all forme of order brake,
So then began her words and thus she spake.

O dost thou thus returne againe to mee?
Are these the triumphs for thy victories?
Is this the glory thou dost bring with thee,
From that vnhappie Irish enterprise?
O haue I made so many vowes to see
Thy safe returne, and see thee in this wise?
Is this the lookt for comfort thou dost bring,
To come a captiue that wentst out a king?

And yet deare Lord though thy vngratefull Land
Hath left thee thus, yet I will take thy part,
I doo remaine the same vnder thy hand,
Thou still dost rule the kingdome of my hart;
If all be lost, that gouernment doth stand
And that shall neuer from thy rule depart:
And so thou bee, I care not how thou be,
Let greatnes goe, so it goe without thee.

[1] 'past' (1595).

And welcome come, how so vnfortunate,
I will applaud what others do dispise,
I loue thee for thy selfe not for thy state,
More then thy selfe is what without thee, lies:
Let that more goe, if it be in thy fate,
And hauing but thy selfe it will suffize:
I married was not to thy crowne but thee,
And thou without a crowne all one to mee.

But what doe I heere lurking idlie mone
And waile apart, and in a single part
Make seuerall griefe which should be both in one,
The touch being equall of each others hart?
Ah no sweet Lord thou must not mone alone,
For without me thou art not all thou art,
Nor my teares without thine are fullie teares,
For thus vnioyn'd, sorrow but halfe appeares.

Ioine then our plaints & make our griefe ful griefe,
Our state being one, ô lets not part our care,
Sorrow hath only this poore bare reliefe,
To be bemon'd of such as wofull are:
O should I rob thy griefe and be the thiefe
To steale a priuate part, and seuerall share,
Defrauding sorrow of her perfect due?
No no my Lord I come to helpe thee rue.

Then forth she goes a close concealed way
As grieuing to be seene not as she was;
Labors t'attaine his presence all she maie,
Which with most hard a doe was brought to passe:
For that night vnderstanding where he laie
With earnest treating she procur'd her passe
To come to him. Rigor could not deny
Those teares, so poore a suite or put her by.

Entring the chamber where he was alone
As one whose former fortune was his shame,
Loathing th'obraiding eie of anie one
That knew him once and knowes him not the same:
When hauing giuen expresse commaund that none
Should presse to him, yet hearing some that came
Turnes angerly about his grieued eies;
When lo his sweete afflicted Queene he spies.

Straight cleeres his brow & with a borrowed smile
What my deare Queene, ô welcome deare he saies?
And striuing his owne passion to beguile
And hide the sorrow which his eie betraies,
Could speake no more but wrings her hands the while,
And then (sweet lady) and againe he staies:
Th'excesse of ioy and sorrow both affords
Affliction none, or but poore niggard wordes.

Shee that was come with a resolued hart
And with a mouth full stoor'd, with words wel chose,
Thinking this comfort will I first impart
Vnto my Lord, and thus my speach dispose:
Then thus ile say, thus looke, and with this art
Hide mine owne sorrow to relieue his woes,
When being come all this prou'd nought but winde,
Teares, lookes, and sighes doe only tell her minde.

Thus both stood silent and confused so,
Their eies relating how their harts did morne
Both bigge with sorrow, and both great with woe
In labour with what was not to be borne:
This mightie burthen wherewithall they goe
Dies vndeliuered, perishes vnborne;
Sorrow makes silence her best oratore
Where words may make it lesse not shew it more.

But he whom longer time had learn'd the art
T'indure affliction as a vsuall touch:
Straines forth his wordes, and throwes dismay apart
To raise vp her, whose passions now were such
As quite opprest her ouerchardged hart,
Too small a vessell to containe so much,
And cheeres and mones, and fained hopes doth frame
As if himselfe belieu'd, or hop'd the same.

# THE COPY FOR *RICHARD II*, 1597 AND 1623

Four of the early texts of *Richard II* are of interest to an editor: the First Quarto printed in 1597 (Q.), the version included in the First Folio of 1623 (F.), the Quarto of 1608, which gives evidence of a recent revival of the play[1], and in which the 'Deposition' scene was first published (Qc), and the Quarto of 1615 (Qd) a copy of which, after undergoing 'correction' in the playhouse, was used by the printers of the Folio text. Moved by the discovery of a new and hitherto unrecorded edition of the play (Qw) in the library of Mr W. A. White of the United States, Dr A. W. Pollard has subjected the Quarto and Folio texts of *Richard II* to the most exhaustive bibliographical enquiry they are likely to receive for many years to come[2]. All I need do here is to set down his findings, with which, except for one matter, I find myself in complete agreement.

Dr Pollard contends that the Quarto of 1597 was printed from Shakespeare's own manuscript (with the 'Deposition' scene cut out) after the play had finished its run upon the stage[3]. This is by far the most important of his conclusions, and though in the nature of the case it remains a theory, it is never likely to be challenged. It marks too a turning-point in the history of the editing of the play. For, though the 1597 text has for long been considered 'the best' (as the Cambridge editors remarked in 1864), the fullness of its authority was not recognized until Dr Pollard wrote, and it has never, I

1 v. *Stage-history*, above, p. lxxviii.

2 *King Richard II: a new quarto*, ed. by A. W. Pollard, 1916.

3 *Ibid.* pp. 96–8.

think, been accepted without qualification as a basic text before the present edition. This is not to say that I have not at times adopted readings from the Folio text. But I have departed from those of Q. (and under the head of 'readings' I include stage-directions, punctuation, verse-lineation, as well as dialogue) only when F. presents an alternative both manifestly superior on aesthetic grounds and justifiable from the bibliographical standpoint[1].

Turning to the Folio text, we may note first that the Cambridge editors declared in 1864 that it 'was no doubt printed from a copy of Q4 [i.e. the Quarto of 1615, which Dr Pollard has labelled Qd], corrected with some care and prepared for stage representation.' This Dr Pollard refines upon and rectifies in his statement that the copy for *Richard II*, 1623, was obtained by someone who corrected a specimen of the Quarto of 1615 with the prompt-book at the theatre; that the process of correction was 'very hastily... performed, and that this imperfectly corrected Quarto of 1615 was the sole authority by which Jaggard's press-corrector had to work, so that if he found anything in it which he thought wrong he had to botch as best he could[2].' To an editor, who, when faced with a reading which seems better in the Folio than in the First Quarto, is anxious to know what authority may lie behind the reading in question, the crux of the theory at this point lies in the character of the prompt-book by which the Quarto of 1615 was so 'imperfectly corrected' for Jaggard's purposes. And here I am compelled to suggest a slight modification of Dr Pollard's conjectural history of the text. He inclines to believe that there was never more than a single

[1] There is no 'bad quarto' of *Richard II*; otherwise I have edited the play on the same principles I followed with *Hamlet*, v. MSH. pp. 175–81.

[2] Pollard, p. 99. But see also his p. 52.

manuscript of the play, viz. Shakespeare's draft, which was in his view used as prompt-copy at the original performances, and when the run was over was then handed to the publisher. And even if, he declares, it be admitted that a special prompt-book was prepared for the theatre, once the author's draft was published in book form, the prompt-book would almost certainly have been destroyed in favour of the printed text with 'its greater handiness and legibility.'

Fifteen years after Dr Pollard wrote, Dr McKerrow published an important article on 'The Elizabethan Printer and Dramatic Manuscripts[1],' in which he succeeded in establishing a strong presumption that manuscripts of plays which reached the hands of a printer at that period were generally not, as Dr Pollard and I had hitherto assumed in the case of good Shakespearian quartos, prompt-books, which the players were unlikely to release, but the authors' original drafts, sometimes called his 'foul papers.' It follows that the appearance of a good dramatic text in print is prima facie evidence for the existence of at least *two* manuscripts: the author's draft, which was handed to the printer, and the prompt-book transcript, which was retained at the theatre. In any case, there is one consideration, of great weight with an acting company, which must never be lost sight of in discussions of this kind. I mean the censor of plays, and his authority to perform a given text. That authority was inscribed by the censor's own hand on the manuscript of the play after he had read it, and the 'allowed book,' as such a manuscript was called, would be jealously preserved as the company's legal protection in the event of trouble over the play, an event that occasionally occurred. If therefore Shakespeare's draft was the only manuscript copy of *Richard II*, that draft must have borne the censor's

[1] *The Librarv*, xii. 253–75.

authorization before performance took place in 1595. And if so, it is exceedingly unlikely, indeed almost out of the question, that this same manuscript should have been sold by the players to the publisher. A printed book might be more legible than a prompt-book in manuscript, but lacking the censor's authorization it would be invalid for performance.

The same argument is relevant to the alternative suggestion, that an original prompt-copy, if one existed, would have been destroyed when the Quarto became available. Even if the prompter found the Quarto handier for use, he would have preserved the 'allowed book' as legal guarantee. But is it at all certain that he would have seen in it that 'greater handiness and legibility' which Dr Pollard posits? On the contrary, might not one accustomed, perhaps for many years, to prompt from manuscript books, in his own hand or in that of a scribe familiar to him, manuscripts too in folio which displayed at a time before the eye twice the quantity of dialogue that an open quarto could show, regard the latter as a somewhat awkward substitute? Whichever way we look at it, the probability seems to be that a manuscript prompt-book for *Richard II* was made out from Shakespeare's 'foul papers' in 1595, was read by the censor and endorsed with his approval, and after having served its turn at rehearsal and performance was then placed in the theatre library, where it remained, except for brief employment in 1601 and more extended use in or about 1608, until it came to be consulted by the scribe commissioned to correct a copy of the 1615 Quarto by the authorized playhouse text for the publication of the First Folio in 1623.

And the probability thus established on general grounds is rendered the more likely when we come to examine the particular circumstances of the texts in question. Reference to my notes on 1. 4. 23 and 52 S.D.

will show that traces of the prompter's hand are almost certainly to be seen at one point in the manuscript from which Q. was printed[1]. Nevertheless, when we contemplate that Quarto as a whole, with its scanty and often misleading or imperfect stage-directions, its scantier punctuation, its textual tangles, and its frequent examples of irregular verse-division, we can hardly believe that it can have served as prompt-copy at any time. On the other hand, the Folio text displays all the stigmata of prompt-copy: playhouse cuts, full stage-directions, far heavier punctuation, and a verse-division which, though still wrong in places[2], is much more regular on the whole than that of the Quarto. Dr Pollard's theory implies that these features were introduced into a copy of the First Quarto after 1597, i.e. presumably at the revival of 1608, since such changes can hardly have been made for the single performance of 1601, and we know of no other occasion; and that the First Quarto represents the prompt-book used during the period 1595–7, i.e.

[1] The alterations there attested were, I conjecture, of a more or less haphazard nature, made by the prompter while first perusing Shakespeare's MS., though after that MS. had been transcribed by the theatre scrivener. In short, I imagine a procedure of this kind: (1) Shakespeare produces his draft of *Ric. II*, (2) this is handed to the scrivener who transcribes the whole dialogue, leaving, however, blanks for the prompter to fill in his own stage-directions, (3) the prompter with the two MSS. before him then constructs his prompt-copy from the transcript, and though making his cuts, pays more attention to the S.D.s than the dialogue. Thus, though he alters the dialogue at l. 23 and not the S.D. at the head of the scene in Shakespeare's draft, he only alters the S.D. in the prompt-book. No doubt he got the line to his liking in the player's part, which was all that mattered.

[2] It may well be that in his careless correction of the 1615 Q. the scribe omitted to rectify the verse lining at a number of points.

while the play was enjoying one of the most successful runs recorded for Elizabethan times. Once again, is it not easier to imagine two manuscripts existing from the beginning of the play's theatrical history? Such an hypothesis seems to extricate us from all difficulties.

It clears up, for example, the problem of the 'Deposition' scene, upon which a word must now be said. These 158 lines, which comprise what many regard as the finest dramatic poetry in the play, were undoubtedly already part of it when it left Shakespeare's hands in 1595, and were almost certainly spoken from the stage both at the original performances and at the command performance of 1601; yet they appeared in no quarto printed during the life-time of Queen Elizabeth, so that we can only suppose that the censor of books found offence in them which had escaped the notice of his brother censor of plays[1]. They were first printed in the Quarto of 1608, obviously from copy acquired by underhand means. Dr Pollard suggests that they 'may have been obtained from some subordinate person employed about the theatre, but were more probably procured by means of

[1] There is a difficulty here that needs clearing up. Dr McKerrow (*Library*, *op. cit.* pp. 266–8) argues that manuscripts already licensed for performance on the stage would commonly receive a licence for publication without being read a second time. The absence of the 'Deposition' scene from the Elizabethan printed texts of *Richard II* is proof, I think, that from 1597 to 1603 the scene was considered dangerous matter. Yet if it was excluded at the instance of the censor of books, he must have read the play before it was printed. Did the publisher submit the very untidy 'copy' for *Richard II* 1597, or did he have a special transcript made for the censor's perusal, or did he borrow the 'allowed book' from the theatre for this purpose and when he had received permission to print (without the 'Deposition' scene) go forward with the other manuscript?

shorthand writers specially sent there for the purpose[1].' Whatever their source, it was clearly decidedly inferior to that from which the Folio text was derived; for when the two texts are laid side by side it is seen that the former is not only full of omissions but frequently divides the verse incorrectly[2]. To the Cambridge editors, indeed, the F. text of the 'Deposition' scene appeared so good that they accounted for it on the hypothesis 'that the defective text of the Quarto [Qd] had been corrected from the author's MS.' Dr Pollard, having cleared the deck of all manuscript copies in 1597, is obliged to suppose that the 'Deposition' could be reconstructed, when required for performance at a later date, from the original actors' parts[3]. This is, of course, possible enough; but is not the hypothetical manuscript prompt-book, once again, the easiest way out of the difficulty? Or rather, is not the absence of the 'Deposition' scene from the Quarto of 1597 one reason more for refusing to believe that the prompt-book was destroyed in that year? A quarto without that scene would hardly have been acceptable in place of a manuscript which still retained it; and marking the trend of opinion as shown by the censor of books, would not our prompter have clung still more tenaciously to his precious 'allowed book' with the licence of the censor of plays upon it, 'Deposition' scene and all?

Yet, superior as the F. text of the scene is to that of Qc and Qd, we are fortunate to possess the latter, since it enables us to correct the F. in three small particulars. One of these is an obvious misprint by the F. printers; the other two may be explained as careless 'correction'

[1] Pollard, p. 64.

[2] Inasmuch as these passages are interspersed with others in which the text is of a distinctly higher quality, it is probable that the copy used in 1608 was composite in origin.

[3] *Ibid.* p. 98.

on the part of the scribe employed to provide those printers with their copy.

Apart from the 'Deposition' scene, an editor's duty, as I have said, is to follow the text of Q. as closely as possible, since he will then be following, after making allowance for the intervening printers, the manuscript of Shakespeare himself. Yet, just as the reported text of the 'Deposition' scene, so far from being worthless, enables us to correct the F. text once or twice, so for the rest of the play the F. text is useful as a check upon that of Q., a check which we can employ with more confidence if we assume that it has the authority of a manuscript prompt-book behind it.

# NOTES

All significant departures from the First Quarto text, including emendations in punctuation, are recorded; the name of the critic who first suggested or printed an accepted reading being placed in brackets. The line-numeration for reference to plays not yet issued in this edition is that used in Bartlett's *Concordance* and *The Globe Shakespeare*.

Q., unless otherwise specified, stands for the First Quarto of *Richard II* (1597), the three extant copies of which exist in different states, owing to correction while the sheets were passing through the press; F. stands for the First Folio; the quartos published between 1597 and 1623 are thus described: Qb (2nd ed. 1598), Qw (3rd ed. 1598, recently identified, v. Pollard, *infra*), Qc (4th ed. 1608, which gives the 'Deposition' scene for the first time), Qd (5th ed. 1615, a copy of which was used in the production of the F. text).

Other abbreviations are as follows:

Abbott = *A Shakespeare Grammar* by E. A. Abbott; Bond = *The Works of John Lyly* by Warwick Bond; Boswell-Stone = *Shakspere's Holinshed* by W. G. Boswell-Stone; Buchon = *Collection des Chroniques Nationales Françaises* par J. A. Buchon; Camb. = *The Cambridge Shakespeare* ed. by W. A. Wright; Chambers, *Eliz. Stage* = *The Elizabethan Stage* by E. K. Chambers; Chambers, *Will. Shak.* = *William Shakespeare* by E. K. Chambers; Clar. = the edition of *Richard II* in *The Clarendon Shakespeare*; Coleridge = *Coleridge's Shakespearean Criticism* ed. by T. M. Raysor (Constable, 1930) 2 vols.; Craig = edition of *Richard II* by Hardin Craig (Tudor Shakespeare); Créton = a reprint by John Webb, with English translation, of Créton's metrical *Histoire du roy d'Angleterre Richard II* (*Archaeologia*, vol. xx); *C.W.* = *The Civil Wars* (v. Daniel); Daniel = *The First Fowre Bookes of the Ciuile Wars* by Samuel Daniel (1595); Franz = *Shakespeare Grammatik* von W. Franz; Froissart = *Berners' Froissart* ed. by W. P. Ker; Gordon = edition of *Richard II* by G. S. Gordon; Hall = *Hall's Chronicle* (1550); Hayward = *The first part of the Life of Henrie IIII* by Sir John Hayward (1599); Herford = edition of *Richard II* by C. H. Herford (Warwick Shakespeare); Hol. = *Holinshed's Chronicle* (2nd ed. 1587); Knight = *The Pictorial Shakespeare* ed. by Charles Knight (1838–45); Le Beau = *La Chronicque de Richard II* by Jean Le Beau; MSH. = *The Manuscript of Shakespeare's Hamlet*, 1934, by J. Dover Wilson; Newbolt = edition of *Richard II* by H. Newbolt and J. C. Smith (Oxford); Noble = *Shakespeare's Biblical Knowledge* by Richmond Noble; O.E.D. = *The Oxford English Dictionary*; Oman = *A History of England*, 1377–1485, by Sir Charles Oman; Pollard = *King Richard II: a new quarto* ed. by A. W. Pollard, 1916; Reyher = *Notes sur les sources de 'Richard II'* par Paul Reyher (Paris: Librairie Henri Didier), 1924; J. C. Smith = Newbolt (q.v.); Tilley = *Elizabethan Proverb Lore* by M. P. Tilley; T.L.S. = *Times Literary Supplement*; *Traïson* = *La Chronicque de la Traïson et Mort de Richart Deux roy Dengleterre* (ed. by B. Williams for the English Historical Society, 1846); Verity = edition of *Richard II* by A. W. Verity (Pitt Press Shakespeare); White = *The Works of Shakespeare* ed. by R. Grant White, 1859; *Woodstock* = *Richard II or Thomas of Woodstock* ed. by Wilhelmina P. Frijlinck (Malone Society Reprint, 1929); S.D. for stage direction; G. for Glossary.

*Characters in the Play*. A list was first supplied by Rowe. The name of the *Queen* is not given in the play; nor is the *Duke of York* spoken of as Edmund of Langley, though many editors describe him so. For the *Duke of Surrey* v. notes 1. 1. 204; 1. 3. 251–52.

*Acts and Scenes.* No such divisions in Q. I have followed, like other editors, those of F. with the exception of 5. 4, which, since Pope, all have printed as a separate scene (v. note 5. 3. 146 S.D.). Dr Johnson comments at the end of 1. 3:

> Here the first act ought to end, that between the first and second acts there may be time for John of Gaunt to accompany his son, return and fall sick....As the play is now divided, more time passes between the two last scenes of the first act, than between the first act and the second.

*Punctuation.* Pollard writes:

> In the set speeches the punctuation of Q., if we remember that it is dramatic and not grammatical, will be found sufficiently complete and intelligent to entitle us to believe that Shakespeare punctuated these portions of his own manuscript with some care, and that Q. reproduces this punctuation with very much the same substantial fidelity that it reproduces the words of the text (pp. 64–5)....But my impression is that Sh. paid little attention to punctuation except in what may be called the set speeches, and along with obviously careful stopping there is a good deal which is equally obviously careless, and many sins of omission (p. 70).

The punctuation of Q., like that of Q 2 *Hamlet*, merits indeed the closest attention. I have followed it as nearly as is possible in a modernized text, and have quoted in the notes many of Pollard's illuminating observations upon various passages, e.g. at 1. 1. 96, 132; 1. 2. 21; 1. 3. 68; 2. 1. 185.

*Stage-directions.* All Q. and F. S.D.s are quoted in the notes.

## 1. 1.

*Material.* The first of Sh.'s historical cycle begins at exactly the same point (viz. the quarrel between Bol. and Mow.) as Hall's *Chronicle*, which covers the same period. It also adopts Hall's reading of the characters of the two men. But whereas Hall says nothing of Glouc. (though Froissart, whom he admittedly continues, says much), Hol. (iii. 508/

1/73) names him as the 'cheefe instrument of this mischeefe,' i.e. the fall of Ric. and the troubles that came after. The Glouc. passages in *Ric. II*, however, are prob. mostly inspired by *Woodstock*. All historians agree that the quarrel between Bol. and Mow. arose from a private talk between them concerning Ric.'s treatment of his great nobles (including his uncles). But there are two versions of what followed: (i) that Mow. accused Bol. of broaching the subject and of uttering treason, and (ii) that Bol. was the accuser and Mow. the accused. Froissart, Hall and Daniel follow (i); Hol., *Traïson* and Sh. follow (ii), which modern history endorses (v. Oman, p. 141). Further, most of the details, including at times the actual words, of the scene are based upon Hol., who gives the fullest account. There is, of course, simplification and compression. The few points in which Sh. departs from this source will be noted below.

S.D. Q., F. 'Enter King Richard, Iohn of Gaunt, with other Nobles and attendants.'

*Windsor Castle* Pope located the scene at 'The Court'; Capell, followed by most edd., at 'London. A Room in the Palace.' Clar. first drew attention to Hol. iii. 493/2/60:

> There was a great scaffold erected within the castell of Windsor for the king to sit with the lords and prelats of his realme: and so at the daie appointed, he with the said lords & prelats being come thither and set in their places, the duke of Hereford appellant, and the duke of Norfolke defendant, were sent for to come & appeare before the king, sitting there in his seat of iustice.

The 'scaffold' would be the upper stage in Sh.'s theatre; cf. note l. 186 below.

1. *Old...time-honoured* The play opens in 1398 when Gaunt was actually 58 years old, and his brother York 57. But both are called 'old' in *Woodstock* (ll. 933, 1312), while York is 'old' in Hall and in *Traïson*, v. note 5. 2 *Material* ii. Gaunt = Ghent, his birthplace.

2. *band* v. G.

3. *Hereford* Sometimes in Q. and nearly always in F. spelt 'Herford,' and always pronounced as a dis-

syllable. It is 'Hereford' in Hol., 'Herfford' in Hall, and 'Herford' in Daniel.

4. *appeal* v. G.

9–14. *ancient malice...inveterate malice* Nothing of this in Hol. or Froissart. R. G. White cited Daniel, *C.W.* i. 60 (ed. 1609):

> Hereof doth Norfolke presently take hold,
> And to the king the whole discourse relate:
> Who, not concepting it, as it was told,
> But iudging *it proceeded out of hate*....

as an instance of the poet's debt to the dramatist, but wrongly assigned the lines to 1595. The parallel was first noted by C. Knight (*Histories*, i. 82–3). Cf. *Introd.* p. xliii.

12. *sift* v. G. *argument* v. G.

13. *apparent* v. G.

15–16. *presence—face...brow, ourselves* Q. 'presence face...brow our ſelues' F. 'preſence face...brow, our ſelues' Edd. 'presence, face...brow, ourselves'

18–19. *High-stomached...fire* Richard promises himself a fine display. v. G. 'high-stomached.'

19. *In rage...sea* Cf. *K. John*, 2. 1. 451 'The sea enragéd is not half so deaf.'

S.D. Q., F. 'Enter Bullingbrooke and Mowbray.'

20–21. *Many...liege* 'The supple and somewhat oily character of Bol. is indicated by his first words' (Newbolt). But there is nothing oily about him at the end of the scene, and a conventional salutation to a sovereign could hardly have expressed less with politeness. Yet the dramatic irony in such words on the lips of one who is to dethrone Ric. and become responsible for his death is obvious.

20. *Many...befal* Coleridge compares 'the apparently defective metre' with Prospero's at *Temp.* 1. 2. 53 and adds: 'The actor should supply the time by emphasis, and pause on the first syllable.'

23. *envying* Pron. 'envýing,' cf. *Shrew*, 2. 1. 18.

24. *Add...your crown* = 'add the title of immortality to that of kingship' (Herford). Cf. *Woodstock*, 43–4 (of the Black Prince):

> but heauen fore stauld his diademe on earth
> to place hime w$^{th}$ a royall Crowne in heauen.

26. *come* = come about. Cf. *Ado*, 5. 2. 46 'Let me go with that I came.'

28. *thou* 'The language of affection between members of a family; changed to the formal *you* (l. 186) when Ric. is displeased' (Verity); after which he avoids addressing him directly. For *object* v. G.

30–33. *First...hate* Bol. begins by formally clearing himself of the suspicions voiced by Ric. in ll. 8–11, and no doubt communicated to him by Gaunt. The suspicions are, of course, well grounded. Bol. is moved in this scene and in 1. 3 not by ambition as some think but by the desire to avenge his uncle Gloucester's death, a purpose he reveals at the appropriate moment (ll. 98–108). Cf. *Introd.* pp. xx–xxi. Coleridge comments:

> I remember even in the Sophoclean drama no more striking example of the τὸ πρέπον καὶ σεμνὸν. Yea the rhymes in the last six lines well express the preconcertedness of Bol.'s scheme, so beautifully contrasted with the vehemence and sincere irritation of Mow. (i. 145).

This, which has led many critics astray, should be compared with his verdict on a different occasion (quoted pp. xx–xxi). Bol. has no 'scheme' but vengeance upon the enemies of his family.

37–38. *My body...heaven* i.e. 'I shall either make good the accusation in body on this earth or, if I am slain, render my account before the judgment seat of God.' For *divine* v. G.

40. *Too good* i.e. in rank. Expanded in ll. 41–2.

'Mow.'s rank is regarded as a permanent *ground*, which his treason disfigures, but cannot destroy' (Herford).

43. *aggravate the note* = emphasize the disgrace. v. G. 'note.'

46. *right drawn* = 'drawn in a right or just Cause' (Johnson).

47. *accuse my zeal* i.e. throw doubts upon my loyalty. v. G. 'zeal.'

48. *trial* Referring to 'trial by combat.' Mow. means: It is blows not words that will settle this dispute.

49. *eager* = sharp, bitter.

51. *cooled* i.e. in death.

54–55. *the fair reverence...speech* Anticipates ll. 57–8.

56. *post* Continues the metaphor in 'rein' and 'spurs.' *returned* Q. 'returnd,'

58–61. *Setting aside...villain* Mow.'s cue being to curry favour with Ric., he begins by feigning hesitation, and does not call Bol. 'traitor' until Ric. gives him permission in l. 123.

58. *Setting...royalty* Cf. 1 *Hen. IV*, 3. 3. 138 'Setting thy knighthood aside, thou art a knave to call me so.'

63. *tied* = bound.

65. *inhabitable* v. G. and cf. below 1. 1. 93–4; 4. 1. 74 'I dare meet Surrey in a wilderness'; *Macb.* 3. 4. 104 'And dare me to the desert with thy sword'; and Beaumont and Fletcher, *The Lovers' Progress*, 5. 2 'Maintain thy treason with thy sword? with what | Contempt I hear it! in a wilderness | I durst encounter it.' The expression was evidently common form, and implied a fight to the death, since in the desert none could part the fighters or help the wounded.

67. *this* i.e. what he says in l. 68.

68. *By all my hopes* i.e. of salvation. Cf. *1 Hen. IV*, 5. 1. 87.

69. *Pale trembling coward* Bol. interprets Mow.'s hesitation as cowardice.

S.D. What the gage was we are not told. But Hol. says that Bol. took off his 'hood' and mentions hoods being used as gages in the challenges described in 4. 1. Hayward (p. 45) calls it a 'glove'; that was probably how Sh. himself thought of it. Cf. note 4. 1. 25.

70–71. *Disclaiming...royalty* Ironical. While Mow. tries to hide behind the K.'s favour, Bol. scornfully refuses any such protection. His attitude to Ric. is one of veiled insolence throughout.

70. *kindred* Q. 'kinred'—an old form.

72. *except....* Q. 'except.' 'He pauses for Mow. to take' up his gage; 'but Mow. does not, and Bol. continues contemptuously' (Pollard, p. 67).

77. *or thou...devise* 'Bol. with careless insolence declares himself ready to prove in arms that any insulting charge that Mow. can suggest is true of him' (Herford).

78–79. *by that sword...shoulder* Another compliment to Ric., whose reply shows that the flattery has gone home.

80–81. *in any...knightly trial* i.e. in any honourable fashion or form of knightly trial, allowed by the laws of chivalry. Cf. 1. 3. 45.

84–86. *What doth...ill in him* Ric.'s attitude of amused contempt for his 'high-stomached' cousin is evident. Here he deliberately incites him to further violence, and in l. 109 applauds the outburst he has provoked. He watches the two as if they were performing animals. Cf. next note.

87–108. *Look what I speak...be spent* The text follows Hol. very closely here, though he puts the words into the mouth of a knight speaking for Bol. As all critics have noted, Bol.'s third charge is subtly intended to strike at Ric., by whose command Glouc. had been murdered. Yet it is not until 1. 2 that Ric.'s complicity is revealed. Cf. *Introd.* p. lxvii. Hol. tells us that the K. 'waxed angrie' at the accusation in ll. 98–103. Sh. gives him a reply which is sarcastic rather than angry.

89. *'lendings'* v. G. Q. 'Lendings'—the capital apparently used 'as we might use inverted commas' (Pollard, p. 72).

90. *lewd* v. G.

93. *verge* Q. 'Verge' Possibly rhetorical emphasis (v. Pollard, p. 71).

95. *these eighteen years* i.e. since Wat Tyler's revolt, 1381, the first disturbance of Ric.'s reign. But, as the words come from Hol., Sh. may not have realized their point.

96. *land...* Q. 'land:' 97. *spring!* Q. 'ſpring,' Pollard (p. 65) instances this speech as an example of Sh. punctuation, and writes:

Plump at the end of l. 96, separating 'treasons' from its verb, the Quarto inserts a colon, and the line 'Fetch... head and spring' comes rushing out after the pause with doubled effect. And at the end of this line, shade of Lindley Murray! there is no full stop—only a comma; for Bol. will not give Mow. a chance to interrupt him, but dashes on with his second accusation, with only an imperceptible pause. In the earlier lines, on the other hand, when he is preparing the way for his rush, Bol.'s measured tones are marked by two stops which the Camb. edd. omit, a comma after 'say' in l. 92, and another after 'here' in the next line. Grammatically a comma after 'here' should entail another after 'elsewhere,' but dramatic punctuation sets no store on pairing its commas and usually omits either one or the other.

Cf. my notes on the punctuation of Hamlet's first soliloquy (*Hamlet*, I. 2. 129–59, and MSH. pp. 197–200).

100. *the Duke of Gloucester's death* i.e. Thomas of Woodstock's murder, Sept. 1397, at Calais by Mowbray, on a charge of conspiracy against the crown.

101–103. *Suggest...blood* Cf. I. 2. 21 and 2. 2. 103 which make it clear that Gloucester met his death by being beheaded. The detail is derived from Le Beau: 'le roi envoya son oncle à Calais, et là fut décollé' (Buchon, xxv. Sup. ii. p. 10). Hol., Frois. and *Woodstock* relate that he was murdered by smothering with towels in a feather-bed. Cf. *Introd.* p. xlvii.

102. *consequently* = later—not 'in consequence of.' *traitor* Q. 'taitour'

104–105. *sacrificing Abel's...earth* This is aimed directly at Ric. who was as closely related to Glouc. as Bol. himself. Cf. *Gen.* iv. 10 'The voice of thy brother's blood crieth unto me from the ground.' Once again, the point presupposes knowledge on the part of the audience, which is not given them until the next scene. The words echo those of *Woodstock*; cf. ll. 2899–902 [Ric. speaks]:

> oh my deere ffreendes the fearefull wrath of heauen.
> sittes heauey on o^r^ heades for woodstockes death
> blood cryes for blood. & that almightie hand
> permittes not murder vnrevengd to stand.

Reyher also cites 'The Tragedy of Gloucester' in *Mirror for Magistrates*, ed. 1571, f. 11. 2:

> Alas, King Richard, sore maist thou rue:
> Which by this fact preparedst the waye,
> Of thy hard desteny to hasten the daye.
> For bloud axeth bloud as guerdon dewe,
> And vengeaunce for vengeaunce is iust rewarde:
> * * * * * *
> Bloud will haue bloud, eyther fyrst or last.

104. *sacrificing* Refers, of course, to Abel's offering of the fruits of the earth, but also glances, I think, at Woodstock's reputation for virtuous life and love of the country.

*Abel's, cries,* Q. 'Abels cries,'

106–107. *To me...my descent* The 'me' is emphatic, while 'my descent' refers to Edward III, the glorious grandfather of himself and of Ric., to whom as king and supreme judge in the land 'justice and rough chastisement' rightly belonged. Bol. has constituted himself 'the family champion' (Craig).

109. *How high a pitch...soars* A metaphor from falconry, v. G. 'pitch.' Herford comments: 'Ric. visibly quails' at l. 109. I think Ric. remains unmoved by Bol.'s insinuations; his words are sarcastic: this falcon, he implies, would swoop at the crown itself! The line is a condensation of 2 *Hen. VI*, 2. 1. 1–20, which should be compared with it.

113. *this slander of his blood* i.e. this disgrace to his royal stock; cf. note ll. 58–61 above.

114. *God and good men* C. T. Onions (corr. *T.L.S.* 13 Aug. 1931) shows that this is a proverbial expression, found again in *Ric. III*, 3. 7. 110 and of common occurrence not only in Middle English but also in old Scandinavian texts. He suggests further that Dogberry's 'God's a good man' (*Ado*, 3. 5. 35) may be derived from it.

116–21. *Were he my brother...upright soul* Behind this plea of impartiality it is not difficult to see at once a reply to the implicit accusation of Bol. and a threat to him, while ll. 116–17 show that Ric. suspects Bol. of designs upon the throne.

116. *Were he...my kingdom's heir* 'A very neat hit' (Newbolt). Cf. 1. 4. 35–6.

117. *my father's brother's son* Ric. states the kinship in terms as distant as possible—and in a contemptuous drawl. His insinuations do not prove that Bol. actually entertains treasonable designs at this point.

118–19. *sceptre's awe...sacred blood* Indications of Ric.'s love of ceremony and exaltation of kingship.

118. *by my sceptre's* (F.) Q. 'by ſcepters'—compositor's omission. Cf. Pollard, p. 84.

121. *The unstooping...soul* Dramatic irony!

126. *receipt* v. G.

*Calais* Q. 'Callice,'—a common spelling.

128. *by consent* In Hol. Mow. merely excuses the retention of the money on the ground that the K. was in his debt. The words 'by consent,' implying that he had the K.'s permission, make all the difference.

130. *Upon remainder...account* = 'on the balance of a heavy debt' (Clar.). Cf. *Rom.* 1. 5. 120 'O dear account! my life is my foe's debt' and *Ado*, 4. 1. 337. v. G. 'dear.' 'The word "dear" is regularly used in Eliz. Eng. for what is extreme of its kind. "My dearest foe" = my most hostile (i.e. bitterest) foe' (Herford).

*account*, Q. 'account:'

131. *to France...his queen* Ric.'s first wife, Anne of Bohemia, died in 1394, and in 1395 Mow. was sent to France with Rutland (the Aumerle of the play) to arrange a marriage with Isabel daughter of Charles VI. The embassy cost 300,000 marks, a sufficiently 'dear account.' For 'last' v. G.

132–34. *For Gloucester's...that case* In Hol. Mow. keeps complete silence on the matter of Glouc.'s death and by thus shielding Ric. makes a bid for his favour. Such a point would escape notice in the theatre. Sh. therefore gives him this embarrassed and ambiguous speech, the effect of which upon the audience is to stress Ric.'s complicity. In history Mow. was Ric.'s agent for the murder (Oman, p. 135); but his denial here, taken in conjunction with 4. 1. 1–13, 80–82 which indicates that he laid the blame on Aumerle, suggests that he may have been intended to be guiltless in the play as originally plotted. The issue, however, is left quite obscure. Cf. *Introd.* p. lxvii.

132. *that lie....* Mow.'s speech has only two internal full stops: this one and a second at l. 141 when he turns from Gaunt to the K. v. Pollard, p. 67.

133. *not, but* Q. 'not but'

135–41. *For you...I had it* From Hol. except for l. 139. Nothing else seems to be known of the incident.

139. *But* (Q.) Q. (some copies) 'Ah but' Pollard (p. 35) suggests that the intrusive 'Ah' was due to someone attempting to read aloud an ill-written line to the compositor and beginning 'er But'

144. *most degenerate traitor* Mow. now has the K.'s

permission (v. l. 123) to abuse his kinsman, a permission which is tantamount to a command; 'degenerate,' of course, refers to the blood royal. Cf. note ll. 58–61.

145. *Which* = And this cause. Cf. l. 62 'Which to maintain.'

*in myself* i.e. in my own person.

*defend* Mow. was the 'defendant,' Bol. the 'appellant.'

150. *In haste whereof* i.e. 'For a speedy settlement of which' (Newbolt).

152–59. *Wrath-kindled gentlemen...your son* In Hol. the K. twice (before hearing them and again after their speeches) appeals to them for peace, pleading and not commanding. The conduct of Sh.'s Ric. is very different—the words much stronger, the action much weaker. The tone is trivial and light-hearted; the rhymes suggest, as often in Sh., slight artificiality.

152. *gentlemen* (F.) Q. 'gentleman'

153–57. *Let's purge...bleed* Reyher cites *Woodstock*, 153–57:

> king Richards wounded w^th^ a wanton humo^r^
> luld & securd by flattering Sicophants
> but tis not deadly yett, it may be curd
> some vayne lett blood. wher the corruptione lyes
> & all shall heale agayne.

153. *purge...choler* A quibble; v. G. 'choler' and cf. *Ham*. 3. 2. 306–308 (note).

156. *Forget...agreed* He addresses them like a couple of quarrelsome school-boys.

157. *no month to bleed* F. 'no time to bleed' The best times for the leeches to bleed their patients were duly noted in the almanacs.

162–63. *When...again* (Pope) Q. reads:

> When Harry? when obedience bids,
> Obedience bids I ſhould not bid againe.

Cf. note 1. 3. 136 for a possible explanation of this repetition.

162. *When...when?* An exclamation of impatience. Cf. *Jul. Caes.* 2. 1. 5.

164. *no boot* v. G. 'boot.'

168. *Despite...grave* i.e. that lives, despite of death, upon my grave. This harsh inversion, edd. tell us, is necessitated by the rhyme. But, as my re-arranged version shows, it would have been easy to avoid the inversion, without sacrificing the rhyme. Prob. Sh. placed 'Despite of death' first for emphasis, in order to contrast with 'dark dishonour,' which is worse than death.

170. *disgraced, impeached, and baffled* Terms of chivalry, each stronger than the last; i.e. publicly dishonoured, accused of treason, treated with infamy like a perjured knight. v. G. 'baffle.'

173. *must* Q. 'muſt'

174. *lions...tame* As Bol. says later, 'The skipping king, he ambled up and down' (1 *Hen. IV*, 3. 2. 60). Edd. quote Marlowe, *Edward II*, 2. 2. 201–202:

> Yet, shall the crowing of these cockerels
> Affright a lion?

Malone notes 'the Norfolk crest was a golden leopard,' but Newbolt comments: 'the heraldic "leopard" was only another word for a lion passant and excluded the notion of spots.'

175. *spots* A quibble: (*a*) referring to *Jer.* xiii. 23, (*b*) spot = disgrace, v. G.

177. *mortal times* i.e. the lives of men in this world—the next has 'purer treasures.' v. G. 'time.'

178. *reputation—that* Q. 'Reputation that' F. 'reputation: that'

180–81. *A jewel...breast* Cf. *Oth.* 3. 3. 155–56:

> Good name in man and woman, my dear lord,
> Is the immediate jewel of their souls.

184. *try* = put to the test of Trial by Combat.

186. *throw up* i.e. to the scaffold (upper stage) on which Ric. and his nobles sit. O.E.D. gives no support for 'throw up' = surrender, as some edd. interpret. But F. reads 'throw downe'

187–95. *O God...Mowbray's face* 'Contrast Mow.'s pleading entreaty with Bol.'s peremptory refusal. The latter disdains to argue; he opposes to the K.'s command no plausible generalities (such as ll. 177–81), merely his own invincible repugnance' (Herford). Nor is any deference or regard shown towards Ric.

187. *sin!* Q. 'ſinne,'

189. *impeach my height* = discredit my lofty rank.

190. *out-dared* v. G.

192. *parle* (F.) Q. 'parlee'

193. *motive* v. G.

194. *And spit...disgrace* Hieronimo 'bites out his tongue' in *The Spanish Tragedy*, 4. 4. 190; cf. also *Tit. And.* 3. 1. 131 and *Euphues* (Bond's ed., i. p. 279) 'Zeno bicause hee woulde not be enforced to reueale any thinge agaynst his will by torments, bitte of his tongue and spit it in the face of the Tyraunt.' Lyly quotes from Plutarch, *De Garrulitate*, ch. 8.

*his* = its. Bol. means: I should entirely disgrace the tongue by spitting it into that abode of shame, the face of Mow.

195. *harbour*, Q. 'harbour'

After this line F. reads the S.D. 'Exit Gaunt,' because Gaunt, being needed for the next scene, could not, acc. to theatrical practice, remain on until the end of 1. 1. The exit is not in Q., is quite unmotived dramatically, and is, in view of Bol.'s direct reference to Gaunt at l. 188, especially awkward from the stage point of view. It can hardly have been Sh.'s original intention.

196–205. *We were not born to sue...alarms* Hol. gives no authority for this speech; cf. note ll. 152–59.

But all Ric.'s character is revealed in 'its combination of arrogance and weakness, of outward dignity and inner want of stamina' (Herford). For *answer*, *arbitrate*, *atone*, *chivalry* v. G.

199. *Saint Lambert's day* Sept. 17.

203. *design the victor's chivalry* = 'mark out the rightful champion by giving him the victory' (J. C. Smith).

204. *Lord marshal* Many edd. suppose 'Lord' to be an interpolation, since the line would gain metrically by its omission. But, as Malone notes, 'the metre is such as the poet has used in innumerable other places.' Others suspect 'Lord' on the grounds that 'nowhere else in Sh. does a king address a marshal by the title "lord"' (Herford). But he is called 'Lord Marshall' by Q. in the S.D. at the head of I. 3 and in the dialogue (by Bol.) at I. 3. 46. Hol. also speaks of 'the Lord Marshall.' The Duke of Surrey was marshal of the realm and acted as such both at Windsor and Coventry (Boswell-Stone, pp. 79, 86). But as Sh. was prob. not aware of this (v. note I. 3. 251–52) I have kept them as separate characters.

205. *home alarms* 'A hint at the Irish wars' (J. C. Smith).

S.D. Q. 'Exit.'

## I. 2.

*Material.* The chronicles provide nothing for this scene, which marks an interval of time between the challenge and the combat and is theatrically convenient, if not necessary, in order to separate two scenes so much alike in action and personnel as I. I and I. 3. The Duchess of Glouc., who never appears again, is a character in *Woodstock*, at the end of which she comes on as a weeping widow calling for vengeance. The talk is all of her dead husband (whom Hol. depicts as turbulent and seditious) and the references to Plashy House have a tone of reminiscence which the audience are clearly intended to share. This they would do had they witnessed the old play *Woodstock*; yet the scene at once overlaps and conflicts with that play. (Cf. *Introd.* p. l and Mal. Soc. *Woodstock*, pp. xxv–xxvi.) On the other hand Gaunt's attitude was prob. suggested by Froissart, e.g. (vi. 338): 'The duke of Lancastre, lyke a sage and a prudent prince, for all that the duke of Gloucestre was his brother, and that the murderyng of hym touched hym nere to his herte, all thynges consydred, and that he coude nat recover agayne his brother, wisely and amiably he apeased all these maters, and the kynge his nephue more feared in Englande than he was before.' Add to this the Tudor conception of divine right and you have Sh.'s portrait, which in 2. 1 again derives from Froissart.

S.D. Q. 'Enter Iohn of Gaunt with the Ducheſſe of Glocester.' F. 'Enter Gaunt, and Dutcheſſe of Glouceſter.' Theobald first read 'The Duke of Lancaster's Palace.'

1. *the part...blood* i.e. my kinship with Woodstock. *Woodstock's* F. reads 'Glouſters' to tally with the title at ll. 16, 36, and later in the play. The change is an indication that 'Woodstock' in time ceased to convey anything to an audience.

4–5. *But since...correct* Cf. ll. 37–9. An unmistakable hint of Ric.'s guilt.

5. *correct...* Q. 'correct:' The pause underlines the hint.

6–7. *heaven...they* Heaven is plural, as often in Sh. Cf. *Ham.* 3. 4. 173.

8. *rain...heads* Cf. *Luke* xvii. 28–9; *Gen.* xix. 24–5; *Ps.* xi. 7 (P.B.V.); cxl. 10.

11. *Edward's seven sons* For a catalogue of these v. 2 *Hen. VI*, 2. 2. 10–20 and cf. note 2. 1. 104–14 for the reference to them in *Woodstock*.

12–21. *Were as seven vials...bloody axe* 'The double metaphor is kept up to the end in Sh.'s early manner' (Newbolt). For 'axe' cf. 2. 2. 103 and note 1. 1. 101–103.

15. *branches...cut* Cf. *Dr Faustus*, Epil. 'Cut is the branch that might have grown full straight.'

20. *faded* F. 'vaded' Cf. *Isa.* i. 30.

21. *axe....*The internal full stop 'tells us, I think, that she breaks down' (Pollard, p. 67).

23. *mettle* (F.) Q. 'mettall' Cf. G. Sh. probably did not distinguish the two meanings in his own mind, but to read 'metal' in a mod. text is misleading.

*self* = identical, selfsame.

25. *consent to* v. G.

28. *model* v. G.

34. *breasts....*The full stop 'preludes her final appeal' (Pollard, p. 67).

37–41. *God's substitute...His minister* Cf. note ll. 4–5 above and *K. John*, 3. 1. 136. Gaunt's words here (i) render his denunciation of Ric. in 2. 1 all the more effective, (ii) condemn in advance the usurpation of his son Bol. after his death. For the doctrine of divine right v. *Introd.* pp. xxiii–xxiv. Glouc. is given similar sentiments in *Woodstock*, ll. 2140 ff. Cf. 1 *Sam.* xxiv. 6, xxvi. 9.

42. *then, alas* (Q.) Q. (some copies) 'then'—compositor's omission.

43. *the widow's...defence* Cf. *Ps.* lxviii. 5 (P.B.V.) 'He...defendeth the cause of the widows,' and *K. John*, 3. 1. 108 'A widow cries: be husband to me, heavens.' There is a strong resemblance between Constance and this Duchess. Cf. note ll. 55–9 below.

46. *cousin* = kinsman.

47–52. *O, sit...sins so heavy...lists* Cf. *Woodstock*, ll. 2734–35:

> & may ther sinns sitt heauey on ther soules
> that they in death this day, may perrish all.

47. *sit* (F.) Q. 'ſet' Cf. Pollard, p. 61 and note 5. 5. 27.

48. *butcher* (Q. some copies) Q. (others) 'butchers': *breast!* Q. 'breſt:'

49. *Or if misfortune...career* i.e. Or if Mow. does not come to grief at the first encounter. v. G. 'career.'

55–59. *With her companion Grief...weight* Cf. *K. John*, 3. 1. 70–73:

> To me and to the state of my great grief
> Let kings assemble; for my grief's so great
> That no supporter but the huge firm earth
> Can hold it up.

The parallel is close.

58–59. *Grief...weight* 'The duchess likens the iteration of her grief, which still asks "one word more," to the bounding of a tennis-ball; but that is light, this heavy' (Newbolt).

58. *it* (Qb) Q. 'is'

59. *empty* (Q.) Q. (some copies) 'emptines'—poss. an anticipation from 'hollowness.' For another explanation v. Pollard, pp. 36–7.

66. *Plashy* or Pleshy, near Felstead in Essex. Glouc.'s country house; made much of in *Woodstock*.

70. *hear* (Q.) Q. (some copies) 'cheere' Malone, arguing that 'offices' = pantries and cellars, made out a good case for 'cheere' before copies of Q. reading 'heare' were known. But '"There see"...is so excellently complemented by "heare there"...that there can be little doubt as to the correctness of the latter reading' (Pollard, p. 36).

74. *The last leave...eye* Surely one of the worst lines in the Sh. canon! I suspect it to be a relic of the old play. Cf. *Introd.* pp. lxx–lxxiii.

S.D. Q. 'Exeunt.'

## 1. 3.

*Material.* Making allowance for dramatic compression and re-arrangement, this scene, like 1. 1, represents essentially the events as related by Hol. But the same events are described, in as detailed and more dramatic form, by *Traïson*, and it is clear that both accounts were used (v. note 4. 1.

92–100). Hall also supplies rather full details, mentioning, however, nothing not found in either of the others. Daniel merely states the fact of the combat and the banishment in a single stanza, and Froissart declares that the banishment took place before the combatants could come to the lists at all. Yet Froissart is an important source, since he alone furnishes the material upon which the terms of the K.'s sentence were based, and accounts for the reduction of Bol.'s banishment from ten to six years. He also makes clearer than others that Gaunt was 'party' to the verdict (v. notes ll. 123–53, 208–12, 234). It is noteworthy that Berners' favourite expression 'upon pain of life' occurs in just this passage (v. note l. 140; *Introd.* pp. liv–lv).

S.D. Q. 'Enter Lord Marſhall and the Duke Aumerle.' F. 'Enter Marſhall, and Aumerle.' Actually the Marshal was Surrey (v. note 1. 1. 204) and Aumerle was High Constable of England.

3. *sprightfully and bold* An instance of the idiom of the extended suffix (v. Abbott, § 397). 'When several adverbs follow each other, it suffices if one, generally the last, has the characteristic adverbial ending' (Franz, § 98). Cf. *Ric. III*, 3. 4. 50 'cheerfully and smooth'; *L.L.L.* 5. 2. 841 'true and faithfully.'

6. S.D. Q. 'The trumpets ſound and the King enters with his nobles; when they are ſet, enter the Duke of Norfolke in armes defendent.' F. 'Flouriſh./Enter King, Gaunt, Buſhy, Bagot, Greene, & others: Then Mowbray in Armor, and Harrold.' I follow Q., adding Gaunt's name, because he speaks later. Hol. and *Traïson* make Hereford, 'the appellant,' enter first, and Mowbray, 'the defendant,' second; which is the correct order according to the laws of chivalry. The play, despite l. 4, reverses the order for stage effect.

9. *orderly* = according to the rules.

11–13. *Say who thou art...quarrel* Cf. Hol. 'demanding of him what he was,' and *Traïson* 'asked him who he was, what he wanted, and for what purpose he was come thither.' Clearly the latter is nearer our text.

Such questions were not purely formal. If the visor was down, the face would be invisible; and since a knight was not bound to fight with his inferior in rank, identification was necessary.

14–17. *thy oath...my oath* The oath here assumed to have been taken was, acc. to Hol. and *Traïson*, sworn in the lists.

18. *God* F. 'heauen'

*defend* v. G. The brackets are Q.'s.

20. *my succeeding issue* (Q.) F. 'his ſucceeding iſſue' 'Mowbray's Issue was, by this accusation, in danger of an attainder, and therefore he might come among other reasons for their sake' (Johnson). Moreover, the 'me' at l. 24 supports 'my' here. A reference to Ric.'s 'succeeding issue' would have no point, not because he had none, but because Mow.'s loyalty in the past and present was at stake, not that in the future.

24. *A traitor...me* The set form in the fourteenth century was 'Comme faulx, traytre et foy mentie que tu es' (*Traïson*, 152 n. 1).

25. S.D. Q. 'The trumpets ſound. Enter Duke of Hereford appellant in armour.' F. 'Tucket. Enter Hereford, and Harold.'

Hol. tells us that the combatants entered the lists on horseback, and after making their declarations set them down in chairs at either end of the lists; Mow. in one of 'crimosen veluet, courtined about with white and red damaske,' and Bol. in one of 'greene veluet.' Cf. l. 120 below.

26. 'The line is defective in metre' (Clar.). But it does not halt.

30. *Depose...cause* i.e. 'take his solemn deposition, that he appears in a just cause' (Herford).

33. *comest* (F.) Q. 'comes' This form of the 2nd pers. sing. is common in Sh. Cf. *Ham.* 1. 4. 53; 1. 5. 84, and MSH. p. 291. But since a dissyllable is required by

the metre, I follow F. Probably the Q. compositor simply omitted the 't.'

39. *he is* (Q.) F. 'he's'

42–45. *On pain of death...designs* Hol. 'upon paine of death.' *Traïson*, p. 154 'on pain of having his hand chopped off.'

43. *daring-hardy* (Theobald) Q. 'daring, hardy'

46–51. *Lord marshal...friends* In Hol. and *Traïson* Bol. and Mow. call to take ceremonial leave of the K. a day or two before the combat. In the theatre the leave-taking is naturally transferred to the lists themselves. Bol. pays the K. all the honour due to him, but not a jot more.

49. *pilgrimage* 'Bol.'s allusion carries a suggestion of future events of which he is unconscious' (H. Craig).

54–58. *We will descend...dead* Nothing of this in the sources. Ric.'s effusiveness is patently hypocritical, and the ill-concealed threat in ll. 57–8 is almost gleeful. The rhymes emphasize the insincerity, as Newbolt notes, 'and Bol. replies to the K. in the same [i.e. in rhyme], falling to blank verse when he turns to bid a more sincere farewell to his father.'

55–56. *as thy cause...fight* 'Studied but unobtrusive ambiguity' (Herford).

58. *thee dead* (Q w) Q. 'the dead'—prob. a copy spelling.

59–60. *O, let no...spear* Bol. replies ironically (v. note ll. 54–8), and indirectly. 'If I am slain by Mow. I am an unworthy knight, for whom it would be profanation to shed a tear' (Rolfe).

63. S.D. Malone reads 'To Lord Marshal.' Cf. ll. 251–52 below.

66. *lusty, young* Wright suggests 'lusty-young.'

67. *as at English feasts* Referring to the custom of concluding ceremonial dinners with elaborate confectionery. Clar. quotes Bacon (*Life and Letters*, ed. Spedding, iii. p. 215 note), 'Let not this Parliament end,

like a Dutch feast, in salt meats; but like an English feast, in sweet meats.'

*regreet* Cf. ll. 142, 186. Not found elsewhere in Sh. as a vb., but as a sb. in *K. John*, 3. 1. 241 and *M.V.* 2. 9. 89; cf. 1 *Tamburlaine*, 3. 1. 37.

68. *sweet...*

In the long third scene, comprising over 300 lines, the first internal full stop comes at l. 68, when Bol. turns to address his father; the second at l. 122, dividing what are really two separate speeches by the K., before and after the flourish of trumpets; the third, at l. 270, preludes a question; the fourth, in Gaunt's farewell to his son (l. 280), once more, I think, suggests a struggle with emotion, which would lend added point to the words which follow (Pollard, p. 67).

69. *author* Q. 'Authour' Possibly rhetorical emphasis (v. Pollard, p. 71).

72. *To reach...head* Deighton cites 1 *Hen. IV*, 1. 3. 202 'To pluck bright honour from the pale-faced moon.'

*head...* The pause adds solemnity to what follows.

73. *proof* v. G.

75. *waxen* Used proleptically: 'that my lance may pierce Mow.'s coat of mail as if it were a coat of wax' (Clar.).

76. *furbish new...Gaunt* A reference to Gaunt's extreme old age (cf. note 1. 1. 1). Sh. is still thinking in terms of the 'coat' (l. 75), i.e. armour. Cf. below 3. 3. 116 'His glittering arms he will commend to rust' and *Meas.* 1. 2. 171 'unscoured armour, hung by the wall.' The 'name' (= honour) and the shield or arms of a soldier were closely associated, while 'lusty haviour' (l. 77) suggests the vigour needed to 'scour' rusty steel.

77. *Even* For the idiomatic use of this word 'in recurring to an obvious fact (previously referred to, or forming a part of the dramatic situation), which explains

a bold or figurative thought just expressed' (Herford), cf. *M.V.* 2. 6. 45, and *A.Y.L.* 2. 7. 57.

80. *redoubled* Herford would make this four syllables; but that would drag out the line and destroy the lightning effect which Gaunt intends to convey.

81. *amazing* v. G.

84. *—Mine...to thrive!* Cf. *Cor.* 4. 6. 23 'Live and thrive!' Bol. completes Gaunt's sentence: he intends to live that his innocence may be proved and that St George (i.e. England) may flourish. The point may have been suggested by *Traïson* which tells us that Bol.'s shield 'was argent, with a cross gules, like unto the arms of St George' (pp. 19, 153).

*innocency* (Capell) Q. 'innocence' The sp. 'innocencie' would give four minims in place of the three of the Q. reading; cf. MSH. pp. 106–108.

85–96. *However God...quiet breast* We are here made to feel that Mow.'s words are sincere and that Ric. has in him a staunch friend, in order that we may the more fully appreciate Ric.'s folly and treachery towards him later. Cf. the effect of Hamlet's speech at *Ham.* 5. 2. 224–42; and v. *What happens in 'Hamlet,'* pp. 216–17, 275.

90. *uncontrolled enfranchisement* = freedom from control. Adj. used as the genitive of a subst. Cf. below l. 241 'partial slander' = reproach of partiality; 2. 3. 79 'absent time' = time of absence.

93–96. *Most mighty liege...breast* The rhymes, customary just before the exit of a character on the stage, here 'give the impression of leave-taking' (Verity), and add to the pathos of the speech.

94. *years:* (edd.) Q. 'yeeres,'

95. *jest* = act in a masquerade or masque of chivalry. v. G. Warburton read 'just,' which the rhyme makes impossible, but the meaning is much the same. Farmer (v. Boswell's *Malone* 1821) explained the word and quoted Kyd's *Span. Trag.* 1. 5. 20–22 (ed. Boas):

> But where is olde *Hieronimo*, our Marshall?
> He promised vs, in honour of our guest,
> To grace our banquet with some pompous iest.

*Enter* Hieronimo *with a Drum, three Knightes, each with his Scutchin: then he fetches three Kinges, they take their Crownes and them captiue.*

> *Hieronimo*, this maske contentes mine eye,
> Although I sound not well the misterie.

This meaning gives point to *Temp.* 4. 1. 242–43 'I thank thee for that jest; here's a garment for't,' and 3 *Hen. VI*, 2. 3. 28 'As if the tragedy/Were played in jest by counterfeiting actors.' For such masques of chivalry v. Chambers, *Eliz. Stage*, i. 139 ff. Later edd. have overlooked Farmer's note.

97. *Farewell, my lord,* Q. 'Farewell (my Lord)'

*securely* Explained as 'surely' (Clar.), and as 'confidently, free from anxiety' by Verity and Newbolt, who take it with 'couchéd.' Cf. 2. 1. 266, which supports the latter. But it is awkward to associate the adv. with 'couchéd.' I take the meaning to be that Ric. trusts Mow. implicitly and relies upon his loyalty ('virtue') as well as his 'valour.'

99. *marshal* Q. 'Martiall' The Q. speech-headings give '*Mart.*'

S.D. Capell reads 'returning to his Seat, with the Lords.'

102. *Strong as a tower in hope* Cf. *Ps.* lxi. 3.

108. *his God* (Q.) Q. (some copies) 'God'—compositor's omission.

117. S.D. F. 'A charge sounded' A 'charge' = a signal for attack. The scene is described by Mow.'s son in 2 *Hen. IV*, 4. 1. 117–22:

> And then that Henry Bolingbroke and he,
> Being mounted and both rouséd in their seats,
> Their neighing coursers daring of the spur,
> Their arméd staves in charge, their beavers down,

Their eyes of fire sparkling through sights of steel,
And the loud trumpet blowing them together....

There were, of course, no horses on Sh.'s stage.

122. *While we return* = Until we declare to. *decree*.... Cf. note l. 68 etc.

S.D. F. 'A long Flourish.' Hol. tells us the council deliberated for 'two long houres'; *Traïson* (p. 21) speaks of 'pres de deux heures.' Sh. is obliged to contract all this into a few moments, and the stage-manager to bridge the interval with a flourish of trumpets.

124–53. *list what...pain of life* Cf. *Introd.* pp. liv–lv. In Hol. the sentence is read by Bushy. Froissart (vi. 313–17) supplies the material. He relates how

'Whan the day aproched that these two lordes shulde do their dedes of armes...certayne of the kynges counsayle' strongly advised him that to permit the combat would be 'ryght peryllous,' inasmuch as a large number of his subjects, 'specially in the cytie of London, whiche is the soveraygne cytie of youre realme,' believed him to be in league with Mow. to destroy Bol. 'Whiche thynge they saye they wyll natte suffre. And if the Londoners rise agaynste you, with suche noble men as wyll take their parte, ye shall be of no puyssaunce to resyst theym....Ye muste dissymule the mater if ye wyll have youre honour saved and to make peace; and, sir, ye ought rather to entertayne the generaltie of your realme than the ydell wordes of two knyghtes.' They therefore counselled him to banish for life the detested and suspected Mow. and for ten years the popular favourite Bol.; 'and whan he shall departe the realme, to please the people withall, release foure yere of the tenne.'...'Sirs,' replied Richard, 'ye counsayle me trewly, and I shall folowe your counsayle.' Accordingly he announced the decision to the 'prelates and grete lordes of Englande,' including 'his two uncles, the duke of Lancastre and the duke of Yorke,' and 'this sentence greatly contented the lordes that were there present, and they sayde: The erle of Derby [Bol.] maye well ynoughe go and sporte hym out of the realme for two or thre yeres. He is yonge ynoughe' and 'he hath two susters, one quene of Spaygne, the other quene of Portugale; he maye well passe the tyme with them.'

'The king's speech is confused, perhaps intentionally, perhaps because it is insincere' (Craig).

123–24. *Draw near/And list* Q. and F. print this as l. 123. Theobald first re-arranged it. Perhaps Sh. wrote it in a single line; cf. MSH. p. 221.

128. *civil* (Q.) Q. (some copies) 'cruell' Possibly 'ciuell' misread 'cruell.'

129–38. *And for we think...kindred's blood* Ll. 129–33 are omitted in F., and form the first of eight cuts in that text. Pollard (p. 91) discussing the whole passage (i.e. ll. 127–39) writes:

> This is surely a passage which Sh. can never have read over, or he would not have left the 'Peace' of l. 137 to be frighted by the 'peace' of l. 132. The omission of the five lines 129–33 leaves the sword which is to plow up civil wounds to be roused up by drums in rather an awkward manner, and it might have been better to sacrifice the following five lines as well. The obvious difficulty is surmounted, though in so clumsy a manner as to make it incredible that the omission was either made or approved by Sh. himself.

But how came the Q. text? Pollard suggests (p. 98 and n.) that Sh. left a tangle in the act of hasty composition, like those found in Q2 *Hamlet* (cf. MSH. pp. 24, 92). But the similarity of ll. 132–33 to l. 137 suggests that we have here two versions left side by side in the MS., and that the prompter deleted the wrong passage. Omit ll. 134–38 and nothing is lost in the sense, while what remains reads straight on, or alternatively omit ll. 129–33 and the same thing happens. Surely the two passages represent different attempts to draft the speech and it looks as if ll. 129–33 was the later one. If so it may have been added at the foot of a page; for, if l. 128 originally finished a page of manuscript, ll. 134–38 would have belonged to another page which would help to account for Sh.'s neglecting to delete them.

129–30. *the eagle-wingèd pride...thoughts* Cf. 1. 1.

109 'How high a pitch his resolution soars!' and 1. 3. 61–2. Ric. is of course especially hinting at Bol. in this.

*eagle-wingéd* Q. 'Egle-winged' Possibly rhetorical emphasis (v. Pollard, p. 71).

131. *rival-hating* (Q.) Q. (some copies) 'riuall hating'—compositor's omission.

*set on you* i.e. set you on—which Pope read and Sh. may possibly have written. Cf. 'Inversions' MSH. pp. 44, 76, 119 and below note 2. 2. 112.

133. *Draws* (Q.) Q. (some copies) 'Draw'

*infant* 'Implying that the land had not long enjoyed peace' (Verity).

*sleep;* (edd.) Q. 'ſleepe,'

134–35. *boist'rous...bray* Cf. *K. John*, 3. 1. 303 'braying trumpets and loud churlish drums.' N.B. the expression in *K. John* (v. note) was suggested by a similar one in *The Troublesome Reign*.

136. *wrathful iron* (Q.) Q. (some copies) 'harſh reſounding' Pollard (p. 36) suggests the duplication may be due to dictation in the printing-house.

140. *upon pain of life* F. 'vpon paine of death' v. G. 'pain of life.' Cf. l. 153. The only occasions on which Sh. uses this phrase, though 'on pain of death' occurs nine times, one of them in this very scene (l. 42). I have not found the phrase in any of the sources except Froissart who frequently uses it (cf. vi. pp. 170, 173, 297), though not actually in connexion with the banishment. Cf. *Introd.* p. lv.

143. *stranger* = foreign. Not the comp. of 'strange.'

150. *sly slow hours* v. G. 'sly' and cf. *Lucr.* 1575.

150–51. *determinate...dateless...dear* v. G. for these.

154–73. *A heavy sentence...breath?* 'While Bol.'s stoical rhymed reply conveys the impression that he was prepared for some such issue, Mow. is unaffectedly aghast, and speaks with genuine emotion' (Newbolt).

155–58. *And all unlooked for...hands* Mow.'s only hint of a secret understanding with Ric. Cf. Hol. 'he was in hope...that he should haue beene borne out in the matter by the king, which when it fell out otherwise, it greeued him not a little' (iii. 495/2/18).

156. *merit* = reward (the opposite of 'maim' = injury). Reward, for what? 'O, the instinctive propriety of Sh. in the choice of words!' (Coleridge).

159. *forty years* Mow. was actually only 33 in 1398.

160. *my native English* Mow.'s love of country contributes to the strong patriotic flavour of the play.

165. *That knows no touch...harmony* Cf. G. 'touch' and *Ham.* 3. 2. 359 'I know no touch of it.'

167. *portcullised* Q. (some copies) 'portculiſt'; (others) 'portculliſt'

168. *barren* Combines 'dull' and 'unfeeling,' v. G.

170–77. *I am too old...endless night* A dramatic premonition of his end; cf. note 4. 1. 92–100.

170. *nurse* i.e. wet nurse, into whose care the infants of gentlefolk were put out, and from whom they learnt their early speech.

172. *then but* (F.) Q. 'but' Pollard (p. 84) includes this among 'accepted corrections.'

174. *compassionate* v. G.

179. *Lay on...sword* Cf. *Ham.* 1. 5. 147 ('Upon my sword,' i.e. on the cross of the hilt), and *Sp. Trag.* 2. 1. 87–93.

180. *you owe* (F.) Q. 'y'owe' One of Pollard's 'accepted corrections' (p. 82).

181. *therein* i.e. in 'the duty that you owe.' It was a moot point whether a banished man owed allegiance to the king or not; Ric. says not. The chronicles apparently give no authority for this remark by Ric.

184–90. *Embrace...face...regreet...hate...meet ...state*. For these fossil-rhymes v. *Introd.* p. lxxi.

189. *plot, contrive, or complot* 'Legal tautology' (Rolfe). Dickens has a good disquisition on this kind of

'formal piling up of words' half-way through ch. lii of *David Copperfield*.

193. *fare* (Q., F.) F2 'farre' i.e. far, which all edd. read, taking 'fare' as a misp. for 'farre.' But the orig. sense is clear: Bol. will not bid Mow. fare*well* but only the 'fare' (= condition of life) he would wish as to an enemy. Cf. 1. 4. 11–19.

196. *sepulchre* Cf. *M.V.* 5. 1. 65 'this muddy vesture of decay.' Pron. 'sepúlchre.'

200. *The clogging...soul* Cf. 5. 6. 20 'With clog of conscience.'

202. *my name be blotted...life* Cf. *Rev.* iii. 5.

206–207. *Now no way...my way* i.e. I cannot ever go astray now; for I am free to wander anywhere in the world, except England. 'Perhaps Milton had this in his mind when he wrote these lines,

> The world was all before them, where to chuse
> Their place of rest, and Providence their guide.'
> (Johnson.)

207. S.D. Q., F. 'Exit.'

208–12. *Uncle...banishment* Hol. (iii. 495/2/21) merely says 'The duke of Hereford tooke his leaue of the king at Eltham, who there released foure yeares of his banishment,' which are also Hall's words. Daniel, following a hint in Froissart (note ll. 123–53 above), states that 'he is faine foure of the ten forgiue' because 'such murmuring...he heares' (i. 66). *Traïson* does not mention any curtailment. Sh. conveys the effect of spineless timidity by placing the remission immediately after Mow.'s pointed warning.

213–15. *How long...kings* 'Admirable anticipation!' (Coleridge). Bol.'s contempt is now undisguised; he does not even tender formal thanks.

216. *in regard of* v. G. 'regard.'

219–32. *For, ere the six years...my breath* This is based upon a passage in Froissart, v. *Introd.* pp. lv–lvi.

222. *night* (Qc) Q. 'nightes' v. Pollard, p. 61.

223. *My inch of taper* Cf. *Macb.* 5. 5. 23 'Out, out, brief candle.'

224. *blindfold Death* i.e. Death extinguishes the taper. The image may be due to the similarity between the shape of a hood (for hoodwinking or blindfolding a man) and that of an extinguisher for candles or links.

230. *stop...pilgrimage* = 'efface no wrinkle that comes with time' (Craig).

*his* i.e. time's.

231. *Thy word is current* Cf. 4. 1. 264 'if my word be sterling.'

234. *party-verdict* Herford writes, 'That Gaunt actually voted for his son's banishment is a trait admirably invented by Sh.' But, as Newbolt and Reyher note, the fact is supplied by Hol. in his account of Carlisle's speech (v. 4. 1 *Material*, ii). It is also mentioned by Créton (Webb, 106/330) and implied in Froissart's statement that the nobles, including Gaunt, were 'greatly contented' with Ric.'s sentence (v. note ll. 124–53 above) and in the saying of Bol.'s supporters 'sithe the duke of Lancastre his father suffreth it, we must nedes suffre it' (vi. 319).

236. *Things sweet...sour* Cf. *Son.* 94 'For sweetest things turn sourest by their deeds.'

239–42. *O, had it...destroyed* The second of the F. cuts in the text. Pollard (p. 92) asks, 'Can any one seriously contend that the passage does not gain dramatically by the omission of the...lines, which add to its length much more than to its effect?' I suspect that a good many of these couplets are survivals of the old play. Cf. *Introd.* pp. lxx ff.

239. *had it* (edd.) Q. 'had't'

241. *A partial slander* = the reproach of partiality. Cf. note 1. 3. 90.

*sought* (Q. some copies) Q. (others) 'ought'

243. *looked when* v. G. Cf. *Son.* 22. 4 'Then look I death my days should expiate.'

244. *to make* = in making.

248. S.D. Q. 'Exit.' F. 'Exit./Flourish.' Capell 'Exeunt Richard, and Train.'

249–50. *Cousin...show* i.e. 'As we cannot meet any longer, write to me if you have anything worth saying.' A curt leave-taking, the first indication of Aum.'s attitude to Bol. I give him an exit (none in Q. or F.) because he can hardly remain on after this adieu, more esp. as he comes on at the beg. of the next scene. Yet there is inconsistency here: why does he take leave, if he is to accompany Bol. 'to the next highway' (1. 4. 4)?

251–52. *My lord...your side* 'The Marshal's courtesy to Bol. is strange, if the Marshal is...the Duke of Surrey. But probably Sh. had not thought of this' (Newbolt). Cf. note 4. 1. 60.

254. *returnest* (Q.) F. 'returnſt'

257. *To breathe* = In breathing. Cf. note l. 244.

258–62. *Thy grief...pleasure* For this stichomythia, or dialogue in alternate lines, common in classical drama, cf. below 2. 1. 88–93, *L.L.L.* passim, *Ric. III*, 1. 2; 4. 4, and *Rom.* 4. 1. 17 ff. It gives a light, almost flippant, tone, to cover the deeper feelings of the speakers, which is very English.

258–59. *grief...grief* v. G. A play upon the two meanings. Sh. makes us feel, behind this dialogue, the real grief that neither will see the other again.

262. *travel*—with a quibble on 'travail.' The words are, of course, the same in origin, and did not differ in form at this date.

266. *foil* That this = (*a*) check, defeat, (*b*) the setting for a jewel, makes the transition of the metaphor from the downcast traveller to the precious stone an easy one.

268–93. *Nay, rather...light* The third F. cut. 'Very good rhetoric; but 26 lines of good rhetoric at the end of a very long scene may be much less good as drama' (Pollard, p. 93). Yet the cut leaves ll. 293–303 entirely in the air.

269. *world* Q. 'world:' There seems no dramatic reason for this pause, esp. with the period at l. 270.

270. *love*.... The pause gives expression to Bol.'s silent emotion.

271–74. *serve...journeyman to grief* It was customary for apprentices to spend a year or term of years in travel, for the purpose of perfecting their skill, between the completion of their service and setting up in business. The apprentice who 'in the end' only became a 'journeyman' (v. G.) instead of a master was reckoned a failure. There is a quibble in 'journeyman.'

275–80. *All places...thou the king*.... Malone cites Lyly's *Euphues* (v. Bond, i. 314), 'Plato would neuer accompt him banished y^t had the Sunne, Fire, Aire, Water, & Earth, that he had before...whereby he noted that euery place was a countrey to a wise man, and all partes a pallaice to a quiet minde....When it was cast in Diogenes teeth that the Synoponetes had banished hym Pontus, yea, sayde hee, I them of Diogenes.' Cf. *Cor.* 3. 3. 120 ff. Herford notes that the passage prob. owes something to *Ed. II*, 5. 1. 1–4 (Leicester to the King in prison):

> Be patient, good my lord, cease to lament;
> Imagine Killingworth Castle were your court,
> And that you lay for pleasure here a space,
> Not of compulsion or necessity.

The occurrence of 'necessity' in both passages increases the probability. But Lyly is the main source (cf. note ll. 294–99).

277. *Teach...to reason thus* Cf. *Meas.* 3. 1. 6 'Reason thus with life.'

278. *There...necessity* Cf. *Two Gent.* 4. 1. 62 'To make a virtue of necessity.'

280. *the king*.... Cf. note l. 68 above.

289. *the presence strewed* i.e. the rush-strewn presence-chamber at Court; cf. *K. John*, 1. 1. 216 (and note).

294–99. *O, who can hold...heat?* This, as Malone also noted, derives from the same passage in *Euphues* in part cited above (ll. 275–80). Lyly's words are:

I speake this to this ende, that though thy exile seeme grieuous to thee, yet guiding thy selfe with the rules of Philosophye it shall bee more tollerable: hee that is colde doth not couer himselfe wyth care, but with clothes, he that is washed in y$^{e}$ rayne dryeth himselfe by the fire not by his fancie, and thou which art bannished oughtest not with teares to bewaile thy hap, but with wisedome to heale thy hurt. (Bond, i. 313–14.)

302–303. *Fell sorrow's tooth...sore* i.e. 'These fantastic consolations only fret a festering ("rankle") wound, instead of lancing it, as the truth would do' (Newbolt).

305. *stay* = linger.

309. S.D. Q. 'Exeunt.' F. omits.

## 1. 4.

*Material.* The scene is composed of the following elements (i) the description of Bol. being 'brought on his way' by friends and weeping crowds; (ii) the first intimation of the Irish rebellion; (iii) Ric.'s shifts to raise money; (iv) the news that Gaunt lies sick at Ely House.

(i) Usually supposed to derive from a brief passage in Hol. (iii. 495/2/27), taken almost verbatim from Hall, describing the people running after Bol. 'lamenting and bewailing his departure.' But Froissart (vi. 319) gives a far more vivid picture; says 'there were in the stretes mo thanne fourtie thousande men, wepyng and cryeng after hym, that it was pytie to here'; speaks of nobles accompanying him, together with 'the mayre of London and a great nombre of the chiefe burgesses'; and adds 'Some rode to Dartforde and some to Dover, and sawe hym take shippyng, and than they retourned.' The last sentence clearly suggested the question with which the scene opens. Bol.'s 'courtship to the common people,' of which Ric. here and Henry IV himself later (v. 1 *Hen. IV*, 3. 2. 50–54) make so much, is

I think developed from a hint in Froissart's companion picture of Bol.'s triumphal return to London (vi. 361): 'and alwayes as he rode he enclyned his heed to the people on every syde'—a touch not found in Hol. (ii) All the sources except Froissart speak of this. (iii) Hol. (iii. 496/1/64) mentions 'the common brute... that the king had set to farme the realme of England' [to Scroop, Bushy, Bagot and Green]; and twice refers to 'blank charters.' But as much more is made of both matters in *Woodstock*, that must be regarded as the main source here, especially in view of note 2. 1. 59–66. The point about Ric.'s extravagance might derive from any of the sources; but v. note 1. 4. 43–4. (iv) Immediately after one of the passages about 'blank charters,' Hol. (iii. 496/1/22) states 'In this meane time, the duke of Lancaster departed out of this life at the bishop of Elies place in Holborne.' Froissart (v. *Introd.* pp. lv–lvi) is far more detailed about Gaunt's death; provides information about Ric.'s joy over it; but does not mention where it took place.

S.D. Q. 'Enter the King with Buſhie, &c at one dore, and the Lord Aumarle at another.' F. 'Enter King, Aumerle, Greene, and Bagot.' There has been some adaptation here; the Q. S.D. is clearly the original, and the '&c' may be taken as equivalent to 'Greene and Bagot,' while ll. 23–4 ('Ourself and Bushy/Observed his courtship,' echoing 'We did observe' (l. 1)), suggest that Bushy was first intended to be on, but was later cut out because he was needed for the entry at l. 52. Cf. notes below ll. 23, 52 S.D. Theobald first located the scene at 'The Court.' For F. scene-division cf. Johnson's comment p. 117.

6. *for me* = for my part.

11. '*Farewell*' Q. and F. print this with the next line. Pope first regularized the verse.

13. *that* i.e. my heart's disdain.

20. *cousin's cousin* (Q.) F. 'Coſin (Coſin)'—which all edd. follow. Pollard (pp. 83–4) justifies Q.: 'Aumerle is reminded with a touch of formality that Hereford is his own cousin, and there is an ironical suggestion of regret that in spite of this he may not be recalled.'

22. *friends....* The 'one internal full stop' in the scene, which 'marks a pause full of meaning after Ric.'s words as to Bol.' (Pollard, p. 68.)

23. *Ourself and Bushy* (Q.) F. 'Our ſelfe, and Buſhy: heere Bagot and Greene' Q. (1634) 'Our ſelfe, and Buſhy, Bagot here and Greene'—which edd. follow, harmlessly, but entirely without justification. The easiest explanation of the Q. and F. readings, taken in conjunction with the S.D.s at the beginning of the scene, seems to be (i) that l. 23 in Sh.'s MS. originally ran

Ourself and Bushy here, Bagot and Green;

(ii) that, when Bushy (i.e. the actor who played him) was needed for the entry at l. 52, 'here' was deleted, probably by the prompter, as no longer correct, together with the rest of the line; (iii) that the F. reading, with its tell-tale colon, is simply the Q. (1615) reading, 'Our ſelfe and Buſhie,' *plus* the original ending, copied out into the printed copy from the prompt-book at the Globe; and (iv) that while the changes evident in Q. were prob. made by the prompter when first reading Sh.'s MS., that MS. had already been copied out by a scrivener, at any rate as far as the dialogue went, otherwise l. 23 could not have been preserved in the transcript entire. Pollard (p. 85) regards the extra words in F. as an addition 'to eke out a line.' He has not observed the connexion with the opening S.D. and l. 52 below.

27. *What* (Q. some) Q. (others) 'With'—perhaps due 'to an original contraction "w$^{t}$"' (Pollard, p. 37) or possibly the compositor's eye caught 'with' from the previous line.

*slaves* 'Note Ric.'s contemptuous attitude towards his people' (Verity); cf. 'oyster-wench' (l. 31), 'brace of draymen' (l. 32).

29. *underbearing* v. G.; cf. *K. John*, 3. 1. 65—the only other instance in Sh.

30. *banish...with him* i.e. carry away their affections (from me) into banishment with him. v. G. 'affect.'

33. *the tribute...knee* 'It should be remembered that *courtesying* (the act of reverence now confined to women) was anciently practised by men' (Steevens). Cf. *Ham.* 3. 2. 59 'crook the pregnant hinges of the knee.'

35. *As were...reversion his* v. G. 'reversion.' Cf. note 1. 1. 116–21. Froissart (vi. 319) reports treasonable talk among Bol.'s friends at his departure.

37. *go* = let them go.

39. *Expedient manage* A link with *K. John*, in which 'expedient' (= speedy) occurs 3 times, and 'expedition' (= speed) once, while 'manage' (= management) is also found, and this last derives from *The Troublesome Reign* (v. note *K. John*, 1. 1. 37). Cf. 'expedience' 2. 1. 287. 'Manage' in this sense is found again in *M.V.* 3. 4. 25 and *Temp.* 1. 2. 70; elsewhere it refers to horsemanship (v. 3. 3. 179).

43–44. *with too great a court...largess* A great deal is made of all this in *Woodstock*; but the source of the words may be *Traïson* (p. 11) 'tint le Roy grant Court et grant feste. Et au souper les heraulx...cryoient largesce.'

45. *farm our royal realm* Cf. notes on *Material* (iii) above, and on 2. 1. 59–66, 113, below. v. G. 'farm.'

*inforced* Q. 'inforſt' F. 'inforc'd' Camb. and many mod. edd. 'inforcéd' omitting 'to'.

48. *substitutes* Cf. 1. 2. 37.

48–50. *blank charters...gold* Cf. note *Material* (iii). *Woodstock* devotes several scenes to this matter. v. G. 'blank.'

52. S.D.–53. Q. reads:

*Enter Buſhie with newes.*
*Buſh.* Olde Iohn of Gaunt...

F. reads:

*Enter Buſhy.*
Buſhy, what newes?
*Bu.* Old Iohn of Gaunt...

—which Pollard (p. 87) feels 'bound to acknowledge ...as prob. originating elsewhere than in Jaggard's printing-house.' It looks to me, however, as if the Q. 'with' here may have been a misprint for 'what,' as at l. 27 above, owing to the use of the contracted form 'w$^t$' which might stand for either word. And if 'Enter Buſhie' was written in the margin against 'w$^t$ newes,' after 'Enter a Messenger' or some such words had been deleted, the compositor would be faced with 'Enter Buſhie w$^t$ newes' which he would naturally take as a S.D. A prob. reason for the change in the MS. would be a desire to save a small speaking part, which suggests that it was made here and at l. 23 (v. note) while the MS. was being read over for casting.

58. *Ely House* v. note 1. 4 *Material* (iv). Cf. *Ric. III*, 3. 4. 33.

59–60. *Now put it...to his grave* Herford notes: 'So Marlowe's Edward II is made to wish that Mortimer and Lancaster "had both caroused a bowl of poison to each other's health"' (*Ed. II*, 2. 2. 235–36).

61. *lining* v. G.—with a quibble on the ordinary sense, to suit 'coats.'

62. *wars*.... The internal full stop 'again comes at the close of a sinister sentence. After which Ric. turns to his favourites' (Pollard, p. 68).

65. *Amen* F. omits. Q. prints without prefix. Staunton first gave '*All*. Amen.'

S.D. Q. 'Exeunt.' F. 'Exit.'

## 2. 1.

*Material*. The scene falls into sections: (i) 1–155, The Death of Gaunt; (ii) 155–214, Confiscation of Gaunt's property; York's protest; (iii) 215–23, York left governor of England; Ric. leaves for Ireland; (iv) 224–300, Nobles' discontent at Ric.'s tyranny; news of Bol.'s landing.

(i) 'Wholly Sh.'s invention' (Herford); 'entirely fictitious' (Newbolt). But, as Reyher notes (pp. 10–11), it is obviously a dramatic rendering of Froissart's account of 'Howe the duke of Lancastre dyed' (cf. *Introd.* pp. lv–lvi). Close parallels with *Woodstock,* which also occur, will be noted below.

(ii) Here Hol. is closely followed; but *Woodstock* is drawn upon for part of York's speech.

(iii) 'he appointed for his lieutenant generall in his absence his vncle the duke of Yorke' (Hol. iii. 497/1/11).

(iv) Again, Hol. is the main, if not the sole, source.

'In joining the two parts of this scene [i.e. 1–155 and 155–end] in one,' comments J. C. Smith, 'Sh. did violence to history, since Gaunt died in Feb. and Bol. did not land till July. Whether he also did violence to art turns upon a different consideration. This scene follows immediately on 1. 4. Now the opening of 1. 4 implies that Bol. has just left England; how then before the close of this scene has there been time for his sojourn in France, his projected marriage, and his preparations for return? The answer is, that the death-bed scene so fills the interval to our imaginations that we do not raise the question.'

S.D. Q. 'Enter Iohn of Gaunt ſicke, with the duke of Yorke, &c.' F. 'Enter Gaunt, ſicke with Yorke.' For 'borne in a chair' cf. *Lear,* 4. 7. 20 S.D. (F.) 'Enter Lear in a chaire carried by Seruants.' The fact that both Q. and F. describe Gaunt as 'ſicke' denotes, I take it, that the theatre chair for the entry of sick persons was to be used. Collier's suggestion 'Bed drawn forth' is disproved by l. 137.

1–4. *Will the king...ear* Herford notes 'the broad yet subtle contrast drawn between the two brothers. Gaunt's loyalty sternly reproves; York's timidity acquiesces or faintly protests.' But v. *Introd.* p. lv n. 1. The contrast in character is already found in Froissart; v. notes on *Material* 1. 2 and 2. 1 above, and cf. Froissart (vi. 371): 'The duke of Yorke laye styll in his castell, and medled with nothynge of the busynesse of Englande [after the capture of Richard]: no more he dyde before, he toke ever the tyme aworthe as it came.'

6. *Enforce...harmony* Cf. *M.V.* 5. 1. 70–82 (for 'attention' and 'harmony'), and *Per.* 5. 1. 234–35 'Most heavenly music!/It nips me unto listening.'

9–12. *He that...close* The quatrain, which here marks 'lyrical exaltation' (Herford) and so characterizes Gaunt's visionary mood, is found in Sh.'s early plays, e.g. *Errors, L.L.L., M.N.D.* Cf. *Introd.* pp. xi–xiii and below note 3. 2. 76–81.

9. *is listened* Cf. *J. Caes.* 4. 1. 41 'Listen great things.'

12. *close* v. G.

13. *As* = Like.

*is* Sing., because it goes separately with 'sun' and 'music.' *last* = at the end.

15. *life's* (F4) Q. 'liues'

16. *My death's sad tale* = What my dying tongue shall utter (cf. l. 5).

17. *stopped* v. G. and cf. *L.L.L.* 4. 3. 335–36, and 2 *Hen. IV*, 1. 1. 78 'Stopping my greedy ear with their bold deeds.'

18. *As praises, of whose taste the wise are fond,* (Collier) Q. 'As praiſes of whoſe taſte the wiſe are found' Qb 'As praiſes of whoſe ſtate the wise are found' Qw 'As praiſes of his ſtate: then there are found'—in which last state it reached F., the misprint in Qb being the source of all the trouble (v. Pollard, pp. 15–17). Collier's emendation, accepted by most mod. edd. and justified on the ground that 'fond' became 'found' by attraction from 'ſoundes' and 'ſound' at the end of ll. 17, 19 (helped perhaps by a sp. like 'fonnd'), makes possible sense, since even the wise are made foolish (or become fond) under the influence of flattery. Cf. *K. John*, 1. 1. 213 'Sweet, sweet poison for the age's tooth.' Yet to attribute wisdom of any kind to Ric. in this context is incongruous and I suspect 'the wise' should be 'th'unwise' as Lettsom conjectured.

19. *Lascivious metres* Cf. Gaveston in *Ed. II*, 1. 1. 51–3:

> I must have wanton poets, pleasant wits,
> Musicians, that with touching of a string
> May draw the pliant king which way I please.

21–23. *Report...imitation* One of the innumerable echoes of Ascham's famous attack on the 'Italianated Englishman' in the *Scholemaster* (ed. Arber, pp. 71–86). Cf. also the description of Gaveston in *Ed. II*, 1. 4. 411–14:

> He wears a short Italian hooded cloak,
> Larded with pearl, and in his Tuscan cap
> A jewel of more value than the crown.

But the immediate source, as Reyher notes, is prob. *Woodstock*, which is full of references to the extravagant fashions of Ric. and his friends; cf. esp. ll. 1104–11 (Malone Soc. rep.). Hol. also dwells upon the same theme.

28. *will...wit's regard* 'Where the will mutinies against what intelligence sees to be right' (Gordon). Cf. *Lucr.* 1299 'What wit sets down is blotted straight with will.' *will* = inclination.

31–32. *inspired...expiring* The word-play is itself a play upon 'breath...breath' in l. 30.

31. *a prophet* Cf. note 2. 1 *Material.*

33–39. *His rash...upon itself* J. C. Smith notes 'the string of metaphors, each consistently worked out' in Sh.'s early manner. Cf. note 1. 2. 12–21. They come near to Lyly's euphuistic style. For 'rash' v. G. and cf. 'rash gunpowder' (2 *Hen. IV*, 4. 4. 48).

33. *blaze* v. G. Denotes a more transient flaming than it does to-day.

34. *For violent fires...themselves* Cf. *Rom.* 2. 6. 9 'These violent delights have violent ends' and *Ham.* 3. 2. 195–96 (Herford).

36. *betimes:* Q. 'betimes' F. 'betimes;'

37. *feeder:* (F.) Q. 'feeder,'

39. *Consuming...itself* = The consumption of what ministers to vanity (e.g. money) soon dies of inanition. The notion of voracity, after consuming everything else, at length forced to eat itself, is a common one in Sh.; cf. *Troil.* 1. 3. 121–24; *Cor.* 1. 1. 191–2; Sh.'s Addition to *Sir Thomas More*, l. 210.

40–68. *This royal throne...death!* For the ultimate origin of this famous speech in Froissart v. *Introd.* pp. lvi–lviii. The Bastard's lines in *K. John*, 5. 7. 112–18, which also show Froissart's influence, read like a first draft of it. Cf. ll. 65–6 here:

> That England, that was wont to conquer others,
> Hath made a shameful conquest of itself—

with ll. 112–14 there:

> This England never did, nor never shall,
> Lie at the proud foot of a conqueror,
> But when it first did help to wound itself.

And these latter themselves derive from the *T. Reign*, II. ix. 45–6:

> Let England liue but true within it selfe,
> And all the world can neuer wrong her State.

Gaunt's speech seems to have become at once popular, and is quoted in *England's Parnassus* (1600), though there attributed to Michael Drayton.

41. *earth* Cf. l. 50 and v. G.

42. *Eden* i.e. a fruitful garden, 'fenced from passion and mishap.'

44–63. *Against infection...Neptune* There is a close verbal connexion here with lines in Book iv of Daniel's *Civil Wars*. Cf. st. 43 (italics mine):

> *With what contagion France didſt thou infect*
> *The land* by thee made proud, to diſagree?
> T'inrage them ſo their owne ſwords to direct
> Vpon themſelues that were made ſharpe in thee?

Cf. again st. 90 and 91, cited in part by Clar. (which speak of the murder of Duke Humphrey brought about by Margaret of Anjou, from which civil war began):

> *Neptune keepe out from thy imbraced Ile*
> *This foule contagion of iniquitie;*
> Drowne all corruptions comming to defile
> Our faire proceedings ordred formally;
> Keepe vs meere Engliſh...
>
> But by this impious meanes that worthy man
> Is brought vnto this lamentable end,
> And now that current with maine fury ran
> (The ſtop remou'd that did the courſe defend)
> Vnto the full of miſchiefe that began
> T'a vniuerſall ruine to extend,
> *That Iſthmus failing which the Land did keepe*
> *From the intire poſſeſſion of the deepe.*

The 'infection' Gaunt means is a moral one, that of bloody-mindedness and civil strife. But as his meaning is not fully clear until Daniel's text is in front of us, it follows, I think, that Shakespeare is the debtor, and had read the fourth book of the *Civil Wars* before setting his hand to *Ric. II* and *K. John*. Cf. *Introd.* pp. lvii–lviii, xliv n. 1, notes ll. 47–9, 61–3 below.

45. *this little world* i.e. this microcosm.

47–49. *Which serves...lands* 'The lines would recall the peril of the Armada' (Verity). Cf. above note ll. 44–63 and *K. John*, 3.4. 1–3 (note). For 'envy' v. G.

48. *as a moat* (Qc) Q. 'as moate' v. Pollard, p. 61.

52. *Feared by* = Feared for.

55. *stubborn Jewry* i.e. Judaea, which resists conquest. 'Stubborn' is usually explained as 'obstinately rejecting Christ,' but the Palestine of the Crusades is in question, not the Jews themselves.

59–66. *Is now leased...of itself* Cf. *Introd.* p. l.

61–63. *England...Neptune* Cf. *K. John*, 2. 1. 23–9 (and note):

Together with that pale, that white-faced shore,
Whose foot spurns back the ocean's roaring tides
And coops from other lands her islanders,
Even till that England, hedged in with the main,
That water-walléd bulwark, still secure
And confident from foreign purposes...

which reads like a first draft of Gaunt's speech, though clearly, like that, deriving from Daniel, v. note ll. 44–63 above. Reyher also cites another passage from Daniel (*Civil Wars*, ii. 49), describing the place near Flint Castle where Richard was ambushed, which may have been in Sh.'s mind as well, when he wrote the lines in *K. John*:

A place there is where proudly raiſd there ſtands
A huge aſpiring rocke, neighbou'ring the skies
Whoſe ſurly brow imperiouſly commands
The ſea his bounds that at his proud feet lies:
And ſpurnes the waues that in rebellious bands
Aſſault his Empire, and againſt him riſe.

64. *inky blots* Herford notes in this play the frequent use of imagery drawn from 'blots' and 'stains'; e.g. 1. 3. 202; 3. 2. 81; 4. 1. 236, 324–25; 5. 3. 66 and cf. 'spots' 1. 1. 175.

68. *death!* Q. 'death?'

S.D. Q. (after l. 70) 'Enter king and Queene, &c.' F. (at l. 68) 'Enter King, Queene, Aumerle, Buſhy, Greene, Bagot, Ros, and Willoughby.'

70. *ragged* Q. 'ragde' F. 'rag'd' Most edd. read 'raged' and take it to mean 'enraged,' but the word is weak, and O.E.D. gives no other example of 'raged' in the trans. sense. 'The ragged colt may prove a good horse' is, however, a common proverb of the time (v. Tilley, 101), and Hall actually puts it into Ric.'s mouth in his abdication speech. Here 'ragged' implies not only 'shaggy' but also 'unruly,' 'not broken-in.' Cf. *Euphues* (Bond, ii. 29), 'The olde Hermit glad to see

this ragged Colte retourned...thought not to adde sower words to augment his sharp woes.' For the sp., which prob. shows that Sh. intended a monosyllable, cf. *M.W.W.* (F.), 4. 4. 31 'Herne the Hunter...with great rag'd-hornes.'

73–83. O, *how that name...bones* If justification be needed for this bitter word-play, Gaunt himself supplies it in l. 85. Sophocles makes Ajax, in his misery, play upon his name after the same fashion (*Ajax*, 430–31). Cf. Coleridge, i. 149, 153, ii. 184–85.

75. *grief...fast* Fasts were kept as an expression of grief as well as for religious observance.

77. *For sleeping...watched* = I have kept wakeful guard long over England as she slept in sluggish peace. For 'watching' (l. 78) v. G.

84. *nicely* v. G. Ric. deliberately uses an equivocal word.

85. *misery...itself* = it is misery (not sickness) that finds distraction in mocking itself. v. G. 'sport.'

86. *kill my name in me* i.e. by banishing his heir.

88–93. *Should dying...thee ill* Stichomythia; cf. note 1. 3. 258–62.

94. *Ill...ill* i.e. I see thee ill (dimly), and I see thee an ill (evil) king.

*in thee,* The comma makes 'thee' emphatic.

100. *A thousand...crown* The crown suggests various images in this play, e.g. Death's court (3. 2. 162), Fortune's well (4. 1. 184), and here a round council chamber. The word is used quibblingly and implies the King's head as well as his diadem.

102–103. *verge...waste* Both quibbles, v. G.

102. *incaged* (F.) Q. 'inraged' One of the F. variants which seems to require knowledge or acumen beyond that of an ordinary printer (Pollard, p. 84).

104–14. O, *had thy grandsire...law* As Reyher notes, this reference to Edward III owes something to the speech in *Woodstock* (ll. 2467–81) by Edward's ghost, which appears to Gloucester on the eve of his murder:

behould me heere. sometymes faire Englandes lord
7 warlicke sonnes I left, yett being gone
no one succeeded In my kingly throne
Richard of burdex, my accussed grand child
Cutt of yo^r titles to the kingly state
& now yo^r liues and all, would ruinate
murders his grand siers sonns: his fathers brothers
becomes a landlord to my kingly tytles
rentes out my crownes reuenewes. rackes my subiectes
that spent ther bloodes w^th me in conquering ffrance
beheld me ryd in state through london streetcs
& at my sturropp lowly footeing by
4 captiue kings to grace my victory
yett that, nor this. his royatous youth can stay
till death hath tayne his vncles all away.

108. *possessed* i.e. possessed by a devil, mad.

111. *for thy world* i.e. for thy domain. Cf. 'earth,' ll. 41, 50 above.

113. *Landlord...not king* Cf. the passage from *Woodstock* (ll. 59–66) cited *Introd*. p. l, and (a still closer parallel) ll. 2826–27 which Gaunt speaks:

& thou no king but landlord now become
to this great state that terro^rd christendome.

*now, not king* (Theobald) Q. 'now not, not King' The Q. capital throws emphasis upon 'king.'

114. *Thy state...law* i.e. Your legal status as king ('in all causes supreme') is now 'amenable to the common law like that of any other mortgagee' (J. C. Smith). As a believer in divine right (v. 1. 2. 37–41), Gaunt complains, not that Ric. is acting illegally, but that he is diminishing the royal prerogative. For 'bondslave' cf. ll. 63–4 'bound in with shame' etc.

115. *lean-witted* i.e. gaunt-witted; cf. ll. 74–83.

118–19. *Make pale....With fury* Ric. trembles and turns pale at his terrible old uncle's reproof, but explains his agitation as fury, and, after a dramatic pause at l. 119, summons up a pompous threat as token of his anger. But Gaunt's next speech, more terrible still, completely silences him. For the changes in Ric.'s face, v. *Introd.* pp. lx–lxi and cf. 5. 1. 8, 3. 2. 75–9, and 1 *Hen. IV*, 1. 3. 175.

119. *residence....* The Q. period denotes a long pause, for recovery.

122. *roundly* A quibble, v. G.

124. *brother* (Q b) Q., F. 'brothers' Cf. 1. 2. 48 (and note) where a similar misprint, resulting in a double negative, has been corrected on the press; and v. Pollard, p. 36 n. 1.

126–31. *That blood...Edward's blood* Cf. 1. 2. 11–21.

126. *pelican* i.e. a young pelican. Alluding to the fable of 'the kind life-rend'ring pelican' (*Ham.* 4. 5. 146), which feeds its young upon its own heart's blood.

127. *tapped* A quibble, suggesting both the tapping of the beak and a tapster at work upon a cask.

*caroused.* Q. 'carowſt,'

128. *plain well-meaning soul* A palpable reminiscence of *Woodstock*, in which Gloucester is constantly described as 'plain,' e.g. ll. 113–14:

> homely & playne. boeth free from pryd & enuye
> & therin will admitt distrust to none.

Hol., Froissart and Daniel, on the contrary, unite in depicting him as 'fierce of nature,' 'most violent' and an intriguer against Ric., a man of 'open malice and repugnant brest,' etc. (Reyher). Nor has *Traïson* a good word to say for him. Cf. *Introd.* pp. lxi–lxii.

130. *precedent* Q. 'preſident'—the usual Sh.n sp. v. G.

*good...* Q. 'good:' The colon marks the pause before the delivery of the blow in l. 131.

133. *crooked age* '"Crooked" suggested the image of the sickle in the next line' (Gordon).

138. S.D. Q., F. 'Exit.'

141–44. *I do beseech...were he here* A 'timid and futile attempt to discount Gaunt's reproof, which York knows to be just' (Herford). But cf. *Introd.* p. lv n.

145–46. *Right...as it is* Ric. wilfully misinterprets York's words. There is swagger in l. 146, but a sense of fatality lurks behind it.

149. *His tongue...instrument* The same image occurs at 1. 3. 161–62.

151–52. *bankrupt...poor* Continuing the metaphor of 'all...spent' (l. 150).

152. *death* = the state of being dead.

153. *The ripest...first* Cf. *M.V.* 4. 1. 115–16.

154. *our pilgrimage must be* i.e. we have still to run our pilgrimage on earth.

156. *rug-headed kerns* Cf. 2 *Hen. VI*, 3. 1. 367 'a shag-haired crafty kern.' Clar. cites Spenser's *State of Ireland* (Globe ed. p. 630), 'They have another custome...that is the wearing of...long glibbes, which is a thick curled bush of heare, hanging downe over theyr eyes, and monstrously disguising them.' v. G. 'rug.'

*kerns* Q. (some) 'kernes' Q. (others) 'kerne' As 'kern' might be used as a collective sb., the sing. may be correct here.

157–58. *where no venom...live* Allusion to the legend of St Patrick banishing the snakes from Ireland. Steevens cites Dekker's *Honest Whore*: 'that Irish Judas,/Bred in a country where no venom prospers/But in the nation's blood.'

158. *live.* So Q.

159. *ask some charge* = demand some expense.

160–62. *we do seize...possessed* Here, and again in ll. 201–204, Hol. is followed almost verbatim.

160. *us...* The Q. colon gives emphasis to the outrageous intention announced in ll. 161–62. Cf. note 1. 1. 96; 1. 3. 68, etc.

162. S.D. v. note l. 185.

163. *How long...patient?* Cf. Hol. iii. 496/1/42:

The duke of Yorke was therewith sore mooued, who before this time, had borne things with so patient a mind as he could, though the same touched him verie neere, as the death of his brother the duke of Glocester, the banishment of his nephue the said duke of Hereford, and other mo iniuries in great number, which for the slipperie youth of the king, he passed ouer for the time, and did forget aswell as he might.

166. *rebukes* v. G.

*private wrongs* i.e. wrongs suffered by private persons (specified in ll. 246–50).

167–68. *the prevention...marriage* Nothing is said elsewhere about this in the play; and it is only explicable by reference to the chronicles, which tell us that when Bol., in exile at Paris, was about to marry the cousin of the French king, Richard

sent the earle of Salisburie with all speed into France, both to surmize by vntrue suggestion, heinous offenses against him, and also to require the French king that in no wise he would suffer his cousine to be matched in mariage with him that was so manifest an offendor' (Hol. iii. 495/2/38).

And Froissart, as is natural, has a great deal more to say about it. Cf. *Introd.* pp. lxv–lxvi.

168. *nor my own disgrace* Another loose thread; but we do not know to what it refers.

171–83. *I am the last...his kin* Reyher cites from *Woodstock*, ll. 33–51, a speech by Lancaster (Gaunt) comparing Ric. with his father, which clearly gave suggestions for these lines, e.g. cf. l. 176 with *Woodstock*, l. 38:

for sweete & louely was his Countenance.

172. *first.* Q. 'firſt'

177. *Accomplished...hours* i.e. when he was in his prime like you (J. C. Smith).

*with the number* (F.) Q. 'with a number'—an obvious correction (Pollard, p. 87).

185. *between....* 'The sentence is not finished, for York breaks down, and the King, who has been paying no attention to him whatever, but has been walking round the room appraising the value of its contents, at the sound of his sob turns round, and with his usual superficial good nature, exclaims "Why, uncle, what's the matter?"' (Pollard, p. 66).

186–88. *O, my liege...withal.* (arr. Theobald) Q. 'Oh...you pleafe,/If not...with all,' F. 'Oh...if not/I pleas'd...with all:' Poss. the passage was crowded by Sh. at the foot of a page of MS.

190. *Hereford?* (F.) Q. 'Hereford:'

192. *true* v. G. Bol. had loyally submitted to banishment.

195–97. *and take from Time...to-day* Cf. *Ham.* 4. 5. 103–105.

198. *thyself....for* Q. 'thy felfe. For'

201. *wrongfully...rights* The word-play must not be overlooked.

201–208. *If you do...cannot think* Hol. hints that York regarded Ric.'s conduct as suicidal. Cf. note l. 211 below.

202–204. *Call in...homage* Cf. note ll. 160–62 above, and v. G. for the legal terms used.

204. *deny...homage* 'deny' = refuse. An act of homage was required of the heir when lands had been delivered to him by his sovereign. Ric. confiscated the lands and 'respited' the homage, in return for a 'reasonable fine,' as Hol. informs us.

209–10. *Think...goods* The rhymes lend a note of finality to Ric.'s decision, and have 'the effect of bringing the situation to a close' (Verity).

211. *I'll not be by the while* Hol. iii. 496/1/50 (following Hall nearly verbatim) tells us that York 'perceiuing that neither law, iustice nor equitie could take place...thought it the part of a wise man to get him in time to a resting place, and to leaue the following of such

an vnaduised capteine, as with a leden sword would cut his owne throat.' J. C. Smith notes a stage reason for his exit here: 'He could not well go out with the King, nor could he stay with the conspirators.'

213. *by* = concerning.

214. *events* v. G.

S.D. Q., F. 'Exit.'

217. *To see* = To see to.

*to-morrow next* 'Gaunt died in February, Ric. sailed for Ireland in May' (J. C. Smith). The dramatist was perhaps conscious of some compression of time for artistic ends; but 'Hol.'s language leaves it open to suppose that he [Ric.] may have departed at once after Gaunt's death' (Herford).

221. *For he is...well* For York's character, v. *Introd.* p. lv n.[1] and notes 2. 1. 1–4; 2. 2. 103.

223. S.D. Q. 'Exeunt King and Queene: Manet North.' F. 'Flouriſh./Manet North. Willoughby, & Roſſ.'

225. *living too* (Qb) Q. 'liuing to'

228–29. *My heart...tongue* Cf. *Ham.* 1. 2. 159 'But break my heart, for I must hold my tongue.'

229. *Ere't* Q. 'Eart'

232. *thou wouldst* (Q.) F. 'thou'dſt'—which I suspect was Sh.'s intention. The Q. line is overlong.

246. *The commons...pilled...taxes* Cf. *Introd.* p. li.

247–48. *And quite lost...their hearts* Cf. note 1. 3. 136. It looks as if the duplication here was due to a similar compositor's blunder, unhappily not detected by the corrector; if so l. 248 is hopelessly corrupt.

247. *hearts.* So F.

251. *this?* Q. 'this:' Was the Q. compositor short of queries?

252–55. *Wars...in wars* This refers to the cession of Brest to the Duke of Brittany, which caused the original quarrel between Ric. and his uncle Glouc., and the passage is clearly based upon the latter's words, as reported by Hol. (iii. 487/2/65): 'Sir, your grace ought to put your bodie in paine to win a strong hold or towne by feats of war, yet you take vpon you to sell or deliuer anie towne...gotten with great aduenture by the manhood and policie of your noble progenitours.' Cf. also the lines cited from *Woodstock* in note ll. 104–14.

252. *Wars hath* (Q.) Rowe reads 'Wars have' and all edd. follow, though Capell conj. 'War hath.' But 'hath' is quite common in sixteenth-century usage in the plur. Cf. O.E.D. 'have' A.d.

257. *king's* (Qw) Q. 'King' v. Pollard, p. 59.

*a broken man* = a failure in business.

258. *Reproach...over him* Reyher cites *Woodstock*, l. 846:

> confusione hangeth ore thy wretched head.

The same thought is expressed by Hall, who says that when York retired to Langley he prayed God 'to deuerte from kyng Richarde the darke clowde whiche he sawe dependyng ouer his hed' (p. 6, ed. 1809).

263–69. *we hear this fearful tempest...wrack* Reyher notes that Hall employs similar metaphors in his account of the arguments used by Archbishop Arundel to induce Bol. to return to England.

266. *strike* = strike sail. But a quibble is prob. intended. For 'securely' v. G.

268. *unavoided* = unavoidable. The suffix -ed most commonly has the force of -ble in words beginning with a negative prefix (J. C. Smith). But cf. 'despised' 2.3.95.

277–90. *Then thus...for Ireland* Hol. is closely followed here, except for certain details noted below.

277–78. *Then thus...intelligence* (Q., F.) Capell and all subsequent edd. divide 'Then thus...bay/ In Brittany...intelligence'—an unnecessary change.

277. *le Port Blanc* Q. 'le Port Blan' F. 'Port le Blan'—which many edd. follow. But Hol. reads 'Le

port blanc' (iii.498/1/9) and Camb. restored Q. reading, noting the name as that of 'a small port in the department of Côtes du Nord near Tréguier.'

278. *Britain* (Q., F.) i.e. Brittany. Cf. l. 285 where edd. read 'Bretagne' for the sake of the metre, and note *K. John*, 2. 1. 156.

280. [*The son...Arundel*] (Malone) Not in Q. or F. As the person who 'broke from the Duke of Exeter' (l. 281) was not Lord Cobham, as the Q. text would imply, but the Earl of Arundel's son 'which was kept in the duke of Exeters house, escaped out of the realme...and went to his vncle Thomas Arundell late archbishop of Canturburie,' as Hol. (iii.496/1/70) states, Malone had not 'the smallest doubt, that a line was omitted in the copy' and 'rather than leave a lacuna' he 'inserted such words as render the passage intelligible.' The matter has an interest apart from Malone's ingenious restoration. The words just quoted from Hol. being drawn from a passage some pages distant from that used for what immediately follows, exhibit a mind respectful of the chronicle in a fashion very remote from the lordly indifference to history displayed in *K. John* or, indeed, in the treatment of the names in ll. 281–84 (v. next note).

283–84. *Sir Thomas...Francis Coint* Hol.'s words are: 'There were also with him, Reginald lord Cobham, sir Thomas Erpingham, and sir Thomas Ramston knights, John Norburie, Robert Waterton, & Francis Coint esquires' (iii. 498/1/15). It is noteworthy that whereas the lines in Q. halt, they would be metrically improved had they followed Hol. more exactly; as thus:

> Sir Thomas Erpingham, Sir Thomas Ramston,
> John Norbery, Robert Waterton and Francis Coint.

Taking these points in conjunction with the mislining of ll. 277–78 and the omission of l. 280, we are entitled to suspect, with Malone, careless copying on the part of a scribe (a compositor would scarcely do such things)

One does not suppose that Sh. himself would trouble to be exact over a string of names whose sole purpose would be to give an *appearance* of historical accuracy to an audience quite incapable of checking them. But he is unlikely, even if working under pressure, to have debased the metre. If Q. then was printed from his MS., it looks as if the play-book it was based upon was a transcript and not the unknown author's original.

284. *Coint* (Hol.) Q. 'Coines' F. 'Quoint'—which most edd. follow. 'Coines' is a term of carpentry (cf. *M.N.D.* p. 102), but the carelessness here is prob. due to the Q. compositor, since F. has it correct, if in a different sp.

285–86. *All these...men of war* This represents one of two conflicting reports recorded by Hol. (iii. 498/1/19) without deciding between them. The other is that Bol. took ship with 'not past fifteene lances...that is to saie, men of armes, furnished and appointed.' The first, as Herford notes, 'whether true or not, was clearly the more fit to be put into the mouth of North. at this crisis. Even Ross and Willoughby might have shrunk from joining a handful of returned exiles.'

287. *expedience* v. note 1. 4. 39.

289–90. *but that...Ireland* Hol. (iii. 498/1/31) does not give this reason for Bol.'s delay, but says that he 'lay houering aloofe, and shewed himselfe now in this place, and now in that, to see what countenance was made by the people, whether they meant enuiouslie to resist him, or freendlie to receiue him.' Boswell-Stone (p. 97) suggests that 'this deviation from his authority accords with Sh.'s annihilation of time in the present, and the preceding, scene.' Reyher (p. 16) writes, 'Le poète a peut-être jugé qu'il y aurait une contradiction au moins apparente entre ces précautions, ces prudents sondages de Bol. et sa popularité relatée dans la dernière scène de l'acte précédent.'

*stay The first departing of the king* = 'wait till the king has first departed' (Herford).

292. *Imp out...wing* v. G. 'imp.'

293. *broking* v. G. 'Q. prints a capital B, which adds a bitter emphasis' (Pollard, p. 71).

294. *the dust...gilt* With a quibble on 'guilt' (as Q. spells the word). Cf. *Troil.* 3. 3. 179 'gilt o'er-dusted.'

296. *Ravenspurgh* 'Otherwise Ravenspurn, or Ravenser, near Spurn Head, was, in the time of Edward I, the most considerable port on the Humber. In the middle of the fourteenth century the sea did it great mischief. Its merchants afterwards removed to Hull' (Clar.). Froissart relates that Bol. landed at Plymouth and gives precise details; such is contemporary history!

297. *if you faint* i.e. if you are faint-hearted. Cf. 2. 2. 32.

300. S.D. Q., F. 'Exeunt.'

## 2. 2.

*Material.* Two sections: (i) 1–40. The Queen's melancholy, (ii) the consternation of York, Bushy, Bagot and Green at Bol.'s landing and rapid advance.

(i) 'This part of the scene is wholly original' (Herford). 'The Queen, Isabel of France, was at this time not yet ten years old. Sh. was either ignorant of, or indifferent to, this fact' (Clar.). Yet Charles Knight had noticed by 1840 the analogy between the Queen in Sh. and the Isabel of Daniel's *Civil Wars*; both poets represent her as a mature woman, and both bring her face to face with Ric. in the streets of London after his downfall. Daniel appears to draw largely upon Froissart, but R. M. Smith does not succeed in his attempt to trace this element of *C.W.* to his influence; on the contrary, while dwelling it is true upon her beauty and grace, Froissart states that 'she was but a yonge chylde of eyght yere of age' when she married Ric. (vi. 159, 190), and it was only 14 years after he first pub. *C.W.* bks. i–iv in 1595 (i.e. in an Epistle Dedicatorie to the 1609 ed.) that Daniel apologizes for 'not suting her passions to her yeares.' Cf. *Introd.* pp. lix–lx.

(ii) The rest of the scene is based on Hol., but the events are re-arranged and in places modified in order to create the effect of disaster crowding upon disaster.

S.D. Q. 'Enter the Queene, Bushie, Bagot.' F. 'Enter Queene, Bushy, and Bagot.' Pope headed 'The Court of England,' other edd. 'A room in the Palace,' Clar. first read 'Windsor Castle,' because Hol. states that the Queen was left at Windsor when Ric. went to Ireland.

3. *life-harming* Because sighing and grief were supposed to impoverish the blood. Cf. *Ado*, 1. 1. 235, *Rom.* 3. 5. 59, 'dry sorrow drinks our blood' and *M.N.D.* 3. 2. 97 (note).

7–8. *guest...guest* The image is suggested by 'entertain' (l. 4), cf. note 5. 1. 13–15.

8–9. *so sweet...Richard* The first step towards capturing our sympathy. 'The amiable part of Ric.'s character is brought full upon us by his queen's few words' (Coleridge).

10–11. *Some unborn sorrow...towards me* With this presentiment cf. *Rom.* 1. 4. 106 ff. 'My mind misgives' etc. and Antonio's melancholy in *M.V.* 1. 1.

11. *inward soul* = secret or inner being.

12. *trembles, yet at something grieves* (Pope) Q., F. 'trembles, at something it grieues' Most eighteenth-century and mod. edd. read 'trembles: at something it grieves.' The colon forces a sense upon the original; but I am persuaded that Pope gives what Sh. intended. It eases the verse; it echoes the 'yet' of ll. 6 and 9, quite after Sh.'s early manner; it points the antithesis between 'nothing' and 'something,' which is impaired by the division 'some thing'; and it greatly clarifies the sense. Nor is the Q. reading difficult to account for. 'Yet' and 'yt' (a Shakespearian spelling of 'it') might be easily confused; and if we suppose that the word was first omitted in proof and then inadvertently inserted in the wrong place, all is explained.

14. *substance...shadows* The contrast is a favourite notion of the age. Cf. *Ham.* 2. 2. 261 'the very substance of the ambitious is merely the shadow of a dream.' v. G. 'shadow.'

15. *shows...is* Pope read 'show...are'; but the sing. is more effective, implying that *each* 'shows' etc.

16. *eye* (F.) Q. 'eyes' 'Dictated by the context' (Pollard, p. 83); cf. 'Sorrow's eye' (l. 26).

18. *perspectives* Two possible meanings, v. G. Sh. is mainly thinking of a perspective-picture, but 'glazed... tears' shows that he has the perspective-glass in mind also. For the quibble in 'rightly' v. G. also; it is continued in 'awry' and forms the pivot of the conceit. Actually, of course, the perspective is 'rightly gazed upon' when 'eyed awry.'

20. *distinguish form* = exhibit distinct form, or divide 'one thing...to many objects' (l. 17).

22. *Find* The subj. is 'you' (understood from 'your majesty').

*himself* i.e. the King.

24. *thrice-gracious queen* (F.) Q. 'thrice (gracious Queene)'

25. *more is not* (Q.) F. 'more's not' The line being an alexandrine, the contraction is unnecessary, and was prob. introduced by the F. compositor who had to overrun the line.

31. *though* (Q. some) Q. (others) 'thought'

*though...I think* 'though I think on thinking on no thought' (J. C. Smith) = though I set myself to think on nothing melancholy. Johnson, who appears to be the only editor to realize that 'thought' = melancholy (v. G.), adds, characteristically, 'The involuntary and unaccountable depression of the mind, which every one has sometime felt, is here very forcibly described.'

34–40. *'Tis nothing less...I wot.* A piece of word-twisting, such as Sh. and his public loved at this period. To paraphrase: My sadness is certainly not imaginary, for the imaginary fears of fanciful people are themselves reflections or memories of earlier sorrows. But mine are not. Whatever my trouble may be, it is not caused by anything that has happened before (? because my life has so far been entirely happy), or if there be such a cause, it is unknown to me; I may come to discover it in the future, but as yet I have not done so; I must call it, therefore, a nameless woe.

34. *nothing less* = anything but. v. G.

38. *in reversion...possess* i.e. I own this grief like a property now held by someone else; I shall not 'realize' it, until I come into actual possession and see what it consists of. v. G. 'reversion.'

39. *known, what* (F.) Q. 'knowen what,'

40. S.D. Q. omits. F. 'Enter Greene.'

50–51. *And with...Ravenspurgh* (F.) Q. prints in one line.

50. *uplifted* v. G.

52. *that* = what.

*worse...* Q. 'worſe:'—marking as usual a pause before a startling announcement.

57. *the rest* (Q.) Qb, F. 'the reſt of the' Cf. 1. 1. 142 'the rest appealed,' which is not quite parallel, since there 'appealed' agrees with 'rest,' whereas here 'revolted' goes with 'faction.' Verity cites *A.Y.L.* 2. 7. 39 'the remainder biscuit.'

58. *Worcester* i.e. Thomas Percy, brother to North. and steward of the royal household.

59–60. *Hath...fled with him* Hol. (iii. 499/2/74–500/1/9) relates that

> Sir Thomas Persie earle of Worcester, lord steward of the kings house...brake his white staffe, which is the representing signe and token of his office, and without delaie went to duke Henrie. When the kings seruants of houshold saw this (for it was doone before them all) they dispersed themselues.

59. *broken* (Q.) Qb, F. 'broke'—which all edd. read.

60–61. *And all...Bolingbroke* (arr. Pope) Q., F. print in one line.

63. *heir* = offspring. Cf. l. 10 above. Cf. ded. to *V.A.* 'the first heir of my invention.' For 'prodigy' v. G.

67. *Who shall hinder me?* etc. This is very close to Constance in *K. John.*

72. *lingers* v. G.

*extremity* v. G.

S.D. Q. omits. F. 'Enter Yorke.' For my S.D. v. next note, and cf. Ford, *Perkin Warbeck*, 3. 1 S.D. 'Enter King Henry, with his gorget on.'

74. *With signs...neck* i.e. in gorget of mail.

75. *careful business* = anxious pre-occupation (Herford). The mod. sense of the words gives exactly the meaning Sh. did *not* intend.

84–85. *Now comes...him* Reyher cites *Woodstock*, ll. 597–98:

> now headstrong Richard shallt thoᵘ reap the fruite
> thy lewd lesentious willfullnes hath sowne.

85. S.D. F. 'Enter a ſeruant.' Q. omits, but heads his speeches 'Seruingman.'

86. *your son...came* i.e. Aumerle who had gone to join the K. in Ireland. But the context does not make this clear; indeed, it gives the impression that Aumerle had deserted with the rest. Créton declares that Aumerle was treacherous throughout and caused Ric. to delay his departure from Ireland.

87. *He was?* (Capell) Q. 'He was;'

*Why, so! go* (edd.) Q. 'why ſo go' F. 'why ſo: go'

88. *the commons cold* (Pope) Q., F. 'the commons they are colde' The repetition seems to be of the same order as those already noted at 1. 3. 136, 2. 1. 247–48 (v. notes). Cf. Hol. (marginal note iii. 498/2): 'The harts of the commons wholie bent to the duke of Lancaster.'

90. *Sirrah* Q., F. and all mod. edd. print this with l. 91. But it is extra-metrical, and the period at the end of l. 89 shows that the old man has fallen into gloomy

silence, from which he rouses himself by turning abruptly to the servingman. Cf. a similar start of recovery in l. 104 below.

91. *Plashy* Cf. note 1. 2. 66.

98. *the duchess died* 'The Duch. of Glouc. died in Oct. not in July; at Barking, not at Plashy; of grief for her son's, not her husband's, death' (Newbolt). Hol. (iii. 514/2/6) mentions the last point, but names neither date nor place.

99–124. *God for his mercy...six and seven* Edd. have differed in the line-arrangement of this agitated speech, and I have made a fresh attempt. The verse may be compared with that of the Nurse in *Rom.*, as an example of Sh.'s early experimentation in the expression of irregularly disposed thoughts by means of metrical form. Between this and the speeches of Leontes in *Wint.* 1. 2 there lies a long road. Q. prints ll. 110–11 as one line, divides ll. 118–20 as 'Wel...coufin,/Ile... your men' and ll. 122–24 as 'I ſhould...permit:/All... ſeauen.' In the last instance I follow Pope.

102. *untruth* v. G.

103. *cut off my head* Cf. note 1. 1. 101–103.

*brother's....* York falls once more into melancholy contemplation, to recover himself with a start. He is a studied portrait of an old man weighed down with perplexity and sorrow, thrust into an office he is quite unable to perform.

104. *What...Ireland?* Not a good line. F. omits 'no,' and Vaughan suggested we should read 'yet dispatched.' Possibly 'What' might stand as an extrametrical exclamation (cf. 'Sirrah,' l. 90), leaving 'Are there...Ireland'—a short but rhythmical line, like ll. 116, 121.

106. *sister* His mind runs upon the dead duchess.

107. *carts* The triviality of this produces an effect of pathos less intense than, but similar in kind to, that caused by Lear's 'Prithee, undo this button.'

112. *thrust disorderly* (Steevens) Q., F. 'disorderly thrust' Cf. note 1. 3. 131.

114–15. *Th'one...th'other* Q. 'Tone...tother'

116. *Is my kinsman...wronged* Many have tinkered at this short line, the best suggestion being Vaughan's 'my kind kinsman,' since, with 'kinsman' following, 'kind' might be overlooked by a compositor.

117. *kindred* Q. 'kinred'—old form.

121. *Berkeley* Q. 'Barkly' F. 'Barkley Castle' Most eighteenth-century edd. follow F., because it regularizes the metre; they may be right.

124. S.D. Q. 'Exeunt Duke, Qu, man, Bush, Green.'

125. *to Ireland* (F.) Q. 'for Ireland' The Q. compositor has repeated the 'for' earlier in the line.

126. *returns* So Q.

127–28. *Proportionable...unpossible* (Pope) Q. prints in one line.

130. *Is near* = implies, involves.

131. *that is* F. 'that's'—which all mod. edd. read.

135. *in them* Refers to 'hearts' (l. 133).

*so do we* i.e. stand condemned.

139. *office* v. G.

140. *hateful* = full of hate.

*The...commons will* (Pope) Q., F. 'Will...commons.'

151. S.D. Q. omits. F. 'Exit.'

## 2. 3.

*Material.* Hol. (iii. 498/2/54) is closely followed as regards facts referred to, and though he states that Willoughby and Ross joined Bol. at Ravenspurgh, and North. and Percy at Doncaster, their entries in the scene give effect to his words: 'And thus what for loue, and what for feare of losse, they came flocking vnto him from euerie part.' According to Hol. York 'came foorth into the church that stood without the castell and there communed with the duke of Lancaster,' while ll. 148–49 are based upon the following (498/2/3): 'At his comming vnto Doncaster...he sware vnto those lords [North. and Percy], that he would demand no more but the lands that were to him descended by inheritance from his father, and in right of his wife.' Hol. however has nothing about York remaining 'neuter' (l. 159).

S.D. Q. 'Enter Hereford, Northumberland.' F. 'Enter the Duke of Hereford, and Northumberland.' Capell and mod. edd. head the scene 'Wilds in Gloucestershire.'

2–18. *Believe me...your noble company* This fulsomeness raises suspicions of the speaker's trustworthiness, which are confirmed in 1 *Hen. IV*.

5. *Draws...makes* Edd. explain that Sh. is thinking of the travelling over 'these high hills' etc. But the sing. form may be due to the compositor. Cf. MSH. pp. 235–38.

9. *Cotswold* (Hanmer) Q. 'Cotſhall' F. 'Cottſhold' Sh. knew the Cotswolds, Stratford being at one end of them, so that the Q. spelling prob. gives us his pronunciation of the name. Cf. *M.W.W.* (F.), 1. 1. 92 'Cotſall,' and 2 *Hen. IV* (Q.), 3. 2. 23 'a Cotſole man.'

12. *tediousness and process* = tedious process.

20. S.D. Q. 'Enter Harry Perſie.' F. 'Enter H. Percie.'

21. *my son* Capell conj. 'my son, my lord,'

28–29. *What...together.* (F.) Q. divides 'What... reſolude,/When...togither?'

30. *lordship* (F.) Q. 'Lo:' which may stand for 'Lord,' as it does in l. 31.

36. *Hereford* (Qw) Q. 'Herefords' Cf. Pollard, p. 59.

*boy* Cf. l. 42. 'The historical Hotspur was two years older than Bol. and twenty-two years older than his son' (Newbolt). In 1 *Hen. IV* he is made of the same age as Prince Hal for dramatic purposes, and the mention of his youth here is one of the links with that play.

41–42. *tender...tender* Wright (Clar.) declares 'Even Sh. could scarcely have meant a pun here.' To Sh. a pun was not an offence but a graceful turn of speech, and he puns upon 'tender' again at *Ham.* 1. 3. 107–109, *Cymb.* 3. 4. 11–12.

43–44. *Which elder...desert* Dramatic irony, in view of what follows in 1 *Henry IV.*

48. *as my fortune ripens* Cf. l. 66 'till my infant fortune comes to years.' Hotspur recalls these expressions in 1 *Hen. IV*, 1. 3. 251–55:

> Why, what a candy deal of courtesy
> This fawning greyhound then did proffer me!
> Look, 'when his infant fortune came to age,'
> And 'gentle Harry Percy,' and 'kind cousin':
> O, the devil take such cozeners!

But it is North. who fawns; Bol. being merely diplomatic with his supporters.

56. S.D. Q. omits. F. 'Enter Rosse and Willoughby.'

61. *unfelt* v. G.

*which* The antecedent is 'treasury.'

63–67. *Your presence...bounty* 'Both the deferential language of Ross and Will., and Bol.'s reply, betray the tacit assumption of the whole party that Bol. is not come merely, as he tells York, "to seek his own"' (Herford). No doubt, Bol. is pleased to find his friends so complaisant; but it is noteworthy that he never once says anything either here or in 3. 3 which might later be interpreted as treason. He came 'to seek his own'; if more than that offered, and offered with security, he would not be averse from taking it. Cf. *Introd.* pp. xx–xxii.

65. *thank's* (Q.) i.e. thank (or 'thanks') is. All edd. follow F. 'thankes,' with which 'the exchequer... poor' is taken in apposition.

66. *my infant fortune* Cf. *C.W.* iii. 13 'his tender raigne/And infant-young-beginning gouernment' and *K. John*, 2. 1. 97 'infant state.'

67. S.D. F. 'Enter Barkely.' Q. omits.

70. *my answer is to 'Lancaster'* i.e. I will answer to no name but Lancaster.

75. *one title* Capell conj. 'one tittle' and there is clearly a play upon that word.

78. *York;* Q. 'Yorke:'

79. *the absent time* = the time of (the King's) absence.

80. *self-borne* Q. 'ſelfeborne' i.e. borne in one's own interest and not the State's. Many edd. read 'self-born,' and explain as 'home-sprung,' 'indigenous,' which would carry on the idea of 'native'; but Sh. is quite capable of echoing that idea quibblingly.

S.D. F. 'Enter Yorke.' Q. omits.

86. *Tut, tut!* Q., F. read this with l. 87.

88–89. *that word 'grace'* etc. Referring to the grace of God.

92. *But then more 'why'* i.e. But other questions follow.

99–105. *Were I but...thy fault!* 'It does not appear that Sh. had any historical authority for this statement' (Clar.). Reyher writes, 'Le poète songeait sans doute au danger couru par le Prince Noir à Crécy. Edouard III refusa d'envoyer des renforts à son fils, entouré d'ennemis et prêt à succomber sous le nombre, pour qu'il gagnât ses éperons.' The incident is treated at length in *Edward III* (1596), but there is no hint of a rescue by the Prince's brothers. Clar., therefore, suggests that York's memories of his former prowess were due to the influence of Homer, since they bear 'considerable resemblance to the speech of Nestor' (*Iliad*, vii. 157 ff.), and though Chapman's trans. was not pub. till 1598, Hall's (1581) was available. The theme is a recurring one with Sh., cf. *M.W.W.* 1. 1. 36; 2. 1. 203–204; 2. 3. 40; *Lear*, 5. 3. 276–77; and *Troil.* 1. 3. 291–301. The last, being Nestor's speech and indubitably based upon *Iliad*, bk. vii, makes it seem possible that all derive from Homer.

99. *the lord* (F.) Q. 'Lord' Cf. Pollard, p. 86.

107. *On what condition stands it* = From what defect in my character does the fault spring? But 'condition' also has its mod. sense (v. G.), and York (l. 108) quibblingly replies, 'Even in the worst circumstance conceivable.'

121. *perforce...* Q. 'perforce;'

123. *king in England* (Q.) Qb 'King of England,' which F. and all edd. follow. Cf. Pollard, p. 55.

128. *rouse...bay* Metaphor from hunting, v. G. The 'wrongs' are the quarry.

129–30. *sue my livery...letters-patents* Cf. 2. 1. 202–203, and v. G.

130, 132. The Q. periods (pauses) mark York's silence in face of Bol.'s strong arguments.

144. *Be his own carver* Cf. *Ham.* 1. 3. 20 'carve for himself' = indulge himself. The expression suggests greed or impoliteness at table.

146. *kind,* (Q.) The slight pause is expressive.

151. *never* (Q.) Qc, Qd, F. read 'ne're' or 'neu'r'

154. *ill left* = badly provided for.

158. *unto you* (Q.) Qb, F. and mod. edd. 'to you'—'a needless tinkering of a quite inoffensive line' (Pollard, p. 56).

163. *win your grace* A polite way of 'attaching' York.

164. *Bristow* The old form of Bristol, used by Holinshed.

165. *Bagot* We have already heard (2. 2. 143) that Bagot has fled to join the King in Ireland, and he is not mentioned in 3. 1. Cf. *Introd.* p. lxv. Theatrically these small fry do not matter.

170. *Nor friends nor foes...are* i.e. I cannot welcome you as either friends or foes.

171. S.D. Q., F. 'Exeunt.'

## 2. 4.

*Material.* This scene is based upon Hol. iii. 499/1/32, which relates that Ric., on news of Bol.'s landing, sent Salisbury over 'to gather a power togither, by helpe of the kings freends in Wales, and Cheshire, with all speed possible,' that an army of 40,000 was assembled, but 'there was a brute spred amongst them, that the king was suerlie dead, which wrought such an impression, and euill disposition in the minds of the Welshmen and others, that...they would not go foorth with him, till they saw the king: onelie they were contented to staie foureteene daies to see if he should come or not; but when he came not within that tearme, they would no longer abide, but scaled and departed awaie.'

The omens spoken of by the Captain are taken partly from Hol. and partly from Daniel. Thus Hol. (iii. 496/2/66) writes: 'In this yeare [1399] in a manner throughout all the realme of England, old baie trees withered, and afterwards, contrarie to all mens thinking, grew greene againe, a strange sight, and supposed to import some vnknowne euent.' As this passage only occurs in the second ed. of Hol. (1586–87), it is clear that this was the ed. used for the drafting of the play (v. p. v. pref. Clar.). The parallels following from *C.W.* i. 114, 115 were first pointed out by Charles Knight:

> Warnings of wrath, foregoing miseries;
> In lines of fire and caracters of blood,
> There fearefull formes in dreadfull flames arise,
> Amazing Comets, threatning Monarches might
> And new-seene Starres, vnknowne vnto the night.
> Red fierie Dragons in the aire doe flie,
> And burning Meteors, poynted-streming lights.

S.D. Q. 'Enter erle of Salisbury and a Welch captaine.' For the Welsh Captain cf. note 3. 1. 43.

## 3. 1.

*Material.* Hol. relates that Bol. etc. marching to 'Bristow' within whose castle 'were inclosed...the lord William Scroope earle of Wiltshire and treasuror of England, sir Henrie Greene, and sir John Bushie knights, who prepared to make resistance: but when it would not preuaile, they were taken and brought foorth bound as prisoners into the campe, before the duke of Lancaster. On the morow next insuing, they were arraigned before the constable and marshall, and found giltie of treason, for misgouerning the king and realme, and foorthwith had their heads smit off' (iii. 498/2/64). The Earl of Wiltshire, mentioned as being in Bristol (2. 2. 138) and as having been beheaded (3. 2. 141–42; 3. 4. 53), is omitted not only from this scene but from the play as a whole.

For ll. 11–15, 43, v. notes below.

S.D. Q. 'Enter Duke of Hereford, Yorke, Northumberland, Bushie and Greene prisoners.' F. adds 'Rosse, Percie, Willoughby' to make up a stage-crowd, and all edd. follow. The heading 'Bristol. Before the Castle' is derived from Capell.

5–6. *to wash...my hands* An allusion to Pilate. Cf. *Ric. III*, 1. 4. 279–80 and below 4. 1. 239–42.

11–15. *You have...foul wrongs* This accusation, to which Hol.'s statement (iii. 508/1/32) that in Ric.'s time 'there reigned abundantlie the filthie sinne of leacherie and fornication, with abhominable adulterie, speciallie in the king,' lends some countenance, is, however, quite inconsistent with the references to the relations between king and queen in the rest of the play. Nor can it be set down as a false charge, since that would ill suit with the character of Bol. Newbolt calls it 'a mere echo of Marlowe's *Ed. II*.' I suspect it to be, like l. 43 below, a loose thread from the old play. N.B. The queen in *Woodstock* (Anne of Bohemia) is no friend of Richard's minions or his extravagance. Cf. *Introd.* p. lxvi.

20. *sighed...clouds* Cf. *Rom.* 1. 1. 139 'Adding to clouds more clouds with his deep sighs.' Prob. a piece of Eliz. science, rather than a 'bold conceit' as most edd. describe it.

22–25. *signories...Disparked...imprese* v. G. On 31 March 1613, Sh. received 44 shillings in gold 'about my Lorde's impreso,' and Burbadge the like sum 'for paynting and making yt'; the payments being recorded in the accounts of the Earl of Rutland, close friend of the Earl of Southampton (Chambers, *Will. Shak.* ii. 153).

35. S.D. Q., F. give no exit; Capell first supplied one.

43. *Glendower and his complices.* Prob. another loose thread, there being nothing more about Glendower in *Ric. II*, though of course much in 1 *Hen. IV.* Clar. showed that the reference is derived from Hol. iii. 518/2/53, which, speaking of the rebellion of Glendower against Hen. IV in 1400, uses the phrase 'Owen and his vnrulie complices' and mentions that he had 'serued king Richard at Flint castell, when he was taken by Henrie duke of Lancaster.' I may add that Hol. also twice refers to Glendower as the 'capteine' of the Welshmen, which suggests the possibility that the Welsh captain in 2. 4, whose superstition closely resembles that attributed to Glendower in 1 *Hen. IV*, was originally intended to be Owen himself. Cf. *Introd.* p. lxvii.

44. S.D. Q., F. 'Exeunt.'

## 3. 2.

*Material.* Hol. as usual provides the canvas; but it is *Traïson* (p. 190) and Créton (p. 97), not Hol., which make Salisbury bring tidings of the desertion of the army. Hol. and Créton mention Sir Stephen Scroop as being with Ric. at this time; perhaps Sh. makes 'Scroop' the messenger from Bristol through confusion with *William* Scroop, the Earl of Wiltshire, whom Hol. reports as being beheaded there (cf. 3. 1 *Material*). All accounts stress Ric.'s 'vtter despaire' (Hol. iii. 499/2 marg.) and Créton notes that 'on all sides, one after another, came pouring in upon him mischief and trouble' (p. 113) which is exactly what happens in this scene.

S.D. Q. 'Enter the King/Aumerle, Carleil, &c.' F. 'Drums: Flouriſh, and Colours./Enter Richard,

Aumerle, Carlile, and Souldiers.' Capell supplied 'Coast of Wales. A Castle in View.'

1. *Barkloughly castle.* Hol. (iii. 499/1/71) speaks of 'Barclowlie castle,' which is a copyist's or printer's error for Hertlowli, which in turn is the form given to Harddlech (mod. Harlech) by the Monk of Evesham in his *Life of Richard II.* Sh.'s spelling suggests derivation from Hol. by ear rather than eye.

4–11. *Needs must...hands* Pollard (p. 69) cites this as a good example of Sh.n punctuation, in which the colons and semicolons represent 'definite instructions for the time at which these lines are to be taken.' 'Clearly,' he adds, Richard 'has sat down on a bank, and between these unrhymed couplets is caressing the earth.'

5. S.D. suggested by Pollard, v. previous note.

9. *Plays...tears and smiles* Malone writes 'There is, I believe, no image which our poet more delighted in than this.' Cf. 5. 2. 32 below; *Lear*, 4. 3. 20; *Wint.* 5. 2. 70–73; *Cymb.* 4. 2. 52 ff.; *Cor.* 1. 9. 3; *Macb.* 1. 4. 35; *Temp.* 3. 1. 75.

14–22. *But let thy spiders...enemies* Cf. *M.N.D.* 2. 2. 9–12, 21–4. Sh. can turn the same material to diverse uses!

23. *senseless* i.e. addressed to things that cannot hear it. 'This earth,' he continues, '*shall* have a feeling' etc.

24. *these stones* Prob. an echo of *Luke* xix. 40 'I tell you that, if these should hold their peace, the stones would immediately cry out,' or of *Luke* iii. 8 'God is able of these stones to raise up children unto Abraham.'

29–32. *The means...redress* F. cut these lines, prob. as Pollard (pp. 93–4) suggests, because the omission of 'if,' or some such word, in l. 30 on Sh.'s part left the sense impossibly obscure. But the cut, by removing one obscurity only added another, since Aumerle is left without any foundation for the meaning he attributes to the Bishop's speech.

29. *heaven yields* (Pope) Q. 'heauens yeeld'

30. *neglected; else, if* (Pope) Q. 'neglected. Elſe'

32. *succour* (Pope) Q. 'ſuccors'

33–35. *He means...power* Aumerle applies the touchstone of chill common sense to Ric.'s fantasies.

35. *power* (Q.) F. 'friends'—which some edd. follow.

36–53. *Discomfortable...his sin* R. Noble (pp. 37–8) cites *Job* xxiv. 13–17 as the source of ll. 36–40, 44–6, and for 'discomfortable' *Ecclus.* xviii. 14 (Geneva) 'speake no discomfortable wordes'. For the comparison of Ric. to the sun v. *Introd.* pp. xii–xiii, notes 3. 3. 63–7, 178; 4. 1. 260–62, 281–83; Spurgeon, pp. 233–35, and Reyher, *Le Symbole du Soleil dans la tragédie de Richard II* (Revue de l'Enseignement des Langues Vivantes, June 1923).

37–38. *the searching eye...lower world* It is clear, as one reads, that 'eye' should be the antecedent of 'that' in l. 38, but no one could tell this in the theatre, and Malone thought the order intended by Sh. may have been:

> That when the searching eye of heaven, that lights
> The lower world, is hid behind the globe.

40. *boldly* Q. 'bouldy' Qb 'bloudy' F. 'bloody' —which many edd. follow.

54–57. *Not all the water...the Lord* Cf. 1 *Sam.* xxiv. 6; xxvi. 9; *Rom.* xiii. 4.

55. *off from* (Q.) F. 'from'

58–61. *For every man...angel* Cf. 1 *Tamb.* 1. 2. 177–80:

> Draw forth thy sword, thou mighty man-at-arms,
> Intending but to raze my charmed skin,
> And Jove himself will stretch his hand from heaven
> To ward the blow, and shield me safe from harm.

60–61. *God...glorious angel* Cf. *Matt.* xxvi. 53 'Thinkest thou that I cannot now pray to my Father, and he shall presently give me more than twelve legions of angels?' Both passages are associated with the drawing of swords. Ric.'s belief in his semi-divine powers is spoken of in Hol. v. *Introd.* p. lii.

62. S.D. Q. 'Enter Salis.' F. 'Enter Salisbury.'

70. *twelve thousand* Acc. to Hol. iii. 499/1/45 'fortie thousand.' But historical arithmetic is of no interest to Sh.; we shall have 'twenty thousand' anon (l. 76), as the verse demands.

72. *O'erthrows* (F.) Q. 'Ouerthrowes'

76–81. *But now...my pride* 'Ric.'s highly emotional speech is in the form of a sestet' (H. Craig). Cf. note 2. 1. 9–12 and *Introd.* pp. xi–xii.

76–79. *But now the blood...pale and dead* Cf. *Introd.* pp. lx–lxi.

79. *dead* v. G.

84. *coward* (Q.) F. 'ſluggard' Both P. A. Daniel and J. C. Smith think 'sluggard' more Shakespearian.

91. S.D. Q., F. 'Enter Scroope.'

107–10. *the silver rivers...fearful land* This image is twice used in *K. John* (3. 1. 23; 5. 4. 53–7); cf. also *Ham.* 4. 5. 99, *M.N.D.* 2. 1. 90–92, etc. Spurgeon (pp. 92 ff.) finds 59 river images in Sh., 26 of them being of a river in flood. As some of these occur in *Titus*, *V.A.* and *Lucr.* she is prob. right in attributing them to memories of the Avon; but Daniel also writes (*C.W.* i. 84):

> Like to a riuer that is stopt his course
> Doth violate his bankes, breakes his owne bed,
> Destroies his bounds and ouer-runs by force
> The neighbour-fieldes, irregularly spread.

114. *female* v. G.

116. *beadsmen* v. G.

117. *double-fatal* Because the berries are poisonous, and the bows death-dealing.

*yew* The Q. sp. is 'ewe.'

122. *Bagot* Cf. notes 1. 4. 23; 2. 3. 165. As Ric. (l. 132) mentions only 'three Judases' and Aumerle does not speak of Bagot (l. 141), Theobald assumed that 'the transcribers must have blundered' here. On this Johnson shrewdly observes: 'I believe the author rather than transcriber, made a mistake.' But no one has suggested how the mistake may have arisen. It was simply, I conjecture, that Sh. identified 'Bagot' with 'the Earl of Wiltshire,' which should be taken in apposition, therefore, in this line. They are distinguished at 2. 2. 138, where Bagot goes off to Ireland and so could not be beheaded at Bristol; but Sh. has forgotten this, just as he forgets that Bagot has been beheaded in 3. 2 when he introduces him at the beg. of act 4! Cf. *Introd.* p. lxv.

129. *vipers, damned without redemption* Cf. *Matt.* xxiii. 33 and *Deut.* xx. 17.

133–34. *Would...hell,/Make...this* (Q.) F. 'Would...warre/Vpon...this Offence.' All edd. follow F., but Pollard (p. 85) writes 'The words "make peace?" are a cry of rage which can only be adequately rendered by giving to each the time of a whole foot. The next two words are pronounced slowly, and after "hell" there is a slight pause marked by the dramatic comma, and then the next line follows with a swift rush. Some one, however, as I think, whether actor, editor, or press-corrector, could only see that the middle line [i.e. l. 133] was short of two syllables, so supplied these from the opening words of the next, and made good the loss by adding a pitifully weak word at the end, thus giving the F. reading.'

153. *model* v. G. and cf. 1. 2. 28; 3. 4. 42; 5. 1. 11. 'The image was suggested...by the raised earth over graves, which appears to mark the length and breadth of the body beneath' (Clar.).

154. *as paste and cover* A metaphor borrowed from *Titus*, 5. 2. 187–90 [1950].

156. *And tell sad stories* etc. Cf. *Introd.* pp. xvii–xviii, and Cf. *Ecclesiasticus*, ch. 11, vv. 5 and 6

160–62. *within the hollow crown...sits* The image, Douce suggests, may have come to Sh. from a print in the *Imagines Mortis*, which depicts a king, sword in hand and enthroned, with a grinning skeleton rising from his crown. But it also clearly owes something to Marlowe, whose Tamburlaine holds the following colloquy with the virgins of Damascus (1 *Tamb.* 5. 2. 45–9):

*Tamb.* Behold my sword; what see you at the point?
*Virg.* Nothing but fear and fatal steel, my lord.
*Tamb.* Your fearful minds are thick and misty, then,
*For there sits Death*; there sits imperious Death,
*Keeping his circuit* by the slicing edge.

Sh. uses 'circuit' for 'crown' at 2 *Hen. VI*, 3. 1. 352. Cf. also *K. John*, 5. 2. 176 'and in his forehead sits/A bare-ribbed death.'

162. *the antic* Steevens cites 1 *Hen. VI*, 4. 7. 18 'Thou antic death, which laugh'st us here to scorn,' and Johnson notes, 'an allusion to the antick or fool of old farces, whose chief part is to deride and disturb the graver and more splendid personages.' Hence 'little scene.'

164. *breath* v. G.

166. *self and vain conceit* = empty self-conceit.

167–68. *this flesh...impregnable* Cf. *Job* vi. 12.

168. *humoured* Clar. and Herford incline to take this absolutely, in agreement with 'the king' understood. But the more direct construction seems to give a far better and grimmer sense, i.e. 'when Death has tired of his whim (which is all that the life of man is, since Death can end it when he will), he comes etc.' Cf. *M.V.* 4. 1. 43.

171. *Cover your heads* No subject might wear his hat in the royal presence.

175–77. *I live with bread...a king* The paradox of

the human frailty and divine attributes of royalty is the constant theme of Sh., as it was doubtless the standing wonder of his contemporaries. Cf. *Hen. V*, 4. 1. 247–301.

175. *I live...want* The brevity of this line adds to its solemnity by making the utterance more deliberate; cf. note ll. 133–34 above.

176. *subjected* 'with a play on the senses "liable to" and "made a subject"' (J. C. Smith).

183. *to fight* = in fighting.

184–85. *And fight...breath* Cf. *Jul. Caes.* 2. 2. 32–3:

> Cowards die many times before their deaths;
> The valiant never taste of death but once.

185. *Where* = Whereas.

186. *power* v. G.

196. *eye*, Q. 'eie:'

198. *by small and small* v. G. A grim glimpse of the procedure of the rack.

204–205. *Beshrew thee...despair!* 'This admirable stroke goes to the core of Richard's artist nature' (Herford).

207–208. *I'll hate him...comfort any more* 'This sentiment is drawn from nature. Nothing is more offensive to a mind convinced that his distress is without a remedy, and preparing to submit quietly to irresistible calamity, than these petty and conjectured comforts which unskilful officiousness thinks it virtue to administer' (Johnson)—a criticism which reveals as much of Johnson as of Sh.

210. *A king...woe obey* Boswell cites *K. John*, 3. 1. 69 'For grief is proud and makes his owner stoop' etc.

212. *ear* v. G.

218. S.D. Q. gives no exeunt.

## 3. 3.

*Material.* Hol., *Traïson* and Daniel relate that Ric., after landing in Wales (Hol. at Barclowlie; *Traïson* at Pembroke), goes to Conway Castle, which is called by some oversight 'the castell of Flint' in Hol.'s margin (iii. 499/2); that (at Bol.'s orders) Northumberland persuades Ric. to leave Conway and go to Flint, *taking an oath* that he should have safe conduct; and that on the way to Flint Ric. is ambushed and taken prisoner. It is Froissart (vi. 364) who says that Ric. rode straight to Flint and occupied it, that Bol. came and found him there, and that he entered in and persuaded Ric. to go with him to London. Yet though Sh. is closer to Froissart than to any one else here, Froissart makes no mention of North. as an actor in the scene. The play borrows North. from Hol. and uses him as a herald, omitting all reference to his treachery, prob. because such conduct would discount the favourable references to Ric. by the Percies in 1 *Hen. IV*. Yet the treachery seems at one time to have formed part of the plot (cf. notes 4. 1. 170, 235–36).

S.D. Q. 'Enter Bull. Yorke, North.' F. 'Enter with Drum and Colours, Bullingbrooke, Yorke, Northumberland, Attendants.' The heading comes from Capell.

11–13. *The time hath been...shorten you* (F.) Q. reads:

*Yorke* The time hath bin, would you haue beene ſo briefe
He would haue bin ſo briefe to ſhorten you, (with him,

Pollard (pp. 84–5), accepting F., writes:

Here also it seems fairly arguable, though not certain, that the acumen required is beyond what we have a right to assume in the editor of the F., and obliges us to presume some external help.

I suggest that the Q. compositor, slightly underestimating the amount of copy for the page, which falls in the inner forme of a sheet tightly packed throughout, was obliged to crowd this passage, overrunning 'with him' and omitting 'with you,' and that for F. the prompt-book was available. Cf. Note on the Copy, pp. 109–112 and note 3. 4. 54–7 below.

14. *taking so the head* i.e. (*a*) 'taking so presumptuous a liberty: as we talk of a runaway horse "taking its head"' (Gordon); cf. *K. John*, 2. 1. 579; (*b*) docking him of his title (J. C. Smith).

17. *mis-take: the heavens* (Rowe) Q., F. 'miſtake the Heauens' Most eighteenth-century edd. followed Rowe. The reading seems to give both better rhythm and greatly superior sense. The Q. punctuation is often scanty elsewhere; v. p. 117 'Punctuation.'

31. *lord*, (F.) Q. 'Lords,' Since Bol. is speaking to Northumberland, F. is almost certainly right.

32. *rude ribs...castle* Cf. *K. John*, 2. 1. 384 'The flinty ribs of this contemptuous city.'

33. *his ruined ears* i.e. the battered loopholes of its 'tattered battlements' (l. 52). Cf. *K. John*, 2. 1. 215 'Your city's eyes, your winking gates.'

35–38. *Henry Bolingbroke...hither come* So Q., though reading 'H. Bull....Richards hand' as one line. F. reads thus:

*Henry Bullingbrooke* vpon his knees doth kiſſe
King *Richards* hand, and ſends allegeance
And true faith of heart to his Royall Perſon: hither come

40–41. *Provided...granted* 'Provided that the repeal of my banishment and the restoration of my lands be freely granted'—a Latin construction (J. C. Smith).

47. *land*, (F.) Q. 'land:'

50. S.D. supplied by Capell.

52. *tattered* (F.) Q. 'tottered'—a mere difference of spelling. Cf. *Ham*. Q2, 3. 2. 11 'tere a paſſion to totters, to very rags.' Bol. implies that the castle may be easily taken; cf. ll. 32–4.

54–60. *Methinks...My waters* The simile gives an interesting pre-scientific account of the supposed causes and effects of a thunderstorm.

57. *heaven.* So Q.

60. *waters—on* Q. 'water's on'

61. S.D. Q. 'The trumpets ſound, Richard appeareth on the walls.' F. 'Parle without, and anſwere within: then a Flouriſh./Enter on the Walls, Richard, Carlile, Aumerle, Scroop, Salisbury.'

62–126. *See, see...kind commends* The speech-heading *Bull.* is needlessly repeated by Q. at the beg. of l. 62, while similarly *King* is repeated at the beg. of l. 127. Between these two points lie 65 ll., i.e. just about what Sh. would normally get on to one side of a leaf of foolscap (v. *Shakespeare's Hand in 'Sir Thomas More,'* p. 116). It looks therefore as if the double repetition was due to a page of the MS. having been written on a different occasion from those that precede or come after. It is the more interesting, therefore, to observe that this same passage contains a number of fossil-rhymes ('bent,' 'occident,' ll. 65, 67; 'bone,' 'done,' ll. 79, 82; 'head,' 'said,' ll. 108, 111; 'rust,' 'just,' ll. 116, 119) which like 1. 3. 184–90 suggest revision into blank verse of dialogue originally in rhyming couplets. Cf. *Introd.* p. lxxi.

63–67. *As doth...occident* Cf. *Ric. III,* 1. 1. 1–2:

> Now is the winter of our discontent
> Made glorious summer by this sun of York.

The sun was commonly the symbol of royalty with Sh. Cf. *Introd.* pp. xii–xiii, and note 3. 2. 36–53.

73. *fearful* v. G.

76. *awful* v. G.

83. *torn their souls, by turning them from us* i.e. 'have incurred the guilt of perjury by transferring their allegiance. The word "torn" would not have been used but for the jingle "torn" "turning," in which the point of the phrase, such as it is, consists' (Clar.). The use of 'torn' is not so forced as this suggests; it commonly meant 'wounded' or 'lacerated' (v. O.E.D. 'tear' 2).

86–87. *Is mustering in his clouds...pestilence* Cf. 2 *Kings* xix. 35 and *M.N.D.* 2. 1. 90; *K. John,* 5. 4. 33; *1 Hen. IV,* 1. 2. 190 [1950].

88. *children yet unborn* Cf. Daniel, *C.W.* i. 90 'The babes vnborne, shall ô be borne to bleed.'

92. *every stride...land* Cf. *C.W.* i. 90 'Stay here thy foote, thy yet vnguilty foote.'

93–94. *open The purple testament...war* The speeches of Ric. are full of Biblical echoes. Here, I think, is an allusion to *Heb.* ix which deals with the Old Testament and the New in connexion with the shedding of blood; e.g. 16, 'For where a testament is, there must also of necessity be the death of the testator'; 18, 'Whereupon neither the first testament was dedicated without blood.' Delius cites *First Part of Ieronimo,* 2. 2. 87 'Then I vnclaspe the purple leaues of war'; but as this was first printed in 1605, it may be imitated from *Ric. II.*

95–100. *But ere the crown...English blood* 'Clearly intended as an unconscious forecast of the civil wars of the next cent., like Carlisle's speech (4. 1. 136ff.)' (Herford).

97. *the flower of England's face* C. Knight cites Daniel, *C.W.* i. 121:

> And theſe beginnings had this impious warre,
> Th'vngodly bloudſhed that did so defile
> The beauty of thy fields, and euen did marre
> The flowre of thy chiefe pride ô faireſt Ile.

98. *maid-pale peace* Clar. cites 1 *Hen. VI,* 2. 4. 47:

> I pluck this pale and maiden blossom here,

of which this passage seems to be a memory.

100. *pasture's* (Theobald) Q., F. 'paſtors' Capell reads 'pastures' which all edd. now follow, though it is surely inferior to Theobald's text. No difference would be perceived upon the stage.

101. *forbid our* (F.) Q. 'forbid: our'

102. *civil and uncivil* A quibbling oxymoron: 'civil' refers to civil war; 'uncivil' = barbarous, v. G.

112. *scope* v. G.

113. *lineal* Cf. *Introd.* to *K. John*, p. xxv. The word is used here in the same unusual sense as there, and both seem to derive from *The Troublesome Reign*. For 'royalties' cf. 2. 1. 190 and G.

114. *Enfranchisement* v. G.

119. *as he is a prince, is just* (F.) Q. 'as he is princeſſe iuſt' Pollard (p. 87, cf. p. 59): 'The new Quarto [Qw] changed "princeſſe" into "a prince," and the F., by inserting "is," finally restored the line.'

136. *sooth* v. G.

137. *lesser than my name* i.e. than the name of king.

143–end. *What must the king do now?* etc. 'Richard, in his agitation, now loses his head and throws himself into his enemy's hand....Shakespeare, finely impartial as ever, takes equal pains to show us Richard's fatuity and to prevent our despising him for it' (Herford).

143–59. *What must the king...my head?* One of the passages which Pollard (pp. 69–70) notes as carefully punctuated by Sh. The Q. pointing is followed exactly.

The germ of this famous speech appears to be the following sentence in Hall's account of Ric.'s abdication:

> And then with a lamentable voyce and a sorowfull countenaunce, delyuered his sceptre and croune to the duke of Lancastre, requiryng euery persone seuerally by their names, to graunte and assente that he might liue a priuate and a solitarie life, with the swetnesse whereof, he would be so well pleased, that it should be a paine and punishement to hym to go abrode (ed. 1809, p. 12).

149. *my gay apparel* Steevens quotes Hol. (iii. 501/2/39) 'he was in his time exceeding sumptuous in apparell, in so much as he had one cote which he

caused to be made for him of gold and stone, valued at 30000 marks.' Ric.'s reputation for luxury forms, indeed, the background to the whole speech.

156. *trade* v. G.

157. *sovereign's head* Dr Johnson notes:

Shakespeare is very apt to deviate from the pathetick to the ridiculous. Had the speech of Richard ended at this line, it had exhibited the natural language of submissive misery, conforming its intention to the present fortune, and calmly ending its purposes in death.

169. *eyes!* Q. 'eies?' A query often stands for an exclamation mark in early print.

175. *a leg* i.e. an obeisance, or (as the Elizabethans called it) a 'courtesy'; cf. l. 193, and note 1. 4. 33.

176, 180, 182. *the base court* Hol. (iii. 501/2/8) 'into the vtter ward'; Froissart, 'downe into the courte' (vi. 368); *Traïson*, 'le Roy descendi du donion en la basse court' (p. 59). Cf. *Introd.* p. lix.

178–79. *Down, down...unruly jades* Reyher finely observes: 'Descendre ainsi, c'est descendre les marches du trône: c'est l'abdication, la déchéance. Il n'a pas su régner; le pouvoir royal, le char du soleil, lui a échappé et passe en des mains plus fermes. Désillusion amère, il se croyait Phébus, il n'est que Phaéton!' (*Le Symbole du Soleil dans la tragédie de Richard II*).

179. *Wanting the manage...jades* Cf. Daniel, *C.W.* i. 43:

And yet I doe not ſeeme herein to excuſe
The Iuſtices, and Minions of the king
Which might their office and their grace abuſe,
But onely blame the courſe of managing.

186. S.D. *come forth* After the fluid fashion of the Elizabethan theatre the locality changes from without the walls to within, in the base court.

187. *Stand all apart* 'So as to give a clear stage to Ric. and himself. Perhaps as Ric. descends the traverse

is opened, disclosing the rear-stage,' as the 'base-court' (J. C. Smith).

189. S.D. Q. 'he kneeles downe.' F. omits. Cf. Hol. (iii. 501/2/9):

Foorthwith as the duke got sight of the king, he shewed a reuerend dutie as became him, in bowing his knee, and comming forward, did so likewise the second and third time, till the king tooke him by the hand, and lift him vp, saieng; 'Deere cousine, ye are welcome.'

192. *Me rather had* = I had rather.

201. *strong'st* Q. (some copies) 'ſtroug'ſt'

204. *Cousin...father* Historically they were both born in 1366, and were therefore 33 years old at this time. 'But Sh. throughout the play conveys the impression that Ric. is young, Bol. middle-aged, v. 1. 3. 159; 2. 1. 69–70' (Newbolt).

209. S.D. Q. gives no exit. F. 'Flouriſh. Exeunt.'

## 3.4.

*Material.* The scene is purely fictitious. But hints may have been given by Froissart (vi. 370–71), who speaking of 'the state of quene Isabell' after the downfall of Richard, says, 'her house was newly furnisshed with ladyes and damoselles, and other offycers and servauntes; they were charged all, that in no wyse they shuld nat speke of the kynge, nat one to another'; while the following remark of King Henry, upon his triumphal entry into London, 'to the prelates, as he sat quietly upon his horse,' which *Traïson* reports (p. 93), seems to be the germ of the gardeners' speeches at ll. 29–54: 'By St George! 'twere a fine sight to see us all here assembled, provided we were all true and faithful one towards another, for certainly there are some traitors amongst us; but I vow to God that I will gather up the weeds and will clear my garden of them, and will sow good plants, until my garden shall be all clean within my ditches and walls, unless some of you repent' (trans. by B. Williams, p. 247).

S.D. Q. 'Enter the Queene with her attendants' F. 'Enter the Queene, and two Ladies.' Capell headed the scene 'Langley. The Duke of York's Garden,' inferring this from ll. 68–70 below, and from 2. 2. 118–19; 3. 1. 36. But the name Langley is not mentioned in the play; Froissart and *Traïson* state that the queen was removed to Wallingford by York; and Hol. does not say what became of her.

7–8. *measure...measure* v. G.

11. *of joy* (Rowe) Q., F. 'of Griefe' The slip may have been Sh.'s; l. 13 proves that 'joy' must be correct.

15. *being altogether had* = 'occupying my whole mind' (Clar.).

18. *complain* v. G.

21. *weep*, Q. 'weepe:'

22–23. *And I could sing...thee* i.e. 'And I could even sing for joy if my troubles were only such as weeping could alleviate, and then I would not ask you to weep for me' (Camb.). Previous edd. followed Pope, who emended 'sing' to 'weep.'

23. S.D. Q. 'Enter Gardeners.' F. 'Enter a Gardiner, and two Seruants.'

26. *pins* (F. 'Pinnes') Q. 'pines'

27. *state, for* Q. 'ſtate for'

28. *change: woe* Q. 'change woe'

*woe is forerun with woe*

The poet, according to the common doctrine of prognostication, supposes dejection to forerun calamity, and a kingdom to be filled with rumours of sorrow when any great disaster is impending' (Johnson).

29. *yon* (Qb) Q. 'yong' F. 'yond' Pollard (p. 56), defending Q., writes:

Surely the picture of the new shoots, as yet only twigs, borne down by the weight of the young green fruit, is vivid enough to stand, and it is the word 'yong' that suggested the comparison of the fruit to 'vnruly children' in the next line.

But the suggestion may have been the other way (to the proof-reader), and the particularizing 'yon' seems required by 'dangling'—the speaker points to a special tree. I conj. that Sh. wrote 'yond,' that the 'd,' accidentally set up 'p,' was corrected to 'g' on the press.

34. *too* (F.) Q. 'two' Cf. Pollard, p. 87. The Q. reading might be defended, but is prob. only an incorrect normalization of the Shakespearian sp. 'to.'

48. *hath* Q. 'htah'

51. *That seemed...up* e.g. the ivy.

54–57. *They are...year* (Capell) Q., F. divide 'They are/And...king/Oh...trimde/And...yeare.' The mislining and omission are closely paralleled at 3. 3. 11–13 (v. note). But as F. does not correct, and no space on the Q. page is saved by the irregularity, the blame prob. rests on the copy and not on the compositor, though the second 'we' may have been deleted by the corrector or proof-reader, confused by defective punctuation, which is very scanty in this scene (cf. note l. 57).

54. *They are,* Q. 'They are.'

57. *garden! We at time* (Capell) Q. 'garden at time' F. 'Garden, at time'

*at time of year* = in season.

59. *over-proud* v. G.

60. *itself.* Q. 'it ſelfe'

63. *superfluous* Perhaps this 'may be accented on the second-last syllable. Otherwise the metre is defective' (Gordon).

67. *think you then* (Pope) Q., F. 'thinke you'

68. *Depressed* v. G.

72. *pressed to death* v. G.

*speaking!* Q. 'ſpeaking' F. 'ſpeaking:'

75. *suggested* v. G.

79. *Divine* A much more solemn word then than now; a 'diviner' was a professional person with pretensions to learning.

80. *Cam'st* (Qb) Q. 'Canſt'

84. *weighed:* (F.) Q. 'weyde'

85. *lord's* F. 'Lords' Q. 'Lo.'

98–99. *What...grace the triumph* etc. 'The queen here recalls the Roman triumph' (Herford). The passage is the germ of Cleopatra's more famous outburst: *Ant. & Cleo.* 5. 2. 207–21.

101. S.D. Q., F. 'Exit.'

105–107. *rue, sour herb of grace...weeping queen* 'This passage is the best comment to Ophelia's words to the queen' (Herford), at *Ham.* 4. 5. 181.

107. S.D. Q. 'Exeunt.' F. 'Exit.'

## 4. 1.

*Material.* Hol. as usual provides the canvas, but evidently most of the other sources have also been drawn upon for the composition of this great and crucial scene, which falls into four sections: (i) 1–106, The Challenges. This incident Hol. relates as taking place, not before Ric.'s deposition, but at a meeting of parliament two days after Henry's coronation; he speaks of '20,000 pounds' and not 100,000 crowns (l. 16), and he does not introduce Percy at all (l. 44). The association of Mowbray with the crusades is derived from *Traïson* (v. note ll. 92–100); (ii) 107–61, The Bp. of Carlisle's speech. This follows the incident of the Challenges in Hol. iii. 512/2/29 but as a reply to 'The request of the commons' for Ric. to be placed upon trial, and not to Henry's assumption of the throne, which had taken place some days before. In *Traïson,* however, the two events are found in Sh.'s order and in similar proximity. But no source makes the speech introductory to the abdication as Sh. does with great dramatic effect (v. note ll. 114–49). Hol. does not mention York, but (as Reyher notes) Hall writes (ed. 1809, p. 12): 'The Duke of Lancastre the nexte daie declared al kyng Richardes hole mind to the coûcel, but especially to his vncle Edmunde duke of Yorke (whose helpe he much vsed) whiche hearyng al thynges to be in a broyle, a fewe daies before was come to London.' Froissart also writes (vi. 378): 'His uncle the duke of Yorke came to London, and the erle of Rutlande his sonne, the erle of Northumberlande, and the lorde Thomas Percy his brother; the duke of Lancastre made them good chere.' Here too is the origin of Northumberland's part (l. 150) in the scene, while possibly this Percy was mistaken for H. Percy (l. 44). The words of Carlisle are nearer to Hol. than to *Traïson*; yet the latter was clearly read for the incident, since the Fr. chronicle places the speech almost immediately after Bol.'s assumption of the throne, and gives the clue for the Abt. of Westminster being charged with Carlisle's custody, and not the Abt. of St Albans (Hall and Hol.). Carlisle's speech also owes something to Daniel (v. note ll. 121–29), though it is linked to yet another occasion in *C.W.* (iii) 162–320, The Abdication. All sources locate this in the Tower, before the meeting of parliament spoken of above. For dramatic purposes it was necessary to transfer it to parliament and combine it with episodes i and ii. This is deftly contrived by introducing York who announces that the abdication had already taken place and by Bol.'s command that Ric. be required to surrender 'in common view' so as to preclude suspicion (ll. 155–57). Hol. (iii. 503/1/65) merely states that Ric. 'being now in the hands of his enimies, and vtterlie despairing of all comfort, was easilie persuaded to renounce his crowne and princelie preheminence, so that in hope of life onelie, he agreed to all things that were of him demanded'; after which he quotes the instruments of resignation. But Froissart, and Daniel after him, describe a formal act of abdication in the hall of the Tower, and Sh.'s scene is clearly derived from one or both of them (cf. Newbolt, head-note 4. 1). Froissart's account runs as follows:

'And on a day the duke of Lancastre acompanyed with lordes, dukes, prelates, erles, barones, and knyghtes, and of the notablest men of London, and of other good townes, rode to the Towre, and there alyghted. Than kynge Rycharde was brought into the hall, aparelled lyke a kynge in his robes of estate, his septer in his hande, and his crowne on his heed. Than he stode up alone, nat holden nor stayed by no man, and sayde aloude: I have been kynge of Englande, duke of Acquytany, and lorde of Irelande, about xxii. yeres, whiche sygnory, royalte, cepter, crowne, and herytage, I clerely resygne here to my cosyn Henry of

Lancastre: and I desyre hym here in this open presence, in entrynge of the same possessyon, to take this septour: and so delyvered it to the duke, who toke it. Than kynge Rycharde toke the crowne fro his heed with bothe his handes, and set it before hym, and sayd: Fayre cosyn, Henry duke of Lancastre, I gyve and delyver you this crowne, wherwith I was crowned kyng of Englande, and therwith all the right therto dependyng. The duke of Lancastre tooke it, and the archebysshop of Caunterbury toke it out of the dukes handes' (vi. 378).

(iv) 321–34, The Abbot of Westminster's plot. This was not hatched until two months later than Bol.'s coronation (Hol. iii. 501–14). The 'sacrament' (l. 328) is mentioned by Daniel alone (*C.W.* iii. 35).

A table of the actual dates of various episodes in the scene:

| | |
|---|---|
| 29 Sept. | Abdication of Richard (Hol. 503, 2). |
| 30 Sept. | The abdication notified to parliament (*id.* 504, 2). |
| 13 Oct. | Coronation of Henry IV. |
| 16 Oct. | Bagot accuses Aumerle (Hol. 512, 1). |
| 18 Oct. | Fitzwater accuses Aumerle (*id.* 512, 1, 2). |
| 23 Oct. | Carlisle's speech (*id.* 512, 2). |
| 17 Dec. | Abbot of Westminster's plot (*id.* 514, 2, 10). |

S.D. Q. 'Enter Bullingbrooke with the Lords to parliament.' F. 'Enter as to the Parliament, Bullingbrooke, Aumerle, Northumberland, Percie, Fitz-Water, Surrey, Carlile, Abbot of Weſtminſter. Herauld, Officers, and Bagot.'

Malone first located the scene in 'Westminster Hall,' noting:

> The rebuilding of Westminster Hall, which Richard had begun in 1397, being finished in 1399, the first meeting of parliament in the new edifice was for the purpose of deposing him.

Had Sh. been aware of these facts, he would assuredly have made dramatic capital out of them.

1–106. *Call forth Bagot* etc. This episode, writes

Herford, 'leaves a strong presumption of Aumerle's guilt; but it is not definitely brought home to him, still less is he punished for it.' Moreover, Henry is unsuspicious enough to receive him alone in private in 5. 3. Clearly Sh. had little interest in the historical relevance of the scene, which was nevertheless useful for dramatic and poetic reasons, e.g. the noisy threats and altercation of the wrangling nobles (i) form an obvious contrast to the bearing of the martyr-king in ll. 162–320, (ii) strike the note of discord and disorder which supplies the burden of 1 and 2 *Hen. IV* and the main theme of the plays which succeed those, and yet (iii) re-introduce the issue of Gloucester's death, for his part in which Richard was being justly punished.

1. *Bagot* Cf. note 3. 2. 122.

S.D. Q. 'Enter Bagot.' F. omits.

9. *delivered.* So Q.

10. *dead time* = fatal (or 'gloomy') period. Cf. *K. John*, 5. 7. 65 'You breathe these dead news in as dead an ear,' and *Ham.* 1. 1. 65 'dead hour.'

12. *restful* Because 'at last free from Gloucester's intrigues' (Verity).

17–19. *Than...death* (Capell) Q., F. 'Then... adding withall,/How...death' Hanmer reads 'Than ...adding/Withal...in this/Your...death' which some may prefer, since it makes a decasyllable of l. 19. Perhaps due to crowding at the foot of a leaf in the MS.

17. *England* A trisyllable—'frequent in pre-Shakespearian drama, especially in Peele' (Herford). Cf. *Ric. III*, 4. 4. 263.

21. *my fair stars* 'The birth is supposed to be influenced by the stars, therefore our author with his usual licence takes stars for birth' (Johnson). Cf. *Tw. Nt.* 2. 5. 156 'In my stars I am above thee.'

22. *give him* (Qw) Q. 'giue them'

25. *my gage* Cf. Hol. (iii. 512/1/62) 'He appealed him of treason, offering by throwing downe his hood

as a gage to proue it with his bodie. There were twentie other lords also that threw downe their hoods.'

But the quibble in 'manual' proves that Sh. had a glove in mind. Cf. note 1. 1. 69 S.D.

*manual seal* v. G. An arrogant assertion that a challenge from him was a death-warrant. Cf. *V.A.* 516 'Set thy seal manual on my wax-red lips.' N.B. both passages refer to lips; perhaps the word 'lips' here (l. 24) recalled the image in *V.A.* to Sh.'s mind.

33. *sympathy* v. G. Often used for agreement or correspondence of any kind; cf. *Oth.* 2. 1. 232 'sympathy in years, manners, and beauties.'

40. *rapier's* An anachronism; rapiers only came into use during Sh.'s life-time.

43. *Fitzwater* (F.) Q. 'Fitzwaters' Q. prints 'Fitzwater' at l. 60, but cf. 5. 6. 12 S.D. where F. prints 'Fitzwaters' as well as Q.

52–59. *I task...such as you* One of the F. cuts. With the misprints in ll. 52, 55 of Qd, the passage may have puzzled the scribe who prepared the F. copy, though prob. as Pollard (p. 95) notes, the scene seemed too long and three challenges were thought enough. The cut also saved a small speaking part, always a nuisance to a producer.

52. *I task the earth* (Q.) Qb, w, c, d 'I take the earth' Clar. explains: 'I lay on the earth the task (of bearing the like gage).'

54–55. *As may be holloaed...sun* Cf. 1 *Hen. IV*, 1. 3. 221–22:

> But I will find him where he lies asleep,
> And in his ear I'll holla 'Mortimer.'

Perhaps both suggested by *Ed. II*, 2. 2. 126–27:

> I'll thunder such a peal into his ears
> As never subject did unto his king.

54. *As may* (Capell) Q. 'As it may'

55. *From sun to sun* (Capell) Q. 'From finne to finne'—a minim-misreading. Capell's emendation has been accepted by all. Cf. *Traïson*, p. 14 'entre deux soleilz' and *Introd.* p. lix.

57. *sets...throw* v. G. Metaphors from dicing.

60. Surrey was Ric.'s nephew and like Aumerle of the Yorkist faction. Cf. note 1. 3. 251–52.

65–66. *Dishonourable...sword* (F.) Qa–d prints in one line. Possibly regularized in prompt-book.

65. *boy* v. G.

67. *vengeance and revenge* Ceremonious tautology.

74. *in a wilderness* Cf. note 1. 1. 65.

76. *my bond* (Qw) Q. 'bond' v. Pollard, p. 60.

78. *in this new world* i.e. created by Bol.'s rebellion.

79. *appeal:* Q., F. 'appeale.'

83. *Some honest Christian trust me* etc. Cf. Hol. (iii. 512/2/17) 'throwing downe an other hood which he had borowed.'

87–89. *Repealed he shall be* etc. This rather self-righteous expression of clemency, immediately followed by the news of Mow.'s death, is prob. intended to convey the suggestion, as Kreyssig notes, that Bol. knows the facts before Carlisle speaks.

89. *he's* (F.) Q. 'he is'

92–100. *Many a time...fought so long* Cf. the sentence of banishment upon Mow. as reported in *Traïson* (pp. 22/158): 'That Thomas of Mowbray, Duke of Norfolk, shall quit the realm for the rest of his life, and shall choose whether he would dwell in Prussia, in Bohemia, or in Hungary, or would go right beyond sea to the land of the Saracens and unbelievers; that he shall never return to set foot again on Christian land,' etc. (trans. B. Williams). Cf. *Introd.* p. lix. Hol. states that the death occurred at Venice and Stow (*Annals*, 1601, p. 525) adds 'on his return from Ierusalem.'

98. *that pleasant country's earth* Cf. 'the pleasant

countree of Italy' (Hall's *Chronicle*, cited *Introd.* p. xxvi above).

103–104. *the bosom...Abraham* v. *Luke* xvi. 22. Bol. with difficulty conceals his delight.

106. S.D. Q., F. 'Enter Yorke.'

108. *plume-plucked Richard* Cf. 3. 3. 7–17, where York uses very different language. For York's entry v. note on *Material.* For 'plume-plucked' cf. *Ant. & Cleo.* 3. 12. 3.

109. *Adopts thee heir* (Qw) Q. 'Adopts the heire'

112. *of that name the fourth* (F.) Q. 'fourth of that name' Edd. try to justify Q. by making a dissyllable of 'fourth,' for which there is no parallel in Sh., except the doubtful one of 2 *Hen. VI*, 2. 2. 55. I suggest that 'the fourth' was accidentally omitted by Q. compositor, and that the line was then miscorrected in proof.

113. *In God's name...throne* Bol. takes his cue with businesslike celerity. He advances no legal claim of any kind. The abruptness of the action is noted by Créton who writes that when Bol. had received the assent to his accession by acclamation in parliament, 'This...put such a flea in his ear that without farther delay he accepted and took possession of the Crown of England' (Créton, 201/391).

114–49. *Marry...against you 'woe!'* Carlisle's speech, at once a glorification of Richard, an assertion of the doctrine of Divine Right, and a prophecy of the national disasters likely to spring from Bol.'s sacrilegious act, forms a perfect dramatic prelude to the 'Deposition' scene that follows, and one calculated to enlist the sympathies of an Eliz. audience on behalf of the fallen monarch. 'It must be observed that the Poet intends from the beginning to the end to exhibit this bishop as brave, pious, and venerable' (Johnson). The doctrine of Divine Right is expressed much more clearly and emphatically here than in Hol. or other sources, and the prophecy is Sh.'s addition (though as

Reyher notes he may have found material for it in Daniel's *C.W.* ii. 122–23, cf. also i. 89–90, 121), and looking forward to the troubles of Henry IV's reign and to the Wars of the Roses, forms a sort of preface to the whole historical dramatic cycle. Cf. *Introd.* p. xxxviii.

115–16. *Worst...truth* i.e. Though I am the least worthy of those present, yet as a priest I am bound to testify to the truth.

121–29. *What subject...not present* The influences of Hol. and Daniel are here nicely blended, as C. Knight noted, viz.:

*C.W.* iii. 22

> Neuer ſhall this poore breath of mine conſent
> That he that two and twenty yeeres hath raignd
> As lawfull Lord, and king by iuſt diſcent,
> Should here be iudgd vnheard, and vnaraignd.
> By ſubiects two [= too]: Iudges incompetent
> To iudge their king vnlawfully detaind,
> And vn-brought forth to plead his guiltles cauſe,
> Barring th'annointed libertie of lawes

and Hol. (iii. 512/2/43)

> And I assure you (said he) there is not so ranke a traitor, nor so errant a theef, nor yet so cruell a murtherer apprehended or deteined in prison for his offense, but he shall be brought before the iustice to heare his iudgement; and will ye proceed to the iudgement of an anointed king, hearing neither his answer nor excuse?

From one is taken the point about subjects and from the other that about thieves.

136–49. *let me prophesy...'woe!'* Carlisle's prophecy balances Gaunt's at 2. 1. 31 ff. and it was England's tragedy that both were right. The lines embody Sh.'s doctrine, derived immediately from Elyot's *Governour*, book i, that once disturb the sacred balance of Degree, and anarchy followed almost inevitably; cf. *Troil.* 1. 3. 81 ff. and the 'Addition' to *Sir Thomas More*.

141. *kin with kin...confound* i.e. son against father and Englishman against Englishman. Cf. *Introd.* p. xxvi, Daniel, *C.W.* i. 1. ll. 5–6:

> Whil'st Kin their Kin, brother the brother foyles,
> Like Ensignes all against like Ensignes band,

and 3 *Hen. VI*, 2. 5. 54 S.D. 'Enter a son that has killed his father'; 78 S.D. 'Enter a Father that has killed his son.'

144. *Golgotha* Cf. ll. 170–71, 239–42.

145–46. *house...division prove* Cf. *Mark* iii. 25.

145. *if you* (Qw) Q. 'if yon'

148. *Prevent't* Q., F. 'Preuent it' Jespersen (*Mod. Eng. Gram.* i. 7. 81) classes this as haplology and cites 'put't' *Lear*, 4. 6. 189 and 'let (it) go' *Cor.* 3. 2. 18. This is better than Abbott's proposal to read ''sist' for 'resist.'

152–53. *My Lord of Westminster...trial* Hall, Hol., *Traïson* all state that Carlisle is consigned to the charge of the Abbot of St Albans. But, Clar. notes:

> It appears however from Rymer (*Foedera*, viii. 150) that on the 23rd of June, 1400, he was transferred from the Tower to the custody of the Abbot of Westminster. Sh. must in this instance have consulted some other source besides his usual authority Holinshed, who does not mention his confinement in the Tower, or his transference to Westminster.

This 'other source' was almost certainly Le Beau's version of *Traïson*, which (pp. 76/228), after stating that Henry had imprisoned Exeter, Surrey, and Aumerle for 9 weeks, and that then the Abbot of Westminster became surety for them (saying to them 'You shall be entertained honourably for King Richard's sake'), immediately goes on to relate the plot at his chambers, a plot involving not only the three lords just mentioned but also 'the good Bishop of Carlisle.' To anyone reading the chronicle, the inference that Carlisle, like the three lords, had been transferred to Westminster would be natural.

154–318. *May it please* etc. This, the so-called 'Deposition' scene, was first printed in Qc (1608). For the text v. Note on the Copy, pp. 112–14. It should be noted that the punctuation of my text is here based upon that of F.

154. *May it...the commons' suit?* Hol. (iii. 512/2/29) writes:

On wednesdaie [Oct. 22, 1399] following, request was made by the commons, that sith king Richard had resigned, and was lawfullie deposed from his roiall dignitie, he might haue iudgement decreed against him, so as the realme were not troubled by him, and that the causes of his deposing might be published through the realme for satisfieng of the people: which demand was granted.

Newbolt notes that North.'s request remains unexplained till l. 222. But Bol.'s command (ll. 155–57) is a direct reply to it, and echoes the language of Hol. just quoted.

165. *knee:* F. 'Knee.' Qc 'limbes?'

167–71. *Yet I well remember...none* Cf. Hol. (iii. 512/2/38):

Which renuntiation to the deposed king, was a redoubling of his greefe, in so much as thereby it came to his mind, how in former time he was acknowledged & taken for their liege lord and souereigne, who now (whether in contempt or in malice, God knoweth) to his face forsware him to be their king.

168. *favours* Prob. a quibble; v. G.

170. *So Judas did to Christ* Cf. *Traïson* (pp. 49/198, 52/201):

The said Earl [Northumberland]...can only be likened to Judas or to Guenelon.

Then turning to his companions, who were weeping, he [Richard] said with a sigh, 'Ah! my good and faithful friends, we are all betrayed, and given without cause into the hands of our enemies; for God's sake have patience, and call to mind our Saviour, who was undeservedly sold and given into the hands of his enemies.'

v. *Introd.* pp. lviii–lix.

173. *clerk*—whose duty it was to say 'amen' after the priest's prayers.

*amen.* So F.

176. *To do...hither?* Note the sudden change of tone; it is as if a somnambulist suddenly wakes up.

178. *tired majesty* Reyher quotes Hall (ed. 1809, p. 12): 'He desyred to be disburdoned of so great a charge and so heauy a burdein.'

181. *Give me...seize the crown* Qc 'Seaſe the Crowne' 'Seize' possesses its legal sense.

182. *Here, cousin,* (Camb.) F. reads this with l. 183. Malone omitted, and read l. 183 'On this side, my hand; and on that side, thine,' remarking:

> It is evident that in the original copy, the words 'Here, cousin, seize the crown,' were misplaced, and erroneously printed—'Seize the crown. Here, cousin'; but these words being properly arranged, all the rest of the first copy is right, and I have followed it.

By 'the first copy' he means Qc, which reads:

*Rich.* Seaſe the Crowne.
Heere Cooſin, on this ſide my hand, and on that ſide yours:

and if we suppose that the prompt-book read as Malone suggests, it is easy to see how the F. text might arise through clumsy conflation on the part of the scribe preparing copy for Jaggard.

I suspect therefore that Malone's text may be correct.

184–89. *Now is this...on high* Ric. here makes use of the well-known medieval figure of Fortune's buckets. Cf. H. R. Patch, *The Goddess Fortuna in Mediaeval Literature* (Cambridge, Mass., 1927), pp. 53–4, which cites Guillaume de Machaut's *Remède de Fortune*, 969–84 (ed. Hoepffner, tome ii. pp. 35–6):

Pren moy deus sëaus en un puis,
Qu'assez bien comparer li puis:
Li uns est pleins, li autres vuis;
Et se l'un monte,

L'autre descent; tout einsi truis
Que Fortune par ses conduis
Monte l'un, l'autre avale, et puis
Rien n'i aconte

A roy, a duc, a per, n'a conte:
L'un donne honneur, et l'autre honte;
L'un desgrade; l'autre seurmonte;
C'est ses deduis;

Tout orgueil amolie et donte.
Mais Boëces si nous raconte
Qu'on ne doit mie faire conte
De ses anuis.

186. *The emptier* Johnson (who knew nothing of Machaut) comments:

This is a comparison not easily accommodated to the subject, nor very naturally introduced. The best part is this line, in which he makes the usurper the *empty* bucket.

190. *I thought...resign* The bluntness of Bol.'s speeches in this scene is noteworthy.

195. *down.* So F.

196–97. *My care...care won* 'Shakespeare often obscures his meaning by playing with sounds' (Johnson). Three senses of 'care' are involved here: sorrow, office or dominion, diligence or attention.

201. *Ay, no; no, ay;* F. 'I, no; no, I:' 'In these syllables we see the whole man' (Brandes). We also see an elaborate quibble, obscured by mod. sp. but clear in the original. This Ric. proceeds to develop in what follows: (*a*) 'No I'...'for I must nothing be,' i.e. because I = no, now I am deposed; (*b*) 'I, no'... 'Therefore no "no," for I resign to thee.' Cf. similar word-play in *Rom.* 3. 2. 47–50.

203. *undo* Another quibble, v. G.

*myself:* F. 'my ſelfe.'

206. *heart;* F. 'Heart.'

210. *duteous oaths* (F.) Qc 'duties rites' = duty's rites, which many edd. read. Cf. pp. 112–14.

215. *are made* (F.) Qc 'that ſweare'—which again many edd. read. Cf. pp. 112–14.

220. *Henry* (F.) Qc 'Harry'

222. *What more remains?* This sudden bored question, after the solemn incantation of the previous lines, is characteristic. Cf. l. 176 (note).

*No more,* F. 'No more:'

223–27. *These accusations...deposed* Hol. sets forth '33 solemne articles' relating to 'manie heinous points of misgouernance and iniurious dealings...laid to the charge of this noble prince king Richard...to the end the commons might be persuaded, that he was an vnprofitable prince to the common-wealth, and worthie to be deposed' (iii. 502/1/8).

228–29. *ravel out...weaved-up follies* Cf. *Macb.* 2. 2. 37 'Sleep that knits up the ravelled sleave of care'—the opposite process. The knots and imperfections of the thread, concealed on the reel, are seen when it is unwound.

229. *follies* (F.) Qc 'Folly'—which most edd. read.

231. *so fair a troop* Bitterly sarcastic.

232. *read a lecture of* v. G.

235–36. *And cracking...heaven* Cf. *Exodus* xxxii. 33 'Whosoever hath sinned against me, him will I blot out of my book.' This is, I suggest, a relic of North.'s perjured treachery towards Ric. in Wales, not mentioned by Sh., but made much of in *Traïson*; cf. note l. 170 above, and *Traïson*, pp. 50/199 'Northumberland, for God's sake be sure you consider well what you have sworn, for it will be to your damnation if it be untrue, and *Material* 3. 3.

237. *upon me* (F.) Qc 'vpon' Clar. quotes *Troil.* 5. 6. 10 in support of Qc.

239–42. *with Pilate...your sin.* Cf. *Matt.* xxvii. 24, 26, and *Ric. III*, 1. 4. 272–73. Reyher cites Hol. (iii. 501/1/24) 'he prophesied not as a prelat, but as a Pilat' (of the Abp. of Canterbury at Flint Castle), and Créton's *Poème sur la déposition de Ric. II* (Buchon, *Collection*, xiv. 417):

Lors dist le duc Henry moult hault aux communes de ladicte ville [viz. London]: 'Beaux seigneurs, ve-cy votre roy, or regardez que vous en ferez ne volez faire.' Et ilz respondirent à haute-voix. 'Nous voulons qu'il soit mené à Westmoustier [Westminster].' Et ainsi il leur délivra. A celle heure il me souvint-il de Pilate, le quel fist batre notre Seigneur Jhésu-Crist à l'estache, et après le fist mener devant le turbe des Juifs disant: 'Beaux seigneurs, ve-cy votre roy.' Lesquelz respondirent: 'Nous voulons qu'il soit crucifié.' Alors Pilate en lava ses mains disant: 'Je suis innocent du sanc juste.' Et ainsi leur délivra notre Seigneur. Assez semblablement fist le duc Henry quant son droit seigneur livra au turbe de Londres, à fin telle que s'ilz le faisoient mourir, qu'il peust dire: 'Je suis innocent de ce fait icy.'

Cf. also Le Beau, *Chronique* (Buchon, *Collection*, xv. Sup. ii. p. 62), and *Introd.* pp. lviii–lix.

246. *a sort of traitors* = a pack of traitors; cf. *Ric. III*, 5. 3. 316.

*here.* So F.

250. *pompous* v. G.

251. *and sovereignty* (Qc) F. 'a Soueraigntie' The F. reading is prob. a misprint. Cf. pp. 113–14.

253–55. *My lord...no man's lord* Cf. *Edward II*, 5. 1. 112–13:

*Winchester.* My lord—
*Edward.* Call me not lord; away, out of my sight!

255. *Nor no* (Qc) F. 'No, nor no' The F. reading is prob. a misprint, due to 'No, not' at beginning of the following line.

256. *No, not that name...font* Though dramatically quite obscure, this refers to the story put about by Ric.'s enemies that he was not the son of the Black Prince but the bastard of a priest in Bordeaux, and that his real name was not Richard but 'Jehan.' This story is not given either by Hall or Hol.; but is related by Froissart, who makes Bol. reveal it to Ric. in the Tower (vi. 377), and is twice spoken of in *Traïson* (64/215, 72/223). The point was first noted by W. A. Harrison in the *New Shak. Soc. Trans.* 1883. Cf. *Introd.* p. lxvii.

260–62. *a mockery king of snow...water-drops* Bol. is now the sun! and he gazes from his throne at Richard while the latter 'undoes' himself so elaborately. Cf. *Introd.* p. xii. The image was prob. suggested by 'winters' in l. 258 and by a memory of *Dr Faustus*, 5. 2. 189–90:

> O soul, be changed into little water-drops,
> And fall into the ocean, ne'er be found!—

while in turn it prob. suggested *Ham.* 1. 2. 129–30:

> O, that this too too sullied flesh would melt,
> Thaw and resolve itself into a dew.

264. *word* (F.) Qc 'name'

*sterling* v. G.

*England* (F.) Qc 'Englang'

267. *his* = its.

268. *Go some...looking-glass* Cf. this prosaic paraphrase with Ric.'s 'command a mirror hither straight,' and you get a measure of the difference between the two speakers. Ric. prob. does not expect to be taken literally.

270. *torments* (F.) Sh. often uses this form for the 2nd pers. sing. pres.

271. *Urge it no more* etc. Herford sees 'absence of personal rancour' in this. Does it not rather denote contempt?

276–86. *Give me...by Bolingbroke?* These lines are full of omissions in Qc and are also there irregularly divided. Nevertheless, ll. 285–86 (cf. note) are rightly preferred by edd. to those in F.

275. S.D. F. 'Enter one with a Glaſſe.'

276. *that glass* (F.) Qc 'the Glaſſe' 'That' suggests that the appearance of the glass is unexpected.

*and therein will I read* (F.) Qc omits.

281–83. *Was this face the face...ten thousand men?* Another reminiscence of *Dr Faustus* (5. 1. 107):

> Was this the face that launched a thousand ships?

281. *Thou dost beguile me* (F.) Qc omits.

*this face the face* (F.) Qc 'this the face'

285–86. *Was this...Bolingbroke?* (Qc) F. reads:

> Is this the Face, which fac'd ſo many follyes,
> That was at laſt out-fac'd by Bullingbrooke?—

which is obviously wrong. Cf. pp. 113–14. I conjecture that Jaggard's scribe, faced with a bad patch in Qd, thought it best to transcribe a few lines from the prompt-book and was careless.

290. *silent king* An important dramatic hint, reflecting both Bol.'s contemptuous taciturnity and Ric.'s consciousness of it. Ric. hastens to pretend that his words are only 'sport,' viz. play-acting.

291. *destroyed my face* Here 'face' stands, I take it, for 'beauty,' 'good looks,' the looks Ric. was so proud of.

292. *The shadow of your sorrow* i.e. your petulant affected sorrow, the sorrow you have played. Cf. *M.N.D.* 5. 1. 213 where the actors are called 'shadows.'

295–98. *my grief...tortured soul* Cf. *Ham.* 1. 2. 83–6.

296. *manners of lament* (Capell) F. 'manner of Laments' Qd 'manners of laments'—which all mod. edd. follow, though it is surely both ugly and awkward. I suggest that the scribe deleted the wrong 's' in his copy of Qd.

305. *I am* (F.) Qc 'why: I am'—which suggests an actor's addition.

311. *I have?* (F.) Qc 'I haue it?'

313. *Then give* (F.) Qc 'Why then giue' Cf. note l. 305.

316. *convey him to the Tower* Cf. 3 *Hen. VI*, 3. 2. 120; *Ric. III*, 1. 1. 45.

317. *convey? conveyers are you all* 'Convey' = steal, cf. *M.W.W.* 1. 3. 32. 'This pun is itself "conveyed" from *Edward II*, 1. 1. 200–201: "*K. Ed.* Convey this priest to the Tower. *Bishop.* True, true!"' (Newbolt).

318. *nimbly* Often associated with thieving; cf. *Wint.* 4. 4. 685 'A nimble hand is necessary for a cutpurse.'

319–20. *On Wednesday...prepare yourselves* (F.) Q. reads

> *Bull.* Let it be ſo, and loe on wedneſday next,
> We ſolemnly proclaime our Coronation,
> Lords be ready all.

This is a patch designed to cover the rent in the text made by the exclusion of the 'Deposition' scene. Cf. pp. 112–14.

319. *On Wednesday next* Henry was crowned on Oct. 13; cf. 4. 1 *Material.*

320. S.D. Q. 'Exeunt./Manent Weſt. Caleil, Aumerle.' F. 'Exeunt.'

321. *A woeful pageant* With the deletion of the 'Deposition' scene the Q. text presents no such pageant.

322–23. *The woe's to come...as thorn* Cf. Daniel, *C.W.* i. 90:

> The babes, vnborne, ſhall ô be borne to bleed
> In this thy quarrell, if thou do proceede.

326. *My lord* Q. prints with l. 327. F. omits.

328. *take the sacrament* R. M. Smith (*op. cit.* p. 152) notes that Daniel alone of the sources mentions this point; cf. *C.W.* iii. 34:

A ſolemne oth religiouſly they make
By intermutuall vowes proteſting there
This neuer to reueale; nor to forſake
So good a cauſe, for daunger hope, or feare:
The Sacrament the pledge of faith they take.

333–34. *I will lay...merry day* (Malone) Q., F. 'Ile lay a plot,/Shall...merrie daie.' It is poss. that Sh. intended no couplet here. The couplets at ll. 322–23, followed by blank verse, suggest revision of an original in couplets. Cf. note 3. 3. 62–126 and *Introd.* pp. lxx ff.

334. S.D. Q., F. 'Exeunt.'

5. 1.

*Material.* Except for ll. 51–2 there is nothing in this scene corresponding with any of the chroniclers. Daniel alone describes a tragic meeting between the fallen Ric. and his queen, and R. M. Smith (*op. cit.* pp. 150–51) plausibly contends that, though the two episodes are differently handled, Sh. is here borrowing from *The Civil Wars*, bk. ii. 71–98, which I print on pp. 99–106 for comparison. Reyher agrees with him, and it is difficult not to; the only alternative being to suppose that both derive independently from *Traïson's* account of the queen's leave-taking, on Ric.'s departure for Ireland, which is too far-fetched for credence.

S.D. Q. 'Enter the Queene with her attendants.' F. 'Enter Queene, and Ladies.'

2. *Cæsar's...tower* Cf. *Ric. III*, 3. 1. 68 ff. A medieval tradition, which, though Stow declared it 'of none assured ground,' lasted down to the time of Gray; cf. *The Bard*: 'Ye towers of Julius! London's lasting shame.'

*ill-erected* = built for ill ends.

3. *whose* Q. 'wohſe'

6. S.D. Q. 'Enter Ric.' F. 'Enter Richard, and Guard.'

8. *my fair rose* v. *Introd.* p. lxi.

9–10. *dissolve...fresh again* Cf. *Shrew*, 2. 1. 174

'As morning roses newly washed with dew' and *Ham.* 1. 2. 130 'resolve itself into a dew' (v. note 4. 1. 260–62 above).

11–15. *Ah, thou...alehouse guest* Cf. a similar hysterical apostrophe in *Rom.* 3. 2. 80–5.

11. *thou, the model...stand* i.e. like the outline of the walls where Troy once stood, or 'thou type of ruined greatness'; v. G. 'model.'

12. *map of honour* i.e. the mere outline of glory. 'Map' and 'model' both = representations in little.

*tomb* Because he had ceased to be 'King' Richard.

13–15. *inn...alehouse* Ric. is the 'beauteous inn,' Bol. the common 'alehouse.' The image is founded upon an unexpressed quibble on 'entertain,' which = (*a*) receive a guest, (*b*) harbour a feeling or thought. Cf. 2. 2. 7–9 where the same metaphor occurs. Clar. quotes Beaumont and Fletcher's *The Lovers' Progress*, 5. 3 (a clear echo of this passage):

and 'tis my wonder,
If such misshapen guests as Lust and Murder,
At any price, should ever find a lodging
In such a beauteous inn.

Cf. note 1. 1. 65 above; either Beaumont or Fletcher seems to have been re-reading *Ric. II* while they were writing *The Lovers' Progress.*

24. *new world's* i.e. heavenly.

25. *throwen* Q. 'throwne' F. 'ſtricken' 'The reading of Q., which is supported by 3. 4. 66, requires us to make either "here" or "thrown" dissyllabic' (J. C. Smith). The sp. 'throwen,' a common one in the sixteenth century, makes all well.

26–28. *What...in thy heart* Craig cites *C.W.* ii. 78:

Let me not see him, but himself; a King:
For so he left me; so he did remoue, etc.

27–28. *Transformed...deposed/Thine* (Pope) Q., F. 'Transformd...Bullingbrooke,/Depoſde thine'

28. *hath he....heart?* Clar. suspects corruption. But the heart was the seat of courage (from 'cor' = heart). Cf. *M.W.W.* 2. 1. 202–203 ''tis the heart, Master Page—'tis here, 'tis here.'

29–31. *The lion dying....o'erpowered* Cf. *K. John*, 3. 1. 258–59 'thou mayst hold...A chaféd lion by the mortal paw,' and *Edward II*, 5. 1. 11–14:

> But when the imperial lion's flesh is gored,
> He rends and tears it with his wrathful paw, etc.

31. *To be* = At being.

32. *Take...rod* (Q.) F. 'Take thy Correction mildly, kiſſe the Rodde,' All edd. follow F., but as Pollard (pp. 56–7) shows Q. gives the better reading.

34. *the king of beasts* (Q.) Qb, F. 'a King of Beaſts' Malone restored Q., but Camb. reverted to F. because of Ric.'s rejoinder, and even Pollard (p. 57) writes: 'Frankly, B's [i.e. Qb's] reading is an improvement.' But does not the difference between the Queen's 'the' and Ric.'s 'a' mark just the distinction between her spirited exhortation and his resignation? She accents 'king' and he 'beasts.'

37. *sometimes* (Q.) Qw 'ſometime' which all edd. follow. Cf. 1. 2. 54; 5. 5. 75; and Pollard, p. 60.

41–42. *tell thee tales...betid* Cf. 3. 2. 156, and *Introd.* p. xvii.

41. *thee* (Qw) Q. 'the'

43. *quit their griefs* = 'cap their tragic tales' (Herford), v. G. 'quit.'

44. *fall* (F.) Q. 'tale' After 'tell' and 'tales' (l. 41) the Q. 'tale' is very weak; but 'fall' might easily be misread as 'tale'; and 'fall,' which Malone preferred (quoting *Hen. VIII*, 2. 1. 135–36 'And when you would say something that is sad,/Speak how I fell'), makes an excellent reading.

46–50. *the senseless brands...king* Cf. *K. John*, 4. 1. 105–11; *Temp.* 3. 1. 18–19.

50. S.D. Q. 'Enter Northum.' F. 'Enter Northumberland.'

51–52. *My lord...Tower* Cf. Hol. iii. 507/2/32.

53–54. *there is order...France* Unhistorical; Bol. retained Isabel for some months; sending her back in June 1401.

55–65. *Northumberland...throne* One of the link passages with *Henry IV*. K. Henry quotes ll. 55–9 at 2 *Hen. IV*, 3. 1. 70–77, though not exactly, the emptiness of ll. 57–8 being too much for Sh. who compresses them into one line.

55–56. *thou ladder...my throne* Cf. *Jul. Caes.* 2. 1. 22, and Daniel, *C.W.* i. 74, ll. 3–4:

> Who will throw downe himſelfe for other men
> That make a ladder by his fall to clime?

and again ii. 15, ll. 7–8:

> Th'aſpirer once attaind vnto the top
> Cuts off thoſe meanes by which himſelfe got vp.

60–68. *Though he divide...death* Reyher cites Daniel, *C.W.* ii. st. 2 and 3.

62. *And he* (Rowe) Q., F. 'He'—'a necessary emendation' (Pollard, p. 57).

*knowest* (Q.) Qb 'know'ſt'—which edd. follow (v. Pollard, pp. 57–8).

66. *men* (Q.) F. 'friends'

75. *a kiss* A kiss formed part of the marriage service in old times.

80. *Sent back...day* i.e. her returning is like autumn or winter.

*Hallowmas* (Malone) Q., F. 'Hollowmas' i.e. Nov. 1; in Sh.'s time 13 days nearer the winter solstice than now.

88. *be ne'er the near* 'To be "never the nigher," or as it is commonly spoken in the midland counties, "ne'er the ne'er," is, to make no advance toward the good desired' (Johnson).

95. *dumbly part* Reyher quotes *Edward II*, 1. 4. 134:

Therefore, with dumb embracement, let us part.

101. *make woe wanton* Cf. 3. 3. 164.

102. *the rest let sorrow say* Cf. *Ham.* 5. 2. 356 'the rest is silence.'

S.D. Q., F. 'Exeunt.'

## 5. 2.

*Material.* (i) Ric.'s ride into London. ll. 1–40. Smith (pp. 147–50) traces this to Daniel (*C.W.* ii. 66–70), and Reyher suggests that the description in *Traïson* (62/212–64/215) lies behind both. Its most interesting passage runs: 'And, as he [Richard] rode through London on a little horse on his way to prison, they kept an open space round him, that every one might see him; and there was a boy behind him, who pointed him out with his finger, saying, "Behold King Richard, who has done so much good to the kingdom of England!" It is true that some pitied him much, and others were exceedingly glad, cursing him loudly in their language, and saying, "Now are we well revenged of this wicked bastard who has governed us so ill." And in this manner was he taken to the Tower of London.' Froissart declares that Bol. did not bring Ric. through London; but his accounts of Bol.'s other triumphal rides into London (viz. on his return from banishment, and after his coronation) have undoubtedly contributed touches to York's description and to that in Daniel, touches which, it should be noted, do not always coincide. Thus, Froissart (vi. 380) and Daniel (ii. 74) both speak of Bol.'s 'white courser,' but whereas Sh.'s ll. 15–16 clearly derive from 'the streates hanged as he passed by' (Froissart, vi. 380), Daniel has nothing corresponding with this point.

(ii) Aumerle and the sealed bond. ll. 41–end. Reyher shows that this is more likely to be based upon 'le récit si vivant et dramatique de Hall' than the tame abridgement of Hol. He also shows that Hall here follows *Traïson* closely. Both state that York is 'pledge' (cf. l. 44) for Aumerle, and both say that the son rode quicker than his old father (ll.

114–15); but whereas Hall says that the bond was detected sticking out of Aumerle's 'bosom' (cf. l. 56), *Traïson* (p. 80) says that as he sat at table with his father 'il mist la lectre de leur conseil deuant lui.' Hall must therefore be regarded as the main source, though touches here and there are, as usual, derived from Daniel. None of the sources introduces the Duchess, cf. note l. 90.

S.D. Q. 'Enter Duke of Yorke and the Dutcheſſe.' F. 'Enter Yorke, and his Ducheſſe.' The heading 'The Duke of York's palace' comes from Pope.

6. *Threw dust and rubbish* Cf. l. 30 and 2 *Hen. IV*, 1. 3. 103. Nothing in the sources about this.

8–9. *a hot and fiery steed...seemed to know* Cf. l. 19 'his proud steed's neck' and 5. 5. 78–84, where it appears that this horse, which bore Bol. 'so proudly as if he disdained the ground,' was Ric.'s favourite 'roan Barbary.' Had Sh. been conscious of this here, York must surely have made use of it, since it would have added much to the pathos of the scene he describes. Cf. *Material* 5. 5.

11. *thee* (F.) Q. 'the'

12. *spake*, Q. 'ſpake:'

15–16. *all the walls...had said* Cf. note on *Material* (i) above. Malone writes:

> Our author probably was thinking of the painted clothes that were hung in the streets, in the pageants that were exhibited in his own time; in which the figures sometimes had labels issuing from their mouths, containing sentences of gratulation.

17. *thee* (F.) Q. 'the'

23–36. *As in a theatre...pitied him* 'The painting of it is so lively, and the words so moving, that I have scarce read anything comparable to it in any other language' (Dryden, *Preface to 'Troilus and Cressida,' Essays of John Dryden*, vol. i, p. 226, ed. by W. P. Ker).

23–28. *As in a theatre...scowl* Cf. Daniel, ii. 70:

> Behind him all aloofe came penſiue on
> The vnregarded king, that drooping went
> Alone, and but for ſpight ſcarce lookt vpon.

28. *Richard* (F.) Q. 'gentle Richard' The excision is a decided improvement, the epithet being extra-metrical in Q. and repeated in l. 31.

*Richard;* Q. 'Ric.' F. 'Richard:'

32. *His face...smiles* Cf. note 3. 2. 9.

35–36. *The hearts...pitied him* Cf. *M.V.* 4. 1. 30–33:

> And pluck commiseration of his state
> From brassy bosoms and rough hearts of flint,
> From stubborn Turks and Tartars, never trained
> To offices of tender courtesy.

Cf. also Créton (p. 116) 'There lives not a man so hard-hearted or so firm, who would not have wept at sight of the disgrace that was brought upon him.'

36. *barbarism itself* = even savages.

38. *To whose high will...contents* = To whose high will we bow in calm contentment. 'This compression of style, which gives the effect as already existing in the causal process, is characteristic of Sh. It is seen in its simplest form in such phrases as "pale Fear," i.e. Fear that makes men pale' (Gordon).

40. S.D. F. 'Enter Aumerle' Q. omits. Camb. for some reason transferred the S.D. to l. 45.

41–43. *Aumerle...Rutland now* Cf. Hol. iii. 513/2/1:

> it was finallie enacted, that such as were appellants in the last parlement against the duke of Glocester and other, should in this wise following be ordred. The dukes of Aumarle, Surrie, and Excester there present, were iudged to loose their names of dukes, togither with the honors, titles and dignities therevnto belonging.

46–47. *Who are...spring?* 'What favourites are blooming in the sun of Bolingbroke?' (J. C. Smith). 'Bol. has already been compared to the sun melting winter snow (4. 1. 261)' (Clar.). Cf. *Introd.* pp. xii–xiii.

48. *nor I...care not* Rowe omitted the 'not'; but cf. the double negative at 4. 1. 255.

50. *bear you well* 'Conduct yourself with prudence' (Johnson).

51. *cropped* i.e. beheaded.

52. *do these...hold?* (Q.) F. 'Hold thoſe Iuſts & Triumphs?'—which all edd. follow. But cf. note l. 57. Pollard (p. 86) writes:

York's speech begins with a rhymed couplet rounding off the previous colloquy. Then come a long line and three short ones in which the dramatic tension and with it the dramatic rhythm are completely relaxed, to be resumed at full pressure when next York speaks.

56. *hangs* 'The seals of deeds were formerly impressed on slips or labels of parchment appendant to them' (Malone). The 'bond' was in Aumerle's doublet, and the seal, red and therefore likely to catch the eye, dangled outside—a good point for the theatre.

57. *Yea...the writing* 'Such harsh and defective lines as this, are probably corrupt' (Johnson). Upon which Malone comments: 'Perhaps, like many other speeches in this scene, it was not intended for verse.'

65. *bond* (F.) Q. 'band' Cf. l. 69.

67. *Bound to himself!* One does not make out bonds to oneself. Any bond into which Aum. had entered would be in the safe keeping of his creditor.

71. S.D. Q. 'He pluckes it out of his boſome and reades it.' F. 'Snatches it.' It is noticeable that Q., which hitherto has been scanty of S.D.s, is from now onwards fuller than is usual in dramatic texts.

74. S.D. 'shouts' Neither Q. nor F. gives any S.D. between ll. 71 and 84. Mod. edd. follow Capell and

read 'Enter a Servant' at this line, and 'Exit Servant' at l. 77. But the delay with the boots and York's consequent impatient cries add to the life of the scene. Cf. the opening of 4. 1 in *Shrew*.

78. *by my life, by my troth* (Q.) F. 'my life, my troth' Pope and some others 'by my life, my troth' Cf. note l. 57.

81. *matter, Aumerle?* (Q.) F. 'matter, Sonne?'

84. S.D. Q. 'His man enters with his bootes.' F. 'Enter Seruant with Boots.'

90. *more sons* The historical York had another son at least, and Aumerle was his son by a former wife. 'But Sh. ignores all that for the sake of sc. iii' (Newbolt).

94. *thee* Q. 'the'

97. *a dozen* Hol., Hall and *Traïson* speak of only six who sign the bond.

*the sacrament* Cf. note 4. 1. 328.

98. *interchangeably...hands* Hol. (iii. 514/2/61) describes the document as 'an indenture sextipartite... sealed with their seales, and signed with their hands, in the which each stood bound to other'; and Clar. quotes 1 *Hen. IV*, 3. 1. 80–81:

> And our indentures tripartite are drawn,
> Which being sealed interchangeably.

The indenture was divided into six parts, each conspirator keeping one part and each part being signed and sealed by all.

*their* (Qb) Q. 'there'

99–100. *He shall...him?* (F.) Q. divides 'He... heere,/Then...him?'

101–102. *Away...him* (Q.) F. prints as prose.

102–103. *Hadst...pitiful* (Rowe) Q., F. divide 'Hadſt...done,/Thou...pittifull.' The irregular lining in ll. 99–103 suggests revision in the margin of the MS. Cf. *M.N.D.* pp. 80–86.

104. *thy* Q. 'rhy'

108–109. *as a man...or any* (Q. some copies) Other copies 'as any man...or a' For a poss. explanation v. Pollard, p. 36.

110. S.D. Q., F. 'Exit.'

111. *mount thee upon his horse* Newbolt suggests that this 'odd touch' may be due to a misreading of Hol.'s (iii. 515/1/32) 'The earle of Rutland...tooke his horsse, and rode another waie to Windsore in post, so that he got thither before his father.' But cf. note ll. 112–15.

112–15. *Spur post...as fast as York* Clar. first pointed out that not Hol. (v. note l. 111) but Hall must be the source for this; his text runs (ed. 1809, p. 18)

The duke of Aumerle seyng in what case he stode toke his horse and rode another way to Windsor, riding in post thither (whiche his father being an olde man could not do).

The parenthesis suggested ll. 114–15.

112. *Spur post,* (F.) Q. 'Spur, poſt,' 'Post' is an adverb, cf. above note.

117. S.D. Q. gives none. F. 'Exit.'

## 5. 3.

*Material.* (i) ll. 1–22. Link scene with 1 *Hen. IV*. Prince Hal was actually 12 years old at this time. The stories of his wildness are traditional, but are referred to by Hol. and Stow. (ii) ll. 23–end. The rest of the scene seems to have been suggested by Hall, who gives some of the conversation between Aum. and Ric. which Hol. does not. In Hall it is the gates of the castle that Aum. has locked. The part of the Duchess is dramatic invention.

S.D. Q. 'Enter the King with his nobles.' F. 'Enter Bullingbrooke, Percie, and other Lords.' Q. now heads Bol.'s speeches 'King H.' or 'King.' It is noteworthy that F. still reads 'Enter Bullingbrooke' and continues to print '*Bul.*' at the head of his speeches. Q. returns to 'Bullingbrooke' in 5. 6 S.D though still heading the speeches 'King.' The Q. stickler for historical accuracy (assuredly not Sh.) makes things awkward for the theatre since Burbadge is 'Bullingbrooke' throughout the play. Theobald headed the scene 'The Court at Windsor Castle.'

1–19. *Can no man...challenger* Cf. *Introd.* pp. lxxi–lxxii.

1. *tell me* (Q.) F. 'tell'—which the eighteenth-century edd. read; it accords better with the almost infantile smoothness of the verse that follows.

*unthrifty* v. G.

10. *While* (Pope) Q., F. 'Which'—which all mod. edd. follow. Malone approved 'the correction,' necessary to render 'so dissolute a crew' explicable. The assumed misprint is one of a common type.

11–12. *Takes...crew* (F.) Q. prints in one line. It is the single instance of overrunning in ll. 1–19 and 'so dissolute a crew' looks like a piece of patchwork by Sh. Cf. *Introd.* p. lxxiii.

16–18. *His answer was* etc. This is unlike the Prince of *Henry IV*, who possesses a sense of decency and always keeps the life of Eastcheap distinct from that of the Court.

20–22. *As dissolute...here?* The verse suddenly becomes rougher—and much more vigorous! I suspect the adapting hand of Sh., at the junction between two dramatic episodes of the old play. Cf. *Introd.* p. lxxiii.

22. S.D. Q. 'Enter Aumerle amazed.' F. 'Enter Aumerle.' For 'amazed' v. G.

24–25. *What...wildly?* Q. overruns 'ſo wildly' instead of printing it in a separate line; poss. because the compositor was short of space at the foot of a page. Cf. note 3. 3. 11–13. F. divides at 'ſtares/And'

28. S.D. Q., F. give no 'exeunt'; first supplied by Hanmer.

30. S.D. Rowe supplied 'kneels' which the sense requires.

*knees grow to the earth* Cf. ll. 93, 106.

31. *My tongue...mouth* Cf. *Ps.* cxxxvii. 6.

34. *If on the first* Cf. l. 20 above ('As dissolute as desperate—yet through both'), where substantives are supplied from the adjectives. Here similarly some sb. like 'condition' is to be understood. Cf. 2. 3. 107.

36. *that I may* (Qb) Q. 'that May'

38. S.D. Q. 'The Duke of Yorke knokes at the doore and crieth.' F. 'Yorke within.'

41. *make thee safe* i.e. put thee out of harm's way. Cf. *Macb.* 3. 4. 25 'But Banquo's safe?' and G. 'safe.'

S.D. Johnson reads 'Drawing.'

43. *secure* v. G.

44. *speak treason to thy face* i.e. call you a fool to your face.

45. S.D. F. 'Enter Yorke.' Q. gives no entry.

46–47. *What is...danger* (Q., F.) Capell and all mod. edd. divide 'What is...speak,/Recover...danger' The original arrangement seems as good.

57. *Forget to pity* = Forget the pardon you have given. An unusual sense of 'pity.' Cf. 3 *Hen. VI*, 2. 6. 74 'Thou pitied'st Rutland, I will pity thee.'

61. *sheer...fountain* Steevens cites *Faerie Queene*, 3. 2. 44 'a fountain sheer' and Golding's trans. of Ovid's *Metamorphosis*, bk. iv 'The water was so pure and sheere.'

61–62. *fountain...muddy* Cf. *Shrew*, 5. 2. 142–43 'A woman moved is like a fountain troubled, Muddy' etc.

68. *And he* (Qw) Q. 'An he'

72. *life—giving* Q. 'life giuing' F. 'life, giuing'

74. S.D. F. 'Dutchesse within.'—after l. 73. Q. omits.

75. *voiced* (Qw) Q. 'voice'—and *e:d* misreading ('voice' for 'voicd').

79–86. *Our scene...confound* This farcical upshot is quite in the manner of *The Troublesome Reign*. Cf. 1. i. 412–15 of that play:

Then Robin Fauconbridge I wish thee ioy,
My Sire a King, and I a landles Boy.
Gods Ladie Mother, the world is in my debt,
There's something owing to Plantaginet.

80. '*The Beggar and the King*' the title of the well-known ballad, *King Cophetua and the Beggar-maid* (cf. *L.L.L.* 4. 1. 66).

85. *This...sound* Cf. *Matt.* xviii. 8.

86. S.D. F. 'Enter Dutcheſſe.' Q. omits.

88. *Love...can* i.e. 'If York does not love his own flesh and blood he cannot love another, he cannot love his King' (Clar.).

93. *walk upon my knees* This has puzzled edd., many of whom follow F. which reads 'kneele' for 'walk.' But to walk upon one's knees was (and still is in Catholic countries) a common form of penance. Cf. the Shakespearian Addition to *Sir Thomas More*, ll. 128–29 'and your vnreuerent knees/make them your feet to kneele to be forgyven.'

97–104. *Unto my mother's...all beside* v. *Introd.* p. lxxi.

99. *Ill...grace* F. omits—prob. by accident, v. Pollard, p. 95.

101. *His eyes...jest* As it stands the line is a jerky alexandrine: Capell omitted the 'in,' and the suggestion is tempting.

106. *shall* (F.) Q. 'ſtill' Pollard (p. 87) writes: 'I am not sure that the slight absurdity of this...as it stands in the Q. must not be debited to Sh. himself'—or, I may add, to his predecessor. Cf. *Introd.* p. lxxi.

109–10. *have...have* The second 'have' seems to have been caught by the compositor's eye from the line above and set up in place of a word, such as 'crave' (S. Walker), that rhymes with it.

115. *I never longed...till now* Referring to the 'longings' before child-birth.

119. *pardonne moy* I retain the Q. form; 'moy'

rhyming with 'destroy' (l. 120). 'Pardonnez-moi' is, of course, a polite way of refusing a request.

122. *sets* (Q., F.) A common form of the 2nd pers. sing. pres.

*sets the word...word* Cf. note 5. 5. 13–14, where the expression is repeated.

125. *to speak* i.e. to speak pity.

126. *thy piteous* (Q. some copies). Other copies 'this piteous'

127. *pierce* Pronounced 'perse.' Cf. *L.L.L.* 4. 2. 87 'Master Person—quasi pierce-one.' For 'rehearse' v. G.

135–36. *With all...him* (Pope) Q., F. 'I pardon him with al my heart.' If 'With all my heart I pardon him' were written in one line in the MS., the compositor or corrector might have re-arranged it, in order to bring 'heart' to the end, and rhyme with 'art.' Or Sh. himself may have overlooked the rhyme in hasty transcription; cf. note 4. 1. 332–34.

137. *our trusty brother-in-law* Edd. explain, rightly, that this is John, Earl of Huntingdon who, Hol. tells us, proposed the tournament at Oxford. But, as there is no other mention of him in the text, the reference here is entirely obscure. Cf. *Introd.* p. lxvii.

139. *Destruction...heels* Cf. *Ric. III*, 4. 1. 40 'Death and destruction dog thee at the heels.'

140. *order several powers* i.e. direct different bodies of troops.

144. *cousin too* (Q. 1634; Theobald) Q., F. 'coufin' The emendation was accepted as Theobald's by edd. until Camb. noticed it in Q. 1634. It completes the line; and though 'cousin too, adieu' is very ugly, it is not at all impossible for this scene.

145. *prove you true* Aumerle, as Duke of York, fell at Agincourt; and Sh. spends himself lavishly in describing his death at *Hen. V*, 4. 6. 3–32.

146. S.D. Q. 'Exeunt. Manet fir Pierce Exton, &c.' F. 'Exeunt./Enter Exton and Seruants.'—but

without marking any change of scene. J. C. Smith, the only ed. apparently to observe this interesting S.D., supposes that it merely indicates the Eliz. practice of treating scenes as continuous. But I know of no parallel of a 'manet' for a character not yet spoken of. Cf. *Introd.* pp. lxviii–lxx.

## 5. 4.

*Material.* A blend of Hol. and Daniel, v. *Introd.* pp. xli–xlii.

S.D. v. note 5. 3. 146 S.D.

7. *wishtly* (Q.) F. 'wiſtly'—which edd. read. But 'wishtly' or 'wishly' is a Tudor and Stuart word (v. O.E.D.), prob. derived from 'wistly' under the influence of 'wish' (v. G.); cf. 'wiſht' in quotation from Daniel (p. xli), 'wistlie on him gazed' *Lucr.* 1355, 'wistly to view' *V.A.* 343, and 'wistly' *Pass. Pilg.* 82—the last three all meaning earnestly or longingly.

11. *rid* v. G.

S.D. F. 'Exit.' Q. gives none.

## 5. 5.

*Material.* In *C.W.* (iii. 65–70), as here, 'Ric. engages in a soliloquy comparing and contrasting the state of the King and of a lowly man...; and in both [versions] a servant rushes in with news from the court, followed instantly by Exton with his murderers' (R. M. Smith, p. 153). The episode of 'roan Barbary' may have been suggested, as Steevens first noted, by the story in Froissart (vi. 369) of the greyhound, Mathe, which deserted Ric. and fawned upon Bol. in Flint Castle. But, with his known dislike of dogs and insistence upon their fawning nature (v. 3. 2. 130 and cf. Spurgeon, pp. 195–98), this is just the tale Sh. himself would have been likely to seize upon and elaborate, while the fact that he makes no capital out of the Barbary version at the opening of 5. 2 suggests that he did not realize the force of the story until he reached 5. 5, or in other words until he found it in the old play which he was revising (v. note 5. 2. 8–9). The murder of Ric. is based upon Hol. or Hall, the latter giving fuller details, especially of Exton's remorse, of which Sh. makes little use (cf. note l. 114).

S.D. Q. 'Enter Richard alone' F. 'Enter Richard.'

1–66. *I have been studying* etc. The soliloquy, though very different in theme, clearly belongs to the same period as those of the Bastard in *K. John*.

5. *hammer it out* i.e. worry it out. A common Eliz. expression.

6. *My brain...female to my soul* Cf. *K. John*, 5. 7. 2–3:

> his pure brain
> (Which some suppose the soul's frail dwelling-house).

Sh. was at this time evidently reading or thinking about what we should now call psychology.

8. *still-breeding* = ever-breeding.

9. *this little world* Most take this to refer to the human microcosm, i.e. to himself, but ll. 1–2, 21 identify the 'world' with the prison.

10. *humours* v. G.

11–17. *the better sort...needle's eye* It seems to have escaped notice that these remarkable reflections might have been suggested by 'The archbishop of Canturburie his oration,' delivered to parliament after the deposition of Ric., and reported at length by Hol. iii. 506/1/25, which, with many quotations from the Vulgate, likens Ric. to a child and concludes thus (iii. 507/1/46):

> In sted of a child wilfullie doing his lust and pleasure without reason, now shall a man be lord and ruler, that is replenished with sapience and reason, and shall gouerne the people by skilfull doome, setting apart all wilfulnesse and pleasure of himselfe. So that the word that I began with may be verified of him, *Ecce quia vir dominabitur in populo.*

12. *As* = Such as.

13–14. *do set...the word* This repeats 5. 3. 122.

Perhaps it was in realization of this that F. here reads 'the Faith it ſelfe/Againſt the Faith.' But the repetition betokens careless haste on Sh.'s part. He seems to have unconsciously transferred the phrase from 5. 3 where he found it in the old play.

13. *scruples* = doubts.

15. *'Come, little ones'* *Matt.* xix. 14.

16–17. *'It is...needle's eye'* *Matt.* xix. 24. The two texts are from the same chapter of the Word (R. Noble). Cf. *K. John*, 5. 4. 11 'Unthread the rude eye of rebellion.'

17. *postern* v. G.

*needle* Pron. 'neeld'; cf. *M.N.D.* 3. 2. 204; *K. John*, 5. 2. 157.

25. *silly* v. G.

26. *refuge their shame* i.e. solace their sense of shame in the thought.

27. *sit* (Qw) Q. 'ſet' Cf. note 1. 2. 47, and Pollard, p. 61.

*there:* Q. 'there.' F. 'there;'

31. *Thus play I...people* Cf. *A.Y.L.* 2. 7. 142 'And one man in his time plays many parts.' Dowden thought the whole soliloquy 'might almost be transferred, as far as tone and manner are concerned, ...to Jaques.'

35. *king;* Q. 'king,' F. 'King:'

36–37. *kinged...unkinged* Cf. 4. 1. 220; *K. John*, 2. 1. 371 'kinged of our fears' and *Hen. V*, 2. 4. 26 'so idly kinged.' The verb is not found elsewhere in Sh.

40. *pleased...eased* 'The internal rhyme suggests a doggerel epitaph' (J. C. Smith).

41. S.D. Q. 'the muſike plaies' F. 'Muſick.'

49. *waste me* Because the sighs etc. that Time brought him cause loss of blood, acc. to the physiology of the day.

51–52. *jar Their watches...outward watch* i.e. His sad and wakeful thoughts, each ending with a sigh, follow one another endlessly like the minutes which, with a succession of ticks, move ever round the face of a clock. *Watches* = 'the marks of the minutes on a dial-plate' (Schmidt), with a glance at 'watch' = sleeplessness. The *outward watch* = the dial. N.B. Seconds were apparently not marked upon clocks in Sh.'s day.

52–54. *mine eyes...from tears* The likeness of a clock-face to an eye suggests a comparison between the marks on the dial which the minute-hand keeps pointing to and passing over and the tears that every minute spring to the eye and are as often wiped away by the finger. Apart from their other likenesses, *K. John* and *Ric. II* possess one main poetic theme in common, that of Grief, upon which the fancy of Sh. plays many variations.

54. *tears.* So Q.

62. *holp madmen to their wits* Generally taken as a reference to Saul; but there were classical examples also, and the notion was an accepted one in Sh.'s day; cf. Burton, *Anatomy of Melancholy*, pt. ii. sec. ii. mem. 6, subsec. 3.

66. *a strange brooch* = a rare jewel or ornament. Cf. *Ham.* 4. 7. 94–5. A brooch, worn in the hat, made a particularly conspicuous jewel.

S.D. Q. 'Enter a groome of the ſtable.' F. 'Enter Groome.' This visit of the faithful groom may have been suggested by the 'constant servant' to whom most of the chroniclers refer, viz.:

> Jenico Dartois a Gascoigne that still ware the cognisance or deuise of his maister king Richard, that is to saie, a white hart, and would not put it from him, neither for persuasions nor threats....This man was the last...which ware that deuise, and shewed well thereby his constant hart toward his maister, for the which it was thought he should haue lost his life, but yet he was pardoned, and at length reconciled to the dukes fauour, after he was king (Hol. iii. 500/2/58).

68. *ten groats too dear* A quibble upon 'royal' or 'rial' (= 10*s.*) and 'noble' (= 6*s.* 8*d.*). As the 'groat' = 4*d.*, the difference between 'royal' and 'noble' was 40*d.* or 'ten groats.' Ric. means, therefore, that 'the cheapest' of them (i.e. himself, the prisoner) has become the 'peer' or equal of a groom. Edd. explain 'the cheapest of us' as the 'noble'; but what is the point of that? Ric. is emphasizing his own depreciation; to call him 'royal' is to price him 'ten groats' too high. Sh. has similar jests upon coins in *K. John*, 1. 1. 94, 143, 153. Clar. quotes the following story of Queen Elizabeth from Hearne's *Discourse of some Antiquities between Windsor and Oxford*:

Mr John Blower, in a sermon before her majesty, first said: 'My royal Queen,' and a little after: 'My noble Queen.' Upon which says the Queen: 'What, am I ten groats worse than I was?'

*dear.* So Q.

76. *erned* Q. 'ernd' F. 'yern'd' v. G.

78. *roan Barbary* v. note on *Material* above.

89. *proud* Q. 'prond'

94. S.D. Q. 'Enter one to Richard with meate.' F. 'Enter Keeper with a Diſh.'

97. S.D. Q. 'Exit Groome.' F. 'Exit.'

99. *Taste of it first* Cf. *K. John*, 5. 6. 28 'who did taste to him.' All food that was to pass royal lips was first tasted by an appointed person, as insurance against poisoning.

100–101. *My lord, I dare not...contrary* This can only be printed as prose, but it was clearly once verse, since it begins and ends with a blank-verse line; e.g. 'My lord, I dare not, Sir Pierce of Exton/Came from the king, commands the contrary.' The text as it stands is prob. the result of adaptation.

104. S.D. Q. 'The murderers ruſh in.' F. 'Enter Exton and Seruants.'

105. *How now...assault* Obscure and perhaps corrupt. Staunton conj. 'How now? What? mean'st death in this rude assault?' which is possible; cf. note 5. 3. 122 above for 's' instead of 'st' in 2nd pers. sing.

107. S.D. Q. 'Here Exton ſtrikes him downe.' F. 'Exton ſtrikes him downe.'

114. *O, would the deed were good!* 'It is said, that sir Piers of Exton, after he had thus slaine him, wept right bitterlie' (Hol. iii. 517/1/46).

118. S.D. F. 'Exit.' Q. gives none.

## 5. 6.

*Material.* Hol. provides most that is necessary, though Bol.'s disavowal of Exton is not mentioned in any of the chronicles and Daniel borrowed it from Sh. in his 1609 ed. of *C.W.* (v. note ll. 38–44).

S.D. Q. 'Enter Bullingbrooke with the duke of Yorke.' F. 'Flouriſh. Enter Bullingbrooke, Yorke, with other Lords & attendants.' Cf. head-note S.D. 5. 3. The return to 'Bullingbrooke' suggests Sh.'s pen; but the speech-headings 'King,' together with the silly rhymes (v. *Introd.* p. lxxiii) in what follows make it prob. that he used scraps of the old play in the composition of this last scene.

4. S.D. Q., F. 'Enter Northumberland.'

7–10. *The next news...here* v. *Introd.* p. lxx.

8. *Spencer* (F.) Q. 'Oxford' 'As Aubrey de Vere, Earl of Oxford, had no share in the rebellion, the reading of F. should be preferred' (Boswell-Stone, p. 127 n. 1). The 'Oxford' was prob. due to careless copying (perhaps on Sh.'s part), owing 'to the frequent mention of the town of Oxford in this incident' (Clar.). The F. correction is interesting, since it implies historical knowledge, and perhaps consultation of Hol. P. A. Daniel, indeed, attached so much importance to it that its acceptance carried with it for him the acceptance of

all other F. variants, not 'otherwise discredited' (p. xviii, Introd. Griggs Facs. *Richard II*, 1597). Cf. Note on Copy, and Pollard, pp. 81–2.

10. S.D. Rowe reads 'Presenting a Paper.'

12. S.D. Q. 'Enter Lord Fitzwaters.' F. 'Enter Fitz-waters.'

18. S.D. Q. 'Enter H. Percie.' F. 'Enter Percy and Carlile.'

20. *With clog of conscience* Cf. 1. 3. 200 'The clogging burthen of a guilty soul.' Hol. iii. 516/2/31 'Shortlie after, the abbat of Westminster...for thought fell into a sudden palsie, and shortlie after, without speech, ended his life.'

21. *grave*. So Q.

25. *reverend room* Q., F. 'reuerent roome' v. G. 'reverend.' J. C. Smith paraphrases: 'Choose some place of religious retirement.'

26. *joy* = enjoy.

29. *High sparks of honour...seen* Steevens cites 'the old Play' *King Leir* (*Six Old Plays*, vol. i. p. 402):

I see such sparks of honour in your face.

S.D. Q. 'Enter Exton with the coffin.' F. 'Enter Exton with a Coffin.' Capell supplied 'Persons bearing.'

38–44. *They love not poison...day nor light* R. G. White cites *C.W.* iii. 78–9 (ed. 1609) as a parallel proving that Daniel borrowed from Shakespeare, but assigned the date 1595 in error to the passage (v. *Introd.* p. xliii):

What great aduancement hast thou hereby wonne,
By being the instrument to perpetrate
So foule a deed? where is thy grace in Corte,
For such a seruice, acted in this sort?

* * * * * * * * *

First, he for whom thou dost this villanie
(Though pleas'd therewith) will not auouch thy fact,
But let the weight of thine owne infamie
Fall on thee, vnsupported, and vnbackt:

Then, all men else will loath thy treacherie,
And thou thy selfe abhorre thy proper act:.
'So th' Wolfe, in hope the Lyons grace to win
'Betraying other beastes, lost his owne skinne.'

41–44. *The guilt...nor light* v. *Introd.* p. lxx.

43. *through the shades* (Rowe) Q. 'through ſhades' Qb, F. 'through the ſhade' Camb. reads 'thorough shades,' but the article is surely better and its omission is one of the commonest of misprints.

47. *for what* (Q.) F. 'for that'—which most edd. read. Cf. Pollard, p. 87.

49. *I'll make...Holy Land* This links on with the opening of 1 *Hen. IV*.

52. S.D. F. 'Exeunt.' Q. gives none.

# GLOSSARY

*Note.* Where a pun or quibble is intended, the meanings are distinguished as (*a*) and (*b*)

ABIDE, endure; 5. 6. 22

ABSENT (adj.), 'absent time' = time of (the King's) absence (cf. *Oth.* 3. 4. 174); 2. 3. 79

ABUSE, ill-use, wrong; 2. 3. 137

ACCOMPLISHED, furnished, endowed, fully equipped (cf. *M.V.* 3. 4. 61); 2. 1. 177

ADVICE, deliberation, consultation; 1. 3. 233

ADVISED, deliberate, intentional; 1. 3. 188

AFFECT (sb.), kind feeling, affection (cf. *L.L.L.* 1. 1. 152, the only other instance in Sh.); 1. 4. 30

AFORE, before; 2. 1. 200

AGAINST, in anticipation of; 3. 4. 28

AMAZED, bewildered, distraught; 5. 2. 85; 5. 3. 22 (S.D.)

AMAZING, stupefying, confounding (cf. *M.N.D.* 4. 1. 145); 1. 3. 81

ANCIENT, (i) long-established; 1. 1. 9; (ii) former; 2. 1. 248

ANSWER, pay for, give account of; 1. 1. 38, 80, 198

ANTIC (sb.), (*a*) clown, mountebank, one who plays a grotesque or ludicrous part, (*b*) grinning face, gargoyle or death's head; 3. 2. 162

APISH, (*a*) imitative, (*b*) brutish; 2. 1. 22

APPARENT (cf. Lat. 'apparens'), plain, manifest; 1. 1. 13; 4. 1. 124

APPEACH, accuse, lay information against; 5. 2. 79, 102

APPEAL (sb.), impeachment of treason, accusation which the accuser is prepared to prove by combat; 1. 1. 4; 4. 1. 45, 79

APPEAL (vb.), accuse of a crime which the accuser undertakes to prove, esp. impeach of treason; 1. 1. 9, 27, 142

APPELLANT (adj.), appealing, accusing; 1. 1. 34

APPELLANT (sb.), one who appeals another, the challenger; 1. 3. 4; 4. 1. 104

APPOINTMENT, equipment (cf. *K. John*, 2. 1. 296); 3. 3. 53

APPREHENSION, thinking, conception; 1. 3. 300

APPROVE, prove, test; 1. 3. 112; 2. 3. 44

APRICOCK, apricot; 3. 4. 29

ARBITRATE, decide; 1. 1. 50, 200

ARGUMENT, subject, theme (cf. 1 *Hen. IV*, 2. 4. 310); 1. 1. 12

AT ALL POINTS, completely; 1. 3. 2

ATONE, reconcile; 1. 1. 202

ATTACH, arrest; 2. 3. 156

ATTAINDER, foul or dishonouring accusation (cf. *L.L.L.* 1. 1. 157); 4. 1. 24

Attend, await; 1. 3. 116

Attorney-general, a legal representative acting under a general power of attorney and representing his principal in all legal matters (*O.E.D.*); 2. 1. 203

Awe (sb.), power to inspire fear or reverence (cf. *J.C.* 2. 1. 52); 1. 1. 118

Awful, reverential; 3. 3. 76

Awry, (*a*) obliquely, (*b*) wrongly; 2. 2. 19

Baffle, subject to public disgrace or infamy, treat with indignity (cf. *T.N.* 5. 1. 369 and 1 *Hen. IV*, 2. 4. 480 'hang me up by the heels' etc.). Orig. to hang up a recreant knight by the heels (cf. *F. Queene*, vi. vii. 27 'He by the heeles him hung vpon a tree, And baffuld so, that all which passed by, The picture of his punishment might see'); 1. 1. 170

Bait (vb.), persecute, worry (as a dog worries an animal); 4. 1. 238

Balm, consecrated oil used in the coronation of a king; 3. 2. 55; 4. 1. 207

Band, bond; 1. 1. 2; 2. 2. 71

Barbed, armed or caparisoned with a 'barb' or 'bard,' i.e. a covering for the breast and flanks of a war-horse, made of metal plates or of leather set with metal spikes or bosses; 3. 3. 117

Barren, unresponsive, stupid (cf. *M.N.D.* 3. 2. 13; *Ham.* 3. 2. 46 'barren spectators'); 1. 3. 168

Base court, the lower or outer courtyard of a castle (with a quibble on 'base,' despicable); 3. 3. 176, 180

Bay (sb.), a hunting term, lit. the chorus of barking raised by hounds in conflict with an animal, hence the animal's last stand; 2. 3. 128

Beadsman, almsman or pensioner (so called, because charged with the duty of offering prayers or 'beads' for his benefactor); 3. 2. 116

Benevolence, a forced loan levied without legal authority by the king, and first so called in 1473 by Edw. IV who exacted it as a token of goodwill (*O.E.D.*); 2. 1. 250

Betid, happened; 5. 1. 42

Betimes, soon; 2. 1. 36

Bias, a term at bowls, signifying the construction of the bowl to impart an oblique motion, or the oblique line in which it runs; 3. 4. 5.

Bill, a weapon consisting of a long staff with a curved blade at the end; 3. 2. 118

Blank (sb.), a document with spaces left blank to be filled up at the pleasure of the person to whom it is granted, e.g. a blank charter; 2. 1. 250

Blaze (sb.), flash, violent outburst (cf. *Ham.* 1. 3. 117); 2. 1. 33

Bleed, let blood; 1. 1. 157

Blemished, stained; 2. 1. 293

Boisterous, rough and violent; 1. 1. 4

Boot, there is no boot = there is no help for it, no alternative; 1. 1. 164; it boots not = it avails not; 1. 3. 174; 3. 4. 18

BOUND (vb.), (i) limit, confine; 5. 2. 38; (ii) recoil, rebound; 1. 2. 58

BOY, knave, varlet. A term of abuse or contempt (cf. *Cor.* 5. 6. 113 and v. *Shrew*, G.); 4. 1. 65; (poss.) 5. 2. 69

BRAVING, defiant; 2. 3. 112, 143

BREATH, breathing-space, interval (cf. *Ric. III*, 4. 2. 24 'some breath, some little pause'); 3. 2. 164

BREED, brood, family, race; 2. 1. 45

BRING, accompany; 1. 3. 304

BROKEN, financially ruined; 2. 1. 257

BROKING, characterized by fraudulent dealing; 2. 1. 293

BROOK (vb.), endure, with some of the original meaning 'enjoy'; 3. 2. 2.

BUSINESS, anxiety, disturbance, serious purpose (cf. *O.E.D.*); 2. 2. 75

BUZZ, whisper busily (*O.E.D.* quotes Stubbes, *Anat. of Abuses*, 36 (1877) 'Hauing buzzed his venemous ṡuggestions into their eares'); 2. 1. 26

BY, on account of; 2. 1. 52

CAITIFF, basely wretched; 1. 2. 53

CAREER, charge, encounter at a tournament or in battle; 1. 2. 49

CAREFUL, full of care, anxious; 2. 2. 75

CATERPILLAR, rapacious person, extortioner (cf. Gosson, 1579, *The Shoole of Abuse, Conteining a plesaunt inuectiue against*...*and such like Caterpillers of a Cōmonwelth*); 2. 3. 166

CHANGE (vb.), exchange; 3. 2. 189

CHECK (vb.), rebuke; 5. 5. 46

CHIVALRY, prowess; 1. 1. 203

CHOLER, (*a*) anger, (*b*) biliousness (cf. *Ham.* 3. 2. 306 and note); 1. 1. 153

CHOPPING, that changes the meaning (still in use in the prov. phrase 'chopping and changing'); 5. 3. 124

CLEAN, completely; 3. 1. 10

CLIMATE, region, country; 4. 1. 130

CLOG, impediment, burden, lit. a block of wood tied to the leg of an animal or prisoner to prevent escape; 5. 6. 20

CLOSE (sb.), the conclusion of a musical phrase, theme or movement, a cadence (cf. *Hen. V*, 1. 2. 182–3; *Tw. Nt.* 1. 1. 4); 2. 1. 12

COAT, coat of arms; 3. 1. 24

COMMENDS (sb.), greetings, compliments; 3. 3. 126

COMPARE BETWEEN, draw a comparison (*O.E.D.* gives no other examples); 2. 1. 185

COMPASSIONATE, displaying sorrowful emotion, (or) moving pity (*O.E.D.*). Not found elsewhere in latter sense before 1630. The context (esp. 'plaining') suggests that 'appealing for pity' is the meaning in Sh.'s mind; 1. 3. 174

COMPLAIN, bewail; 3. 4. 18

COMPLAIN ONESELF, bewail oneself, utter one's lamentations (cf. *Lucr.* 598); 1. 2. 42

COMPLOTTED, conspired; 1. 1. 96; 1. 3. 189

COMPOSITION, bodily structure or condition (cf. *K. John*, 1. 1. 88); 2. 1. 73

CONCEIT, fancy, fantasy; 2. 2. 33

CONCLUDE, come to final terms; 1. 1. 156

CONDITION, (*a*) personal quality (cf. *L.L.L.* 5. 2. 20); 2. 3. 107; (*b*) condition, circumstances; 2. 3. 108

CONFINE (sb.), territory; 3. 2. 125

CONFOUND, destroy; 3. 4. 60; 4. 1. 141; 5. 3. 86

CONJURATION, appeal, 'senseless conjuration' = appeal to inanimate things; 3. 2. 23

CONSENT TO, be accomplice in; 1. 2. 25

CONSORTED, associated, leagued (cf. *L.L.L.* 1. 1. 253); 5. 3. 138; 5. 6. 15

CONTRIVE, plot, scheme; 1. 1. 96

CONVERT (vb. intr.), change, undergo a change (cf. *Macb.* 4. 3. 229); 5. 1. 66; 5. 3. 64

CONVEYER, (*a*) one that transports or transfers, (*b*) a thief; (v. note) 4. 1. 317

COUSIN, kinsman; 2. 1. 109; 2. 2. 118

CRAFT, (*a*) guile, deceit, (*b*) a manual art; 1. 4. 28

CROSSLY, athwart, adversely; 2. 4. 24

CROWN (sb.), (*a*) the King's crown, (*b*) head; 3. 3. 95, 96

CUNNING, skilfully contrived, that which requires skill (to play); 1. 3. 163

CURRENT, valid, having currency (like coin); 1. 3. 231

DATE (sb.), period; 5. 2. 91

DATELESS, limitless, eternal; 1. 3. 151

DEAD, pale as death (cf. 2 *Hen. IV*, 1. 1. 71 'so dead in look'); 3. 2. 79

DEAR, (i) of great value; 2. 1. 57–8, (ii) dire, grievous; 1. 3. 151; (iii) 'a dear account' comprises both meanings; 1. 1. 130

DECEIVABLE, deceitful, deceptive; 2. 3. 84

DEFEND, forbid; 1. 3. 18

DEGREE, (i) manner; 2. 3. 109; (ii) one 'step' in direct descent; 1. 4. 36; (iii) 'in any fair degree' = to any reasonable extent according to the code of chivalry; 1. 1. 80

DEPOSE, examine on oath; 1. 3. 30

DEPRESS, bring low, humble; 3. 4. 68

DESIGN (sb.), project, enterprise; 1. 1. 81; 1. 3. 45

DESIGN (vb.), indicate, designate; 1. 1. 203

DESPISED, despicable; 2. 3. 95

DETERMINATE, a legal term = set a limit to, terminate (cf. *Son.* 87. 4 'My bonds in thee are all determinate'); 1. 3. 150

DETESTED, detestable; 2. 3. 109; 3. 2. 44

DIGRESSING, transgressing (cf. *Tit.* 5. 3. 116); 5. 3. 66

DISCOMFORTABLE, destroying comfort or happiness; 3. 2. 36

DISPARK, convert land where game is preserved to other uses; 3. 1. 23

DISTAFF-WOMAN, spinning-woman; 3. 2. 118

DIVINE, immortal (cf. *Lucr.* 1164); 1. 1. 38

DOUBT ('TIS), 'tis feared; 3. 4. 69

DUTY, homage, an expression of submission, deference or respect; 3. 3. 48, 188

EAGER, sharp (cf. *Ham.* 1. 4. 2); 1. 1. 49

EAR (vb.), plough, till; 3. 2. 212

EARTH, country, land, domain; 2. 1. 41, 50

EFFEMINATE, self-indulgent, voluptuous; 5. 3. 10

ENDOWMENT, property from which one derives income; 2. 3. 139

ENFRANCHISEMENT, (i) liberation; 1. 3. 90; (ii) admission (here restoration) to political rights; 3. 3. 114

ENSUE, follow, succeed, approach (cf. *Lucr.* 502, *Ric. III*, 2. 3. 43); 'Used of something about to happen, not necessarily regarded as a consequence' (Gordon); 2. 1. 68, 197

ENTREAT, treat; 3. 1. 37

ENVY (sb.), malice, enmity; 2. 1. 49

ERNE, grieve. Mod. edd. follow F. and print 'yearn' (= desire) with which it was often confused in Eliz. Eng. (cf. *M.W.W.* 3. 5. 45); 5. 5. 76

EVENT, outcome, consequence; 2. 1. 214

EXACTLY, in express terms, precisely (*O.E.D.* quotes from 1646); 1. 1. 140

EXCEPT (vb.), take exception to (*O.E.D.* but cf. *O.E.D.* 3, allege as an objection); 1. 1. 72

EXCLAIM (sb.), exclamation, outcry; 1. 2. 2

EXPEDIENCE, speed; 2. 1. 287

EXPEDIENT, speedy (cf. *John*, 2. 1. 60); 1. 4. 39

EXTINCT, extinguished, quenched; 1. 3. 222

EXTREMITY, IN, to the utmost (cf. *M.N.D.* 3. 2. 3); 2. 2. 72

FACE, (*a*) brazen out; (*b*) give countenance to; 4. 1. 285

FAINT (vb. and adj.), (be) faint-hearted; 2. 1. 297; 2. 2. 32

FALL (vb.), let fall, drop; 3. 4. 104

FANTASTIC, existing only in imagination; 1. 3. 299

FARM (sb.), the letting out of public revenue for a fixed payment; 2. 1. 60 (with a quibble on 'farm' = farmstead), 256

FARM (vb.), lease the right of taxing to the highest bidder, on consideration of a fixed cash payment; 1. 4. 45

FAVOUR (sb.), (*a*) countenance, (*b*) good-will; 4. 1. 168

FEARFUL, timorous; 3. 3. 73

FEMALE, small and weak, like a woman's; 3. 2. 114

FETCH, derive, draw as from a source; 1. 1. 97

FIGURE, image; 4. 1. 125

FLATTER, (i) try to please by obsequious speech; 2. 1. 87, 90; (ii) inspire with hope on insufficient grounds (*O.E.D.* quotes Fleming cont. Holinshed iii. 1351/1 'My lord, you are verie sicke, I will not flatter with you'); 2. 1. 89

FLATTER WITH, fawn upon (cf. *Tw. Nt.* 1. 5. 307); 2. 1. 88

FOIL (sb.), (*a*) defeat (orig. a term in wrestling), (*b*) that which sets off something to advantage; 1. 3. 266

FOND, foolish; 5. 2. 95, 101; 5. 1. 101 (with a quibble on 'tender')

FONDLY, (i) tenderly; 3. 2. 9; (ii) foolishly; 3. 3. 185; 4. 1. 72

FOR ME, for my part; 1. 4. 6

FOR WHY, because; 5. 1. 46

FRANTIC, lunatic, mad; 3. 3. 185

FREE, without constraint; 1. 3. 115

FRET (vb.), form by wearing away; 3. 3. 167

GAGE (sb.), pledge, usually a glove or gauntlet; 1. 1. 69, 146; 4. 1. 25 *etc.*; 'in gage,' in pledge; 4. 1. 34

GLASS, lens of the eye (cf. *Wint.* 1. 2. 268 'eye-glass'; *Cor.* 3. 2. 117 'the glasses of my sight'); 1. 3. 208

GLISTERING, glittering; 3. 3. 178

GLOSE, talk smoothly and speciously, flatter; 2. 1. 10

GNARL, snarl (cf. 2 *Hen. VI*, 3. 1. 192 'And wolves are gnarling who shall gnaw thee'—the only other instance in Sh.); 1. 3. 292

GOLGOTHA, graveyard, charnel-house; 4. 1. 144

GRIEF, hardship, suffering; 1. 3. 258

GRIPE, seize, grasp tightly (cf. 1 *Hen. IV*, 5. 1. 57); 2. 1. 189

HAPPILY, (either) haply (or) happily. The two forms are both found in Sh. and were practically interchangeable; 5. 3. 22

HAPPY, well-endowed; 3. 1. 9

HARDLY, with difficulty; 2. 4. 2

HATEFUL, full of hatred; 2. 2. 140

HAUGHT, haughty; 4. 1. 254

HAVIOUR, bearing, carriage; 1. 3. 77

HEIGHT, high rank; 1. 1. 189

HEIR, offspring; 2. 2. 63

HIGH-STOMACHED, haughty (cf. *Ps.* ci. 7, Prayer-book ver. 'a proud look and high stomach'); 1. 1. 18

HUMOUR, whim; 5. 5. 10

IMP (vb.), a term of falconry, meaning to engraft feathers in the wing of a bird to restore or improve its powers of flight; hence, enlarge, extend, eke; 2. 1. 292

IMPEACH, discredit, disparage (cf. *M.N.D.* 2. 1. 214); 1. 1. 170, 189

IMPRESE, for Ital. 'impresa,' a heraldic device, impressed, engraved or painted upon a shield with an attached motto or 'word'; much affected by noblemen of fashion at this time; 3. 1. 25

INCONTINENT (adv.), straightway, at once; 5. 6. 48

INDIFFERENT, impartial; 2. 3. 116

INFECTION, evil or corrupting influence, contamination, moral or physical (v. *O.E.D.* 6 and 7); 2. 1. 44

INHABITABLE, uninhabitable (cf. Jonson, *Catiline*, 5. 1. 54 'some inhabitable place'); 1. 1. 65

IN HASTE WHEREOF, to hasten which; 1. 1. 150

INHERIT, (i) *trans.* put in possession, lit. make heir; the only instance of this use in Sh.; 1. 1. 85; (ii) *intrans.* hold, possess; 2. 1. 83

INJURIOUS, wilfully inflicting injury, 'almost = insolent' (Gordon); 1. 1. 91

INTERCHANGEABLY, mutually, reciprocally; 1. 1. 146; 5. 2. 98

JACK OF THE CLOCK, an automatic figure which strikes the quarters, etc., on a bell; 5. 5. 60

JADE, vicious or unreliable horse; 5. 5. 85

JAR (vb.), tick; 5. 5. 51

JAUNCING, prancing (*O.E.D.* with a query; cf. Q2 *Rom.* 2. 5. 53); 5. 5. 94

JEST (vb.), to play a part in a pageant, masque, masquerade or the like (v. note); 1. 3. 95

JOURNEYMAN, (*a*) traveller, (*b*) one who works under a master-craftsman for day wages; 1. 3. 274

JOY, enjoy; 5. 6. 26

KERN (derived from Irish 'ceithern' = a band of foot-soldiers), a light-armed Irish foot-soldier; 2. 1. 156

KNOT (sb.), a flower-bed or garden laid out in an intricate design; 3. 4. 46

LARGE (AT), in full; 3. 1. 41; 5. 6. 10

LARGESS, lavish expenditure in gifts; 1. 4. 44

LAST, lately, recently; 1. 1. 131

LEARN, teach; 4. 1. 120

LENDINGS, 'money advanced to soldiers when the regular pay cannot be given' (*O.E.D.*); 1. 1. 89

LETTERS-PATENT, an open letter from a sovereign conferring some right, privilege, title, property or office; 2. 1. 202; 2. 3. 130

LEWD, base; 1. 1. 90

LIBERAL, free; 2. 1. 229

LINEAL, transmitted by lineal descent; 3. 3. 113

LINGER, prolong (cf. *M.N.D.* 1. 1. 4 'lingers my desires,' *Oth.* 4. 2. 231); 2. 2. 72

LINING, contents (cf. *A.Y.L.* 2. 7. 154 'belly with good capon lined'); 1. 4. 61

LODGE, throw down on the ground, beat down (cf. *Macb.* 4. 1. 55); 3. 3. 162

LOOK UPON, look on, as a mere spectator (cf. 3 *Hen. VI*, 2. 3. 27); 4. 1. 237

LOOK WHEN, expect that; 1. 3. 243

MAIM (sb.), mutilation or loss of some essential part, serious injury (cf. 1 *Hen. IV*, 4. 1. 42); 1. 3. 156

MAKE, do; 5. 3. 89

MANAGE (sb.), (i) management, conduct of affairs (cf. *M.V.* 3. 4. 25 and *John*, 1. 1. 37); 1. 4. 39; (ii) the directing of a horse in its paces; 3. 3. 179

MANAGE (vb.), wield; 3. 2. 118

MANNER (IN), so to speak, as it were; 3. 1. 11

MANUAL SEAL, authorized warrant, lit. document sealed by the hand of the competent authority; 4. 1. 25

MAP, epitome, embodiment; 5. 1. 12

MEAN (adj.), poor, humble; 1. 2. 33

MEASURE (sb.), (i) a stately dance; 1. 3. 291; (ii) (*a*) a dance, (*b*) moderation, temperance; 3. 4. 7, 8

MEASURE (vb.), traverse; 3. 2. 125

MERELY, purely; 2. 1. 243

MERIT, due reward; 1. 3. 156

METTLE, essence, stuff (cf. *Ric. III*, 4. 4. 302 'Even of your mettle, of your very blood'); 1. 2. 23

MODEL (sb.), (i) copy; 1. 2. 28; (ii) representation or facsimile on a small scale; 3. 2. 153; 3. 4. 42; (iii) ground plan; 5. 1. 11

MOE, more; 2. 1. 239

MORTAL, deadly; 3. 2. 21

MOTIVE, moving organ, instrument (cf. *Troil.* 4. 5. 57); 1. 1. 193

NATIVE, by right of birth (cf. 3 *Hen. VI*, 3. 3. 190 'native right'); 3. 2. 25

NEAR, nearer; 3. 2. 64; 5. 1 88.

NICELY, (*a*) subtly, (*b*) triflingly (cf. *Rom.* 5. 2. 18; *Caes.* 4. 3. 8); 2. 1. 84

NOBLE = 20 groats or 6*s.* 8*d.*; 1. 1. 88

NOTE, stigma, mark of disgrace. From Lat. 'nota' = 'the technical term for the official and public reprehensions of private persons by the Censor' (Herford) (cf. *Lucr.* 208, *L.L.L.* 4. 3. 122); 1. 1. 43

NOTHING LESS, anything but. Obsolete idiom; cf. Fr. rien moins que (*O.E.D.* 'less' B. 3); 2. 2. 34

NUMBERING, which counts the hours; 5. 5. 50

OBJECT (vb.), bring as a charge; 1. 1. 28

OBSCENE, repulsive, foul; 4. 1. 131

OFFICE, service; 2. 2. 139

ORDER, direct, regulate; 5. 3. 140

OSTENTATION, display; 2. 3. 95

OUT-DARED, dared down, cowed (Herford); 1. 1. 190

OVER-PROUD, too luxuriant. 'Proud' and 'pride' often denote hot-bloodedness in men and animals (cf. *L.L.L.* 5. 2. 66, *Lucr.* 712, *Two Gent.* G. and *Errors* G.); 3. 4. 59

OWE, own, possess; 4. 1. 185

PAIN OF LIFE (ON), on pain of death. The expression 'on pain of,' now 'followed by the penalty or punishment incurred,' was also formerly followed by 'that which one is liable to pay or forfeit' (*O.E.D.* 'pain' 1 b); 1. 3. 140 (v. note), 153

PALE (sb.), fence, enclosure; 3. 4. 40

PARLE, a meeting to discuss terms under a truce, a trumpet-call to such a meeting; 1. 1. 192; 3. 3. 33

PARTIAL SLANDER, accusation of being partial; 1. 3. 241

PARTIALIZE, render partial or one-sided; 1. 1. 120

PARTY, part, side; 3. 3. 115

PARTY-VERDICT, one share in a joint verdict; 1. 3. 234

PASSAGE, wandering, travel; 1. 3. 272

PASSENGER, passer-by; 5. 3. 9

PAWN (sb.), pledge or gage of battle; 1. 1. 74

PEACEFUL, unopposed; 3. 2. 125

PELICAN. The female bird is said to feed or revive her young with her blood (cf. *Ham.* 4. 5. 146) but here Shakespeare puts the initiative on the young; 2. 1. 126

PELTING, paltry, petty; 2. 1. 60

PERSPECTIVE, (*a*) any sort of glass for aiding or distorting the sight; cf. *All's Well*, 5. 3. 48 'his scornful perspective ...Which warped the line of every other favour'; (*b*) 'a kind of relief in which the surface was so modelled as to produce, when seen from the side, the impression of a continuous picture, which, when seen from the front, disappeared' (Herford); 2. 2. 18

PHAETHON. The type of youthful presumption. The son of Helios, who, having obtained from his father permission to drive the sun's chariot for a day, lost control of the steeds, and was struck down by a thunderbolt of Jupiter, to prevent his setting the earth on fire; 3. 3. 178

PILL (vb.), plunder, despoil; 2. 1. 246

PINE (vb.), torment, afflict; 5. 1. 77

PITCH (sb.), the height to which a falcon rises; 1. 1. 109

PITY (vb. and sb.) (have) mercy, pardon; 5. 3. 57 (2)

PLAINING, lamentation, complaint; 1. 3. 175

PLATED, armed (cf. *Ant. & Cleo.* 1. 1. 4); 1. 3. 28

POMPOUS, magnificently apparelled, dressed for ceremony; 4. 1. 250

POSSESSED, (*a*) in possession of, (*b*) dominated by an evil spirit; 2. 1. 107–8

POST (adv.), at express speed; 5. 2. 112

POST (vb.), ride fast, hasten; 1. 1. 56

POSTERN, small back (or side) door; 5. 5. 17

POWER, body of troops; 3. 2. 186, 211; 5. 3. 140; 2. 2. 126

PRECEDENT, instance proving a fact; 2. 1. 130

PRESENCE, reception-room, presence-chamber at court; 1. 3. 289

PRESENCE (IN), present; 4. 1. 62

PRESENTLY, at once; 1. 4. 52; 2. 2. 92; 3. 2. 179

PRESS (vb.), force to serve in the army; 3. 2. 58

PRESS TO DEATH, kill by placing heavy weights on the chest (the punishment for a felon who refused to speak); 3. 4. 72

PREVENTION, baffling or stopping another person in the execution of his designs; 2. 1. 167

PRICK, urge, incite; 2. 1. 207; 2. 3. 78

PROCESS, onward movement in space, progress; 2. 3. 12

PRODIGY, a monstrous or unnatural birth; 2. 2. 64

PROFANE (vb.), (i) misuse (cf. 2 *Hen. IV*, 2. 4. 391); 1. 3. 59; (ii) commit sacrilege; 3. 3. 81

PROOF, invulnerability, lit. strength tested or proved (cf. mod. 'rain-proof'); frequently used of armour (cf. *Ham.* 2. 2. 494; 3. 4. 38); 1. 3. 73

PROPERTY, characteristic or essential quality; 3. 2. 135

PROUD, v. *over-proud*; 3. 4. 59

PURCHASE, acquire; 1. 3. 282

PURGE, (*a*) purify the body of disease or humours, by bleeding or purgatives, (*b*) a legal term = clear from accusation of guilt; 1. 1. 153

QUIT, requite, repay; 5. 1. 43

RAGE (sb.), (i) (*a*) flood, sudden rising of the sea, (*b*) violent passion; 3. 2. 109; (ii) fury, violence; 3. 3. 59

RAGGED, rugged, rough, untamed; 2. 1. 70 (v. note); 5. 5. 21

RANKLE, cause a festering wound (cf. *Ric. III*, 1. 3. 291); 1. 3. 302

RAPIER, long pointed sword for thrusting (superseded the shorter 'broadsword' for hacking, c. 1590); 4. 1. 40

RASH, operating quickly or strongly (cf. 2 *Hen. IV*, 4. 4. 48); 2. 1. 33

RAVEL OUT, disentangle, make clear (cf. *Hamlet* G.); 4. 1. 228

RAW, crude, unripe; 2. 3. 42

RAZE, obliterate; 3. 1. 25

READ A LECTURE, deliver a lecture or sermon; 4. 1. 232

REBUKE, shame, disgrace; 2. 1. 166

RECEIPT, a sum of money received (not an acknowledgment of receipt); 1. 1. 126

RECORD (sb.), witness; 1. 1. 30

RECREANT (sb. and adj.), one who yields in combat, hence cowardly, craven; 1. 1. 144; 1. 2. 53; 1. 3. 106, 111

REFUGE (vb.), shelter, shield; 5. 5. 26

REGARD (sb.), thoughtful attention, consideration; 1. 3. 216; 2. 1. 28

REGREET, greet, salute; 1. 3. 67, 142, 186

REHEARSE, recite in a formal manner; 5. 3. 128

REMEMBER, remind; 1. 3. 269

REPEAL (vb.), recall from exile; 2. 2. 49; 4. 1. 85

RESTFUL, peaceful; 4. 1. 12

RETIRE, withdraw, lead back; 2. 2. 46

RETURN, 'state by way of a report or verdict' (*O.E.D.* 16); 1. 3. 122

REVERSION (IN), a legal term: lit. 'conditional upon the expiry of a grant or the death of a person' (*O.E.D.*) but in Sh. generally = (i) prospectively (cf. *Troil.* 3. 2. 100); 1. 4. 35; (ii) to be realized in the future; 2. 2. 38

RID, make away with, kill (cf. *Temp.* 1. 2. 364); 5. 4. 11

Right (adv.), righteously; 1. 1. 46

Right (sb.), that which justly accrues to anyone, what one may properly claim; 2. 1. 190, 201; 2. 3. 120

Rightly, (*a*) directly, from in front, (*b*) properly; 2. 2. 18

Roundly, (*a*) glibly (*O.E.D.* 6), (*b*) bluntly, unceremoniously (*O.E.D.* 3); 2. 1. 122

Rouse, start an animal from its lair; 2. 3. 128

Royalty, royal prerogative or right granted by the sovereign to an individual; 2. 1. 190; 2. 3. 120; 3. 3. 113

Rub (sb.), a term at bowls meaning an impediment or obstacle; 3. 4. 4

Rue (vb.), repent; 1. 3. 205

Rug, lit. 'a sort of coarse frieze,' hence = shaggy material of any kind; 2. 1. 156

Ruth, pity; 3. 4. 106

Safe, 'placed beyond the power of doing harm' (*O.E.D.* 10) (cf. *Macb.* 3. 4. 25); 5. 3. 41

Scope, (i) object, aim; 3. 3. 112; (ii) opportunity, 'room' to act; 3. 3. 140, 141

Scruple, doubt; 5. 5. 13

Secure, careless, over-confident; 5. 3. 43

Securely, without care or apprehension; 1. 3. 97; 2. 1. 266

See, see to, attend to (cf. *Shrew*, 1. 2. 145 and *Ant. & Cleo.* 5. 2. 368); 2. 1. 217

Seize, (i) take possession of; 2. 1. 160; (ii) (*a*) take hold of with the hands, (*b*) take forcible possession of; 4. 1. 181

Self, same; 1. 2. 23

Self-borne, borne for oneself, i.e. in civil war; 2. 3. 80 (v. note)

Senseless, v. *conjuration*; 3. 2. 23

Set (vb.), (i) hold, regard; 1. 3. 293; (ii) put up a stake, (here) challenge; 4. 1. 57

Several, distinct, various; 1. 3. 51; 5. 3. 140

Shadow, delusive semblance or image (*O.E.D.* 6*a*); 2. 2. 14

Sheer, clear, unpolluted; 5. 3. 61

Shrewd, hurtful, injurious; 3. 2. 59

Sift, discover a man's 'true... designs by dexterous questioning' (Herford) (cf. *Ham.* 2. 2. 58); 1. 1. 12

Signory, domain, estate; 3. 1. 22; 4. 1. 89

Silly, simple; 5. 5. 25

Sly, stealthy; 1. 3. 150

Small and small (by), little by little; 3. 2. 198

Solicit, petition, importune; 1. 2. 2

Sometime (adj.), former; 5. 1. 37

Sometime(s) (adv.), formerly; 4. 1. 169; 5. 5. 75

Sooth, used as a sb. of 'soothe' = blandishment, flattery (cf. *Per.* 1. 2. 44 'Signior Sooth' and *K. John*, 3. 1. 121 'soothe up'); 3. 3. 136

Sort, set, crew, pack (cf. *M.N.D.* 3. 2. 13 'that barren sort' and *Ric. III*, 5. 3. 316); 4. 1. 246

SOUR, bitter; 4. 1. 241

SPORT (MAKE), provide amusement, take pleasure; 2. 1. 85

SPOT (sb. and vb.), disgrace, stain; 1. 1. 175; 3. 2. 134

SPRIGHTFULLY, spiritedly, with great spirit; 1. 3. 3

STAGGER, cause to reel; 5. 5. 109

STAND ON, be contingent on; 4. 1. 33

STAND OUT, hold out; 1. 4. 38

STAND UPON, be incumbent on (cf. *Ham.* 5. 2. 63); 2. 3. 138

STAR, rank (v. *Ham.* G.); 4. 1. 21

STATE, (*a*) government, (*b*) majesty; 1. 3. 190; 3. 2. 72, 117, 163; 3. 4. 27; 4. 1. 179, 192, 209, 252; 5. 1. 18; 5. 5. 47; 5. 6. 6

STERLING (BE), have value, be current; 4. 1. 264

STOP (the ear), render deaf to something (*O.E.D.* 8 *a*); 2. 1. 17

STRANGER, alien, foreign; 1. 3. 143

STREAM (vb.), cause to float in the wind; 4. 1. 94

STRIKE, (*a*) furl sails, (*b*) deal or aim a blow; 2. 1. 266

SUBSCRIBE, put one down for (a sum of money); 1. 4. 50

SUBSTITUTE, deputy; 1. 4. 48

SUE LIVERY, institute a suit for the delivery or surrender of lands which were in the hands of the feudal suzerain until the heir could prove he was of age; 2. 1. 203; 2. 3. 129

SUGGEST, prompt to evil, tempt; 1. 1. 101; 3. 4. 75

SULLEN, melancholy. 'Sometimes with the notion of passing heavily, moving sluggishly' (*O.E.D.*); 1. 3. 227, 265; 5. 6. 48

SULLENS, a morbid state of sullenness, sulks (cf. Dryden, *Troil. & Cress.* 4. 2 'I'll e'en go home, and shut up my doors, and die o' the sullens, like an old bird in a cage'); 2. 1. 139

SUPPLANT, root out, 2. 1. 156

SYMPATHIZE, answer or correspond to; 5. 1. 46

SYMPATHY, consonance, equality (in rank); 4. 1. 33

TAP OUT, draw out (i.e. liquor from a cask); 2. 1. 127

TARDY, slow, making little progress; 2. 1. 22

TEAR, wound, lacerate; 3. 3. 83

TEEMING, fruitful, productive; 2. 1. 51; 5. 2. 91

TENDER (vb.), (*a*) be concerned for or solicitous about, (*b*) offer, allege (cf. *Ham.* 1. 3. 107); 1. 1. 32

TENEMENT, land or real property held of another by any tenure; 2. 1. 60

THOUGHT, melancholy consideration (cf. *Ham.* 3. 1. 85; 4. 5. 187 and G.); 2. 2. 31; 5. 5. 51

THRIVE TO, succeed in; 2. 2. 146

THROW, cast dice; 4. 1. 57

TIED, bound, obliged; 1. 1. 63

TIME, (i) the life of a man (cf. *Ant. & Cleo.* 3. 2. 59 'the time'); 1. 1. 177; (ii) season; 1. 3. 220

TIMELESS, untimely; 4. 1. 5

TOILED, exhausted with toil; 4. 1. 96

TOUCH, fingering (of a musical instrument), note; 1. 3. 165

TRADE (sb.), passage to and fro, resort; 3. 3. 156

TRESPASS (sb.), a violation of the law, properly one not amounting to treason or felony; 1. 1. 138; 5. 2. 89

TRIUMPH (sb.), a public festivity, esp. a tournament; 5. 2. 52; 5. 3. 14

TRUE, loyal; 2. 1. 192

TRUTH, loyalty (cf. *untruth*, 2. 2. 102 and 'truth' *K. John* G.); 5. 2. 44

TWAIN (vb.), divide, hence weaken; 5. 3. 134

UNAVOIDED, unavoidable (cf. *Ric. III*, 4. 4. 217); 2. 1. 268

UNCIVIL, barbarous, uncivilized (cf. *F. Queene*, II. vii. 3 'An vncouth, saluage, and vnciuile wight'); 3. 3. 102

UNDEAF, restore hearing to; 2. 1. 16

UNDERBEARING, endurance; 1. 4. 29

UNDO, (*a*) ruin, (*b*) undress; 4. 1. 203

UNFELT, intangible (cf. *Lucr.* 828), 'not accompanied by any palpable proofs' (Wright); 2. 3. 61

UNGRACIOUS, graceless, profane; 2. 3. 89

UNHAPPY (vb.), make unhappy or unfortunate; 3. 1. 10

UNPEOPLED, without servants (cf. *L.L.L.* 2. 1. 88, note). 'People' commonly = servants, retinue in Sh. (cf. *M.W.W.* 2. 2. 52, *Tw. Nt.* 1. 5. 112); 1. 2. 69

UNTHRIFTY, profligate as well as prodigal; 5. 3. 1

UNTRUTH, unfaithfulness, treason (cf. *truth*, 5. 2. 44 and 'truth' *K. John* G.); 2. 2. 102

UPLIFTED, taken up in defence; 2. 2. 50

URGE (vb.), insist on; 3. 1. 4; 4. 1. 271; 5. 4. 5

VANTAGE, profit; 5. 3. 132

VENOM (adj.), venomous; 2. 1. 19

VENOM (sb.), poison, esp. that secreted by snakes; 2. 1. 157

VERGE, (*a*) rim or circle of metal (cf. *Ric. III*, 4. 1. 59 'The inclusiue Verge of Golden Mettall, that must round my Brow'), (*b*) 'the compass about the king's court, which extended for twelve miles round' (Clar.); 2. 1. 102

WANTON (adj.), (i) trifling, frivolous; 5. 1. 101; (ii) spoilt, pampered; 5. 3. 10

WANTONS (PLAY THE), dally, trifle; 3. 3. 164

WARDER, a staff or truncheon used to give the signal for the commencement or cessation of hostilities; 1. 3. 118

WASTE, with a play on the legal term = 'destruction of houses, wood, or other produce of land, done by the tenant to the prejudice of the freehold' (Wright); 2. 1. 103

WATCH (sb.), (i) 'the marks of the minutes on a dial-plate' (Schmidt); (ii) dial, clockface; 5. 5. 52

WATCHING, sleeplessness (cf. *Ham.* 2. 2. 148); 2. 1. 78

WHERE, whereas; 3. 2. 185
WHILE, until (cf. *Macb.* 3. 1. 44); 1. 3. 122
WILL, inclination, desire; 2. 1. 28
WISHTLY, earnestly, intently and longingly (v. *O.E.D.* 'wishly'); 5. 4. 7
WIT, sound sense or judgment; 2. 1. 28
WORTHY, merited (cf. *All's Well*, 4. 3. 7); 5. 1. 68
WRACK (sb.), (*a*) shipwreck, (*b*) an instrument of torture; 2. 1. 267, 269

ZEAL, devotion, loyalty (often 'religious fervour,' cf. *K. John*, 2. 1. 565); 1. 1. 47